Clive James was born in Sydney in 1939, and educated at Sydney University and at Cambridge, where he was President of Footlights. He has published three books of literary criticism, *The Metropolitan Critic*, *At the Pillars of Hercules* and *From the Land of Shadows*; four mock-epic poems, *Peregrine Prykke's Pilgrimage*, *The Fate of Felicity Fark*, *Britannia Bright's Bewilderment* and *Charles Charming's Challenges*, a book of verse letters, *Fan-mail*; and the autobiography *Unreliable Memoirs* (also available in Picador). He was television critic of the *Observer* between 1972 and 1982, and has published two selections from his column, *Visions Before Midnight* and *The Crystal Bucket* (also available in Picador). He himself has made frequent appearances on television, most notably in *Saturday Night People*. *The Clive James Paris Fashion Show* was nominated for an Emmy and *Clive James at the Movies* for a BAFTA award.

Glued to the Box

Clive James

Television criticism from the *Observer* 1979–82

PICADOR

published by Pan Books

First published 1983 by Jonathan Cape Ltd
This Picador edition published 1983 by Pan Books Ltd,
Cavaye Place, London SW10 9PG
© The *Observer* 1979, 1980, 1981, 1982
Introduction © Clive James 1983
ISBN 0 330 28174 7
9 8 7 6 5 4 3 2

Printed in Great Britain by
Cox & Wyman Ltd, Reading

Humanity will surpass the first dirigibles as it has surpassed the first locomotives. It will surpass M. Santos-Dumont as it has surpassed Stephenson. After telephotography it will continually invent graphies and scopes and phones, all of which will be *tele* and one will be able to go around the earth in less than no time. But it will always be only the temporal earth. And it will even be possible to burrow inside the earth and pierce it through as I do this ball of clay. But it will always only be the carnal earth.

Charles Péguy in 1907

Contents

CONTENTS

Author's Note

As in previous collections, to avoid repetition I have cut individual columns severely and left many out altogether. But certain themes, such as the Barbara Woodhouse phenomenon and the remarkable behaviour of John McEnroe, recurred so hauntingly at the time that it would be a falsification to mention them only once. In the case of the Royal Wedding I have restored certain small cuts which had to be made for production reasons. The Wimbledon column for 5 July, 1981, went unpublished because of a strike and now appears in its proper place as part of the continuing story of Harry Carpenter's elocution.

All the people at the *Observer* whom I thanked in the introduction to *Visions Before Midnight* I can only thank again now that my race is run, while adding a special acknowledgment to Deborah Shepherd at Jonathan Cape, who with such care for detail saw all three volumes through the press. To the task of criticising the critic, my wife has always brought scholarly precision as well as infinite patience, while my daughters grew increasingly valuable as an early warning system: they were the first to spot the vital importance of *Tiswas* and if it had not been for their keen eyes I might have been much slower to notice that Lucy in *Dallas* had no neck.

Introduction

With the last piece selected for this volume I complete a ten-year tour of duty as the *Observer*'s television critic. *Visions Before Midnight* and *The Crystal Bucket* were the first and second volumes of selections from a column written almost every week during that period. This volume is the third and last. By the time it is published I will have moved on to other things, and probably already started regretting that I ever walked away from such a cushy number. More and more often, as the years wore on, people who felt compelled to encourage me in the delusion that I was a hard-working and useful member of the community would ask me how I planned my viewing week. Wasn't it tiring, deciding what to watch and then sitting there watching it? Dutifully I would pretend that it was back-breaking labour, but neither I nor my interlocutor was ever fooled.

As the television critic sits there night after night, year after year, other men are inhaling toxic dust down coal mines, testing for hair-line cracks in the top rims of cooling towers, talking in squeaky voices as they breathe helium at the bottom of the North Sea. Women stuntpersons are doing box-falls down oubliettes in Hammer horror movies. Policewomen with punk hairstyles are out acting as decoys to catch psychopathic rapists who will be fined a hundred pounds and bound over to keep the peace. The greatest risk to the television critic is bedsores, or a sprained wrist as he reaches too suddenly for the thin mints. The present writer once spilled a tray of ice-cubes into his lap when he saw Barbara Woodhouse kissing a horse, but apart from that he got through a whole decade unscathed. Indeed there isn't any reason why a ten-year stint as a television critic should not be extended to embrace the rest of a long life, provided that due attention is paid to diet and exercise. The muscles atrophy, like those of an astronaut too long aloft. Couple that with the almost inevitable acquisition of fatty tissue and you can end up looking like a bean bag, or, dare I say it, a television pouffe.

But though the television critic's body might conceivably be said to be at some slight risk, there is no longer any real reason to think that his cerebral cortex is in danger – unless one has sustained terminal brain damage without knowing it, and has been locked up in a special ward where they encourage the patient to pretend he is writing the introduction to a volume of criticism while they watch him through one-way glass. When I started as a critic there were plenty of wise voices to tell me that I was wasting my prose on the exaltation of ephemera. By the time I was able to contemplate giving the job up, most of the same wise voices were ready to tell me that I was renouncing my true *métier*. Either they thought that my prose had sunk to the level of what it was criticising, or else they thought that what I was criticising had risen to meet my prose. In effect, self-congratulatory though it might sound to say so, the latter was what had happened – in the sense, not that television had significantly improved, but that their estimation of it had. Nowadays it is much less common for educated people to scorn television. Even some of the Cambridge dons now have television sets standing bare-faced in the living room instead of hidden behind an antimacassar. General statements about the culturally deleterious effect of television are nowadays less likely to go unchallenged.

Philosophy, some philosophers say, leaves things as they are but gives them a thorough airing first. Television, I think, is more like that conception of philosophy than it is like those things which until recently it was regularly accused of being – a plague, an apocalypse or a universal solvent. It brings out the histrionic element in otherwise decorous people; it is least of all to be trusted when it purports to show the unvarnished documentary truth; but on the whole it looks at the world while leaving the world as it is. It is not an art form in itself, any more than the telephone is an art form in itself. If people who would realise the folly of deploring the telephone's artistic limitations nevertheless deplore television's artistic limitations, their foolishness is not the fault of television. Television is not even a medium – at least not in the sense that

McLuhan and lesser pundits tried to call it a medium, with special properties shared by no other medium. Television is a medium only in the sense that a window is a medium. A window might limit our perception of the world according to how it restricts the panorama within its frame, blunts our feeling for the movement of the air, and gives us little idea of how things out there actually smell. But unless we have spent our lives ill in bed then we have been out there, and know the world for what it is. That is how we know the window for what *it* is: because we know that it does not very much shape the world – only, temporarily, what we see.

There are welcome signs at long last that the kind of punditry which declaims so glibly about how television distorts life is being asked to show its credentials. The chief qualification required ought to be the ability to give an indication, preferably un-prompted, that life itself has been apprehended as something hard to pin down, sum up or explain away. Ten years ago it was still possible to acquire a reputation as a profound analyst of popular culture by pointing out how the homogeneous 'flow' of television programming imposed the values of a consumer society on the increasingly defenceless population. Today anyone marshalling such a set of assumptions would at least be obliged to argue his case. Beyond that, if his readers were sufficiently on the *qui vive*, he might be asked to explain what he thought a less homogeneous flow of programming might look like, or even what a non-consumer society might be conceived as being, always supposing that it could be that and still be free.

Apart from those programmes which set out to be something better than trivial but end up as trivial because of deficient inspiration, there is indeed a good deal that is deliberately trivial in British television. Even those of us who profess to find junk edifying are likely to draw the line at, say, *Sale of the Century*. But it is a nice question whether such programmes debase their viewers. It is at least as likely that the viewers debase the programmes, in the sense that the programmes are tailored to the requirements of those who watch them. If you believe, as Brecht pretended the East German government believed, that the population needs to be dissolved and a new one elected, then you must say so. Failing that, you must take people as they are. Triviality is one of the things that free people like to consume. Any free society is a consumer society, because it is bound to contain a lot of people who consume things that we don't approve of. Other people consume. You and I eat.

In this context it is a legitimate argument, if not an especially convincing one, to compare ITV with the BBC, deplore the presence of commercials on the former, and regret the former's influence on the latter. But it is not a legitimate argument to compare British television with television in, say, the Soviet Union and cry up the latter's alleged freedom from advertising pressure. The whole of Soviet television is one enormous commercial for single party government. Visitors who come back from the Soviet Union and tell you how marvellous it is to be able to look at public buildings without advertisements stuck all over them are just telling you that they can't decipher the cyrillic alphabet. Every large building in Moscow carries a naked plug for the infallibility of the Central Committee. One of the great wonders of intellectual life in the Western world is the way that those who proclaim themselves disillusioned with a supposedly materialist society are content to recommend, as paradigm cases of societies which are not materialist, societies which are not only materialist in every respect but actually *say* they are.

Back in the free world, the variations in quality between the television systems of different countries are admittedly sharp enough, although they point away from, rather than towards, the sole responsibility of the cathode tube. American television is undoubtedly worse than British television, but the glaring difference is evidence against, rather than for, the culpability of the medium itself. If television is relatively civilised in Britain, and relatively degraded in the United States, then with the medium appearing as a constant in both sums it is very likely that other factors have decided the issue. What is wrong with American television is the way the networks have been set up. (The organisational flaw is even more serious in France, but because it leads merely to political subservience rather than to rampant philistinism it attracts less attention from cultural doomwatchers.) In America people are free to view what they like but the programme makers are not so free to make programmes of which they can be proud. One of the results is a strong film industry. Another result is an embattled Public Service Broadcasting network with low funds but high *esprit de corps*. A probable future result will be independently produced programmes of high quality made available on video disc or cassette – together, alas, with independently produced programmes of bloodcurdling prurience made available the same way. But the main result, here and now, is a daily nightmare and a nightly daydream on all three main channels, producing an effect on the constant viewer likely to reduce him to a zombie. It is not the fault of the television set, but of what is happening in the studio. The window is clear enough but the world behind it has been obscured by a wall of trash.

At one point I was asked to contemplate setting up as a television critic in New York. The first image that flashed into my head was of Christ cleansing the temple. The second was of Hercules cleaning the Augean stables with his bare hands, water rights to the river Alpheus being unavailable. He would have got a Green Card out of it, but that would be about all. I turned the offer down because seriousness would have been impossible to maintain, and without the possibility of seriousness the kind of humour I like must quickly deteriorate to mere jokes. British television provides enough worthwhile programming, week in and week out, to convince even the most demanding viewer that he is not necessarily committing mental suicide by tuning in regularly. Those demanding viewers who say otherwise are usually doing more demanding than viewing. In America the sceptical critic would have nothing left to say after running through his repertoire of mockery, which would be all used up in about six months. His liking for *Hill Street Blues* and *Lou Grant* would scarcely sustain him. Even his affection for Willard the Weatherman on *The Today Show* would rapidly degenerate into whimsy. He would either have to quit or else become a cynic – and a cynic is not the same thing as a sceptic. A sceptic finds *Dallas* absurd. A cynic thinks the public doesn't.

In Britain the sceptical critic can go on being sceptical because when he is offered mutton dressed as lamb he can always point to real lamb. If a big bad classic drama series has been taken at the estimation of its producers and is being ridiculously overpraised, he can compare it with the finely judged play that went comparatively unnoticed last week. If the famous playwright has forgotten how to write, the critic can draw on the example provided by a new comedy series in which the sketches have been composed with real observation and invention. In other words, British television is not homogeneous. A homogeneous 'flow' is just what it does not impose. British television is heterogeneous. It is a culture, or at any rate part of one, and can thus be reduced to a socio-political formula only at the price of distortion. When applied to television, such formulaic voodoo shows itself up clearly, since anybody can compare it against what he knows. As a result the practice has been largely given up by those with a sufficient sense of the absurd to be cagey about their personal reputations. The younger and less cautious have reformulated the same position in the language of semiotics, where it remains safely unexamined by anyone except themselves. The older breed of pundit thought he was protecting cultural authenticity. The newer model is protecting nothing except his own salary, but at least he isn't clouding the issue.

The first duty of the critic is to submit. Not to knuckle under, but to submit. After that he must stay alert. It is not easy to do both, but to do the second without the first is nearly as bad as doing the first without the second. In this respect there is not much to choose between the dumb critic who likes everything and the smart one who likes nothing. The first is tube-struck, in the way that some theatre critics are stage-struck. The second is a purist in the way that some neurotic parents try to keep their precious child free of germs, only to see it die of a cut finger. The Roman Catholic Church, which has had long experience of playing to a mass audience, has often been obliged to remind its intellectual converts that their objections to plastic statuettes of Christ, with a battery-powered Sacred Heart that lights up in the dark, are objections to the universality of the faith. The Church is there for simple people too. Moderate intelligence is frequently prey to a kind of snobbery which genuine intellectual superiority is careful to avoid. Einstein, a profound appreciator of classical music, would introduce it to those who knew nothing about it by playing them a track or two from a Mantovani record. Quite apart from the matter of elementary human charity, people who complain that the common people are not intelligent enough or not politicised enough should ask themselves what life would be like if everyone were highly intelligent and fully politicised. But there could be no such life. Intelligence is nothing if not comparative and a society in which everybody cared exclusively about politics would be one long meeting. Common decency should be valued, not patronised. It shows contempt, rather than respect, to demand that the people's repressed creativity should be freed from its bonds. The people's creativity is already free, and occupied with the business of the day.

Television is simultaneously blamed, often by the same people, for worsening the world and for being powerless to change it. That the world is what it is has never been easy for sensitive souls to accept, and gets harder as faith ebbs. This is not to say, however, that television, or anything else, is without effect. It is just that the effect is never easy to isolate from the cataract of events. People in television must live to the same rules as people who write articles and books. You can't change things as you would like, but nothing you do will be quite without result: that the consequences of your actions are strictly incalculable should make you more responsible, not less. That is what it means to act from principle. Most people in British television do so, and indeed are encouraged to do so. (As people in French television, for example, are not – a difference between democracies which certainly indicates that France is that much less democratic and probably helps make it so.) Meanwhile the world changes at its own pace, or in some of its more depressing aspects obdurately stays the same.

When I started as a television critic, Northern Ireland was a frightening and seemingly intractable issue. As I cease to be a television critic, Northern Ireland is still a frightening and seemingly intractable issue. For ten years I have done, in this respect, what everybody else has had to do – look on helplessly while the little screen fills with masked men, angry young faces, broken bodies and loops of flame. For a long time there were complaints that television was not telling enough of the story. The complaints were justified. Programmes were indeed suppressed, whether because it was thought they would exacerbate bitterness and abet the terror, or because it was thought that they would simply help the IRA to win. Gradually more and more programmes were screened, telling more and more of the truth. Eventually two complete series provided an education in Irish realities which at least one viewer was glad to have. At the beginning of the current outbreak of troubles I was only sketchily aware that the Northern Ireland Catholics were a minority in their country, or that the Northern Irish Protestants had reason to fear for their chances in a United Ireland. To know what one had not known before was an absolute good. But apart from the education-al aspect, there was no denying that the increased television coverage of Northern Ireland did little which was observable to affect the struggle either way. There were frequent complaints that the presence of television cameras made young people more inclined to throw petrol bombs, but this was wishful thinking. Film of a burning soldier horrified all who saw it, but only a dreamer could believe that the soldier would not have been on fire if the camera had not been there. Both sides in Northern Ireland will make propaganda if there are cameras around: they would be foolish not to. But they also go on making war in the dark. The typical deaths in Northern Ireland are not staged for the camera. They happen when a man is shot down in his own hallway with his wife and children looking on, or when a man with a sock over his head drills a squaddie through the flak-jacket with a bullet from an Armalite with a night-sight, so that when he lowers the rifle not even he can see the man who has just been killed.

There is no way of assessing accurately whether television coverage, or access to television by politicians, or the natural propensity of officials and pressure groups to state their case on television if they can – whether any of these things, or any com-bination of them, necessarily entails the debasement of politics. What would undebased politics be like? All we can be sure of is that in certain countries not notable for laying out the details of public life on television, politics is considerably more debased than it is with us. As the time approached for me to hand in my quill, martial law was declared in Poland. The Polish crisis went on being reported by British television but there were few pictures except those that General Jaruzelski's military government allowed. Lech Walesa, in his brief period as the natural leader of his country, had done his best to ensure that television both domestic and foreign – and by foreign could only be meant Western – saw as much as possible of what was going on. Television was synonymous with freedom in Poland and if one were obliged to make a single statement about the connection between politics and television then the first thing to say would be that television is synonymous with freedom anywhere. Sophisticated arguments can be made for television's effectiveness as a repressive tool but those are not arguments about television, only about repression.

From the political angle, television is probably more effective as a scapegoat than as an instrument of debasement. When the Social Democratic Party emerged seemingly out of nowhere, the Labour Party's right wing were even more ready than the Labour Party's left wing to call it a creation of the media. Yet if you were setting out to choose a telegenic front-man for a political party of media darlings, Roy Jenkins would scarcely be ideal casting. Television worked in favour of the Social Democrats mainly by showing, with awful clarity, something of what was going on in the Labour Party. The hubbub was deafening but you could take some comfort from the thought that demagoguery had become, on this evidence, harder to get away with. A first-class television performer is more likely to have ambitions as a television performer than as a politician. The old style rabble-rouser might still get somewhere in the streets but on television the odds would be against him. As Sir Oswald Mosley inadvertently demonstrated towards the end of his misspent life, the spell-binding tones of mob oratory sound like rant when the face is in close-up. Tyrants, said Camus, conduct monologues above a million solitudes. The operative word being 'above'. Aspiring tyrants there will always be, and a million solitudes as well. But television makes it that much harder to be above people. It is not a podium from which you can talk down. On television, arrogance betrays itself very quickly. Giscard d'Estaing, a de Gaulle without the stature, by conducting a monologue on television helped engineer his own downfall.

Anyone afraid of what he thinks television does to the world is probably just afraid of the world. As this world goes he has good cause to be, but sympathy with his distress should not make us forget to ask him what he thinks the modern age would now be like if television were not in it. What does he think, for example, that all those helplessly malleable punters would actually be up to if they were not watching Bruce Forsyth on one mass channel or Larry Grayson on the other? Granting for the moment that it is possible to impose tripe on people who don't want it, it is an even larger and more questionable assumption to suppose that they would want art if tripe were taken away. The history of the Western world offers no encouragement for the view that there is a naturally wholesome form of entertainment which people would seek out if they were not distracted by the manipulators supposedly controlling the mass market. Even Dr Leavis, who believed in an Organic Society from which the society we now live in represents a catastrophic departure, must have been given pause by the thought of all those people who raced to see bears being baited or a cut-purse broken on the wheel. Nor is there a lot to be said, in retrospect, for such up-market pastimes as forming an after-theatre party to go and taunt the lunatics in Bedlam. People who reel back in horror after accidentally switching on Nicholas Parsons should reflect that the world has had worse things to offer. In the nineteenth century it was a big deal when they brought a dead whale to town.

But an apparently more serious indictment of television as art's enemy comes from those who say that it is never more inimical than when trying to be art's friend. This argument can be said to have something to it, if you don't mind dressing up a mutable set of contingencies as a deterministic inevitability. The BBC has indeed had trouble, since letting go of the original *Omnibus*, in coming up with an arts magazine programme that does not sound like a desperate attempt by a bazaar proprietor to buttonhole a topee-clad tourist in a hurry to get back to his ship. On the other hand *Arena* has been well able to keep the Corporation's conscience in that field, and on commercial television Melvyn Bragg's *The South Bank Show* eventually graduated from itty-bittiness to a format in which a single subject could be examined at full, sometimes disproportionate, length. If this latter opportunity has not always been taken well, that is less likely to be the fault of the medium than the fault of the people involved, who would perhaps be more likely to do better if they were criticised in specific terms instead of continually being told that television is the enemy of art, etc. There is a way of talking about art when you are on television, so long as you realise that time is limited. But time is limited in any medium, even the printed page.

There are limits to the amount that a television programme can contribute to the understanding of a work of art, but within those limits there is every reason to believe that at least something useful can be said, and the evidence that a television programme can provide an unbeatably immediate *introduction* to a work of art is overwhelming. For my own part, the clearest case has been provided by opera. During the course of ten years I have seen a dozen operas on television which I might have been very slow to catch up with in the opera house or even on record if I had not been won to their cause by a presentation on the little screen. Before its television presentation in late 1981, Saint-Saëns's *Samson et Dalila* was known to me only through a single aria sung by Callas on one of her anthology records of plums from the French repertoire. I might never have got round to hearing the whole thing until I was old and grey. But before the first act of the television presentation was over I was already enslaved for life, and not just because Shirley Verrett was the ideal physical incarnation of the role on top of wielding the perfect voice for it.

Opera began as a democratic art. In Italy it still is: you can stand at the back of the gods during a production of *Andrea Chenier* and watch truck drivers all around you mouthing the words along with the singers. The economic conditions of the pre-television twentieth century tended to put live opera out of reach of the wider public. Now television has democratised it again – which doesn't mean that all people will end up wanting it. But it will be there for them if they do, and I can't see how television can seriously be asked to do more for an art form than that.

It *is* asked to do more, of course. Michael Holroyd, in a long article published by the *Observer* (10 January, 1982), said that the typical television drama series tended to miss all the nuances of the written work on which it was based and often resulted in the restoration of commercial life to a book already dead from natural causes. Melvyn Bragg dealt with Holroyd's general attitude in fine style the following week, but even when you consider that the occasional series, such as the exquisite dramatic adaptation of Muriel Spark's *The Girls of Slender Means,* actually manages to have *more* nuances than the original book, nevertheless it has had to be conceded that there is some truth in the first of Holroyd's two points. The adaptation of *Brideshead Revisited,* for example, was greeted with excessive quantities of awe, gratitude and worshipful prostration. Any funeral moving at such a pace would have been dispersed by the police before it got to the graveyard. The gifted producer, Derek Granger, has accomplished a great deal during his career and all of it has been more coherent than *Brideshead Revisited*. But only the most incorrigible art-snob would have argued that it would have been better for people not to have seen it. For one thing, it made the book a best-seller all over again. We can assume that Mr Holroyd does not think it to be a book whose life should be regarded as over. We can assume, come to think of it, that Mr Holroyd does not think that about his own books either, and would be glad enough if Derek Granger rang him up tomorrow to discuss the possibility of a thirteen-episode series about Lytton Strachey. It would be interesting to see if Mr Holroyd could bring himself to say no even if Rowan Atkinson were proposed for the title role.

But operas begin, and adaptations at least half begin, in another medium. The case is less equivocal when we come to works of art, or would-be works of art, which are created directly for television. Here the critic had better be sure of his own judgment, because he will be judged upon it in his turn. From the reviews given to this volume's two predecessors I have grown used to finding out that I don't take the real achievements of television seriously – the real achievements being plays devoted to what their authors conceive of as the decaying social fabric of contemporary Britain. On the other hand I take such meretricious, commercially motivated travesties as *Holocaust* far too seriously. If I may be permitted the indulgence of a cross-reference to myself, what I actually thought about *Holocaust* is recorded in *The Crystal Bucket*. What I *should* have thought about it was explained to me in *The Times Literary Supplement* by an Oxford don who disapproved of the series almost as much as Dr Steiner did. The don particularly objected to my notion that historical truths have to be vulgarised before they can be transmitted. He chose to think that I was recommending vulgarisation, instead of just regretfully stating a commonplace. He also chose to ignore that in the case of *Holocaust* the historical truth *was* transmitted, to the people of West Germany, with a degree of success that nobody would have dared predict. A proposed statute of limitations on Nazi war crimes was staved off as a direct result of the programme's effect on public opinion. None of this means that *Holocaust* was a model of artistic integrity. (Although it demonstrated, among the clumsily managed dramatic foreshortenings, a much more detailed and sensitive awareness of the historical facts than most of its detractors proved capable of appreciating, but let that pass.). What it does mean, however, is that *Holocaust* was effective on at least one level – the very level on which television is so often accused of being ineffective, the level where the memory of political experience is preserved and delivered to our successors in some intelligible form. You might assume that such a point would, in this context, be thought of as crucial by a serious academic critic writing in a reputable literary weekly. But it is easier to get on a high horse, especially if your pride depends on believing that only an intellectual can understand genocide. Not even Dr Steiner, who knows a lot about the subject, can quite divest himself of the idea that the annihilation of the European Jews is a tragedy impossible for ordinary mortals to imagine in its essence. Yet the undoubted fact that its scale makes it hard to grasp does not make it impossible to imagine in its essence. Anybody can imagine it in its essence. Its essence is the massacre of the innocent. All you have to imagine is having your children taken away from you and killed. *Holocaust* caught something of that in dramatic form, passed it on to a lot of people who did not know much about it, and moved them. To assume that they were the kind of people not worth moving was to assume a lot – but it was an assumption, I noted with interest, that many riders of high horses made.

In the last ten years I have spent a lot of time looking at programmes about the Nazi era and comparing them with what I have learned from other sources. I can appreciate that *Holocaust* is outpointed for finesse by Arthur Miller's *Playing for Time* (reviewed in this volume, 18 January, 1981) and that both are left looking histrionic by Resnais's documentary *Nuit et brouillard* – which in its turn is not invulnerable to the charge of being unequal to the event. But as well as the issue of the work of art being equal to the event, there is the issue of how the event is to be brought home, in at least some of its importance, to those who know little about it and less about art. It is not wholly an aesthetic issue. Nor, on the other hand, is it merely a sociological issue. It is a cultural issue, taking place in the contentious area where art and politics must be talked about together. To my mind it is the most serious issue that television raises. There is some prestige to be won by pointing out how the original works of art produced by the box are very few and that even those are not up to much. But to see the originality and truth in what was never meant to be art at all is the television critic's real task. To see the inadequacy and bogusness of much that claims the status of quality is the same task from a different aspect. The literary critic, or the critic of any other specific form of artistic expression, may detach himself from the world for as long as the work of art he is contemplating appears to do the same. But the television critic is dealing with the world itself and can no more get free of it than jump up into his own arms. He must judge everything he sees against what he knows the world to be, while never forgetting that what he sees is helping to make him the person who does the knowing.

But nobody ever set out to write the script for a television series with the intention of blocking a proposed West German statute of limitations on Nazi crimes. If he had, it probably wouldn't have happened. The effect we want is seldom the effect we get. Concerned students of television have long worried about how the image of the police as projected on the little screen might affect the police force's conception of itself and the people's attitude towards law and order. When I started as a critic, a son of *Z Cars* called *Softly, Softly* was still portraying the police as incorruptible paragons, only one degree more shop-soiled than Dixon of Dock Green. In the course of the decade, the image roughened, by way of *The Sweeney*, all the way to *Law and Order*, in which police corruption was taken for granted. Then *Juliet Bravo* put the clock back to Dixon in skirts. Pundits who think they know all about the rough side of life tell us that *Law and Order* was the show closest to reality. Not a few of these pundits live in Barnes or Putney, where Dixon and Juliet Bravo are either on the beat or will turn up in a Panda car at the first sign of trouble. The likelihood seems to be that the nice areas are full of nice policemen, the nasty ones are full of nasty ones, and that the demography of British privilege and deprivation has very little to do with television programmes. There are some subjects about which you can tell the truth until your voice gives out and see nothing for your trouble.

On the other hand, you can never be sure that telling the truth won't have an effect, sometimes a profound one. Feminism in Italy started as a component of the radical theoretical discussion which goes on perpetually over the people's heads. But when feminism came to dominate the women's magazines such as *Grazia* and *Amica* it changed the way of life of a whole country in remarkably short order, and with unquestionably beneficial effect. Popular forms of communication can be regarded as passive only by the kind of analyst who is himself asleep. In any free society they are permanently full of information about changes getting ready to happen. Television, especially, is teeming with relevant signals. But you must learn when and where to look. When I came to television criticism it was big news if the BBC appointed a female newsreader. Later it was even bigger news when ITV did the same, because the Fleet Street tabloids (already on a survival diet of television's leftovers) could endlessly cobble stories about what Angela had that Anna hadn't and vice versa. As I leave the job there are half a dozen female newsreaders and the latest recruits take up the post without any fuss at all. To that extent feminism might appear to have won a victory. But it might equally have been a victory for tokenism, and tokenism is not always the best indicator of real developments. The true sign of feminism's triumph on television has been the much more recent, and probably irreversible, rise to prominence of the women comedians. They are there by the right of a much more formidable social law than mere tokenism. They are there because of the law of supply and demand.

The same applies in the case of racial minorities. It is no reflection on Trevor McDonald – whose summaries of the Polish crisis for ITN were models of the craft – to say that the news programmes could go on appointing people with black skins to a point well beyond positive discrimination and still prove nothing except a wish to be just. But when a black comedian on *OTT* sings a bad-taste, talking blues version of Trevor McDonald reading the news then a real change has occurred. Probably that was the secret reason why *OTT* aroused so much critical hatred, with fond memories of *TW3* being invoked to ward off the interloper. Only briefly an innovation and all too soon an institution, *TW3* attacked, or pretended to attack, everything that was recognisable about British life. *OTT* shows you what you don't recognise, or perhaps do but don't want to. Where did these people come from? Hardly anybody on the programme seems able to tell an adverb from an adjective. And they're all so *young*.

Which is the cue for an incipient oldster to pack his gear. George Sanders suicided when he found himself making the same films again. By now, because of television's high burn-out rate, there is a whole new generation of programme makers eagerly coming up with fresh ideas that I recognise in every detail. I suppose that if I were sufficiently professional I would be able to give a pristine response twice. But I have never thought of television criticism as a career. It is the sort of thing one goes into with a whole heart but not for one's whole life. Shaw said that three years as a theatre critic was the maximum before insanity set in – the implication being that anyone who lasted longer than that was too dull to be unbalanced by his nightly ordeal. Shaw also limited his turn as a music critic to about the same span of time. From his few years of criticising music and theatre in London came the six volumes of the Standard Edition which constitute the greatest critical achievement in the English language. He did it all while on the way through to doing something else.

Kenneth Tynan, in the theatrical field the nearest we have so far seen to being Shaw's critical successor, felt the same. He was not a placeman. He did not love criticism as a career: he loved the theatre, which he thought was life. In the introduction to *Visions Before Midnight* I told the story, suitably dramatised to make my part in it less dull, of how Tynan placed the idea in my head that the presumptuousness of publishing a television column in book form was the very reason why it should be done. That was how I began, and if he wasn't exactly at my shoulder as I wrote, he was certainly in my mind, just as he was in the mind of every other critic in Fleet Street who aspired to something better than mere hack work. Somewhere in the middle of the following decade Tynan asked me to collaborate in a theatrical venture based on Willy Donaldson's *Both the Ladies and the Gentlemen*. I would write it and Tynan would produce it. The project foundered when we discovered that our disagreement about the political role of sexual liberty was fundamental. I thought it had no political role and Tynan thought it was the gunpowder of social revolution. But the joint enterprise fell apart in the nicest possible way. If he thought I was hide-bound he didn't say so. He was also generously ready to turn a deaf ear when I lectured him in print about his defection from the critical task. We usually want our mentors to go on being what we first admired them for, and neglect to realise that if they had always done what their admirers wanted they would never have done anything to admire. Tynan understood all this very well and customarily forgave his emulators their savagery. Perhaps he was just secure in the knowledge that he could write better than anybody. At any rate, he was always hospitable, always himself, always there: immortal already but handily still alive, so that you could drop in for tea.

Then he got so sick in the lungs he had to move to California. In the summer of 1979 I was visiting Los Angeles and the Tynans asked me to lunch at their house in Coldwater Canyon. I went there by cab from where I was staying in the Hollywood Hills. In the Raymond Chandler novels the canyons were dark places where Philip Marlowe got sapped at night. Nowadays they are prime real estate and all the trees belong individually to the ranch houses that crouch expensively among them. At the Tynans' house, just off the main road through the canyon, lunch was a fruit and vegetable salad served at a table out in the brilliant sunlight. Tynan asked me if I had thought of doing more television and less criticism. I said I had. He said, in the self-examining way which some people misinterpreted as defensive, that those who had always badgered him to go back to theatre criticism had never realised that he would not have been the critic he was if he could have contemplated doing nothing else for ever.

When Tynan left theatre criticism it was to go further into the theatre. He took his critical sense with him and it made him what he was as a dramaturge. Some people thought he would have done even better in that role if he had been more critical and less easily excited by the stage, but they wanted a lot, since the capacity to be excited is the first requirement of any critic of anything – although ideally it should be followed as closely as possible by the second requirement, the ability to collect one's thoughts. Once, when directing a Footlights revue on the Edinburgh Fringe in the late 1960s, I had read Tynan's first book *He That Plays the King* night after night, wondering how to make what was happening on stage half as thrilling as what the prodigious young critic had made happen in print. 'This is a book of enthusiasms,' he said in the preface to that most dazzling of all first volumes, 'written . . . out of an almost limitless capacity for admiration.' In the last days of his life he was still like that. I can remember eating a lot more than my fair share of the melon. Tynan ate nothing but smoked instead – the very thing he was supposed not to do. We were talking about Hemingway and whether success had ruined him. I mentioned what Dwight Macdonald had said on the subject in *Against the American Grain*. Tynan said that it was better to go and fish for big game than to sit in New York like Dwight Macdonald, reviewing other people's books. He went inside and instantly emerged with an anthology of Hemingway's fugitive prose. He read a glittering passage about how the Gulf Stream is so clear that it soon absorbs whatever trash and offal is dumped into it. The passage was from a pre-war article published in *Esquire*. Therefore the stylistic purity Tynan was praising counted as early work. But to score such a small point did not obviate the larger issue. There was a lot in what Tynan was saying. Better, when the right time came, to be doing one's own work than taking in other people's washing.

Tynan had helped give me the courage to start and now he was helping give me the courage to stop. From that hour in the canyon, under the hot sun, it was only a matter of choosing the right day to pack it in. I can remember clearly how the thought occurred, and how I mentally cursed myself even at the time for thinking of my own concerns instead of his fate. Because no matter how you willed it otherwise, fate was obviously on its way to meet him. The words he quoted had more resonance than you could wish. As he read out that scintillating evocation of the clear river in the sea, it was impossible not to think of what he would have given for just a few days of easy breathing. But in the bright sunlight of the canyon not even he, surely, could really believe that he was going to die quite yet. So I put off until another day the little speech that would have told him how much I had always respected his example. I hope he guessed it but experience suggests that saying these things outright works better than leaving them to be deduced. Anyway, it is too late to make the same speech now, unless this is it.

Too soon afterwards he was dead. At the memorial service in London, Tom Stoppard, characteristically word perfect, spoke for us all. 'Ken', he said, 'was part of the luck we had.' He was certainly part of mine. Apart from a misguided assumption that I would be keen to meet Jeff Thomson and Dennis Lillee, he had the knack of reading my mind. He could do that for a lot of people. It was because he took them as seriously as they took themselves. He flatteringly assumed that one was a critic for the same reason he had been a critic: out of the impulse to excel, to give what he called a high-definition performance. He thought that such an impulse was a kind of inspiration and that when it went – or, rather, just before it went – it was time to move on to other things.

Well, now it's time, although I shall look a precious fool if all other sources of income suddenly dry up and I have to sit down in front of the set again for another ten years' hard. That would be the only good reason for coming back. One has a sense of duty but nobody is indispensable. There were good television critics before I got there, the number has grown in my time, and as I take my leave the woods are full of them, all leaning forward and scribbling notes, with their faces lit up by that spectral glow. Unless brain fever kills them all off overnight, we veterans need never return. So there are no excuses left for not making one's own programmes instead of sprinkling Ajax on other people's. When the domestic VCR machine arrived, the last cop-out was gone. Until recently, the serious writer was always able to say that writing for television was the same as relieving himself down the sink. The use of videotape by the television companies should have changed all that but the BBC still somehow managed to wipe its stockpile of plays by Harold Pinter and other names almost as illustrious, thereby convincing everyone all over again that to write for television was to write in water. Nowadays, however, the matter is no longer in the hands of the television companies. The people at home can store anything they like the look of. Not only will you reach the supposedly anonymous millions, but what you say will be preserved by the happy few. If, of course, they like it. The fact that you might actually be judged on your merits is the ineradicable deterrent. But it was always that.

If people don't like you, they can always switch you off. To that extent, they are all critics. What really scares those deep thinkers who cherish theories about the alienated masses is the possibility that the masses might be composed of individuals. A truly popular medium such as television will always, provided it is not artificially restricted, make this possibility seem more likely instead of less. Hence the fear among those harbouring delusions of superiority: because if the anonymous masses prove to be nothing except a convenient hypothesis then the theorist about mass psychology is out of business, and the aspiring tyrant is reduced to being what he can least bear – one voice among many.

GLUED
TO THE BOX

All the Anthonys

Rather less trite and even more expensive than his epic documentary drama about Churchill, Ian Curteis's *Suez* (BBC1) was an epic documentary drama about Sir Anthony Eden. It added to one's growing impression that recent British history has tended to resemble a not very inspired epic documentary drama.

Somewhere in the early 1950s, it is the end of the line for the British in the Middle East. The writing is on the wall, and it is in Arabic. Glubb Pasha is pwetty angwy at the pewemptowy manner in which he is thwown out of Jordan. One strives to sympathise, but can't help noting that this understandable fit of pique is emanating from an actor who is pretending to have a speech impediment while balancing a tea-towel on his head. No doubt the original Glubb Pasha had a speech impediment which the actor is only copying, but while you are admiring the accuracy of the details it is impossible not to notice a certain cartoon-like simplicity in the general drift.

Back in London, Eden is not well. 'We wed in the papers in Jordan,' says a man with a red face, 'that he'd been pwetty ill.' Straight away you recognise the speaker. It is Glubb Pasha without his tea-towel! Unfortunately Glubb Pasha soon fades back into history. From now on it will be harder to match up the actors with their originals.

Even though he looks more like Harold Macmillan, you can tell Michael Gough is supposed to be Anthony Eden. Always at the centre of the stage, he is addressed either as 'Prime Minister' or 'Anthony'. Thus it is usually possible to pick him out, even when he starts calling other people 'Anthony' in his turn.

Anthony Eden has an assistant called Anthony Nutting and there is at least one other Anthony in the Cabinet. Anthonys are coming out of the woodwork. This is one way of telling that you are watching an epic documentary drama about real life, instead of a play. In a play all the people have different names, with a maximum of one Anthony to any given cast.

So 'Anthony' is most often Eden. But who is 'Bobbity'? When

the Anthony who is usually Eden calls someone Bobbity, one searches the screen desperately for an actor who might conceivably be impersonating the character thus dubbed. Meanwhile the plot is advancing. It does this by means of old newsreel clips and doomy voice-overs. '5.00 pm. The Paris Bourse closes.' Nasser nationalises the Canal. Eden thinks Nasser is Hitler, but we know he is Robert Stephens. Blacked up with dubbin, Stephens shrieks defiance at the British.

Yet Mr Curteis, to do him justice, made the essential points. Eden had no legal justification whatsoever for launching the Suez adventure. On top of that, he had misjudged Britain's real strength entirely. Piling Pelion on Ossa, he handed the Soviet Union a moral advantage, which they were able to exploit when crushing the Hungarian rebellion. Eden's fabled statesmanlike qualities were left looking questionable, even though no reference was made to his disastrous post-war initiative by which many thousands of Soviet nationals were shipped home to be massacred. Eden made *that* blunder with his gall-bladder still reasonably healthy. By the time of Suez he was, apparently, a cot-case.

How did Eden, who had been right about Hitler, get everything so wrong later? Those fond of theorising about the British ruling class could put it down to insularity. People who call each other Bobbity and assume that Egyptians will run away are perhaps unusually prone to attacking the wrong canal. But it seems more likely that *any* ruling class becomes insulated, simply because it rules. Habitual power is a bad vantage point.

Suez was not the last gasp of the British Empire, which was already dead. It was the moment when even Britain's rulers caught up with the truth about their country's reduced capacity to influence events by force. They learned the hard way and might possibly have taken the whole world down the drain with them if Eisenhower had not known what to do. Eisenhower was no great visionary but he was, at least, a realist, especially about modern war.

The one possibility Mr Curteis did not cover was that the Soviet Union, thanks to Philby and the rest of the lads, knew about the whole Suez plan from the day of its inception and made their own preparations accordingly. But to deal with that subject in dramatic form you would need a big enough sense of humour to avoid unintentional farce, since all your leading characters would be either fools or spies. In real life this might well have been true, but to make it convincing as fiction would take a sure touch with language. Mr Curteis gives his British characters American things to say and vice versa. He has a tin ear. But he can cook up a watchable epic documentary drama.

The difference between documentary drama and drama is the difference between ordinary intelligence and that unfathomable combination of intelligence and intuition which the literary critics call sensibility. *Testament of Youth* (BBC2) is drama. It is based on history, just like *Suez*, but it lives an independent life. By now four episodes have gone by. I have watched each of them twice and never ceased to marvel at the writing, directing and acting.

Last week Vera Brittain, played by Cheryl Campbell, was suddenly joined by another nurse of even more heroic stature, one Sister Milroy, played by Frances Tomelty in a high-spirited, long-striding style that recalled a Homeric goddess stepping down a mountain. One of the marks of a living drama is that a new principal character can enter at a late stage without unbalancing the story. Another mark is that it can display any amount of frankness without seeming sensational. In the latest episode mustard-gas victims were carried in, coughing yellow froth. Vera got a telegram announcing her brother's death. That makes it a clean sweep: all the men in her life are gone.

Nancy (BBC2) portrayed Lady Astor as a sacred monster. Here was yet another opportunity for those fond of theorising about the British ruling class to do their stuff. Like Vera Brittain, Lady Astor saw a lot of ruined young men during the First World War. It made an appeaser out of her, but there is no reason to think she admired dictators. She thought that if Ribbentrop were invited to Cliveden and allowed to win at musical chairs then Hitler would moderate his demands. Plainly, like many instinctively virtuous people, she was an innocent. Equally plainly, everyone who knew her misses her like mad.

2 December, 1979

Quite slim indeed

As if in answer to a madman's prayer, *Ski Sunday* (BBC1) was back, fronted as ever by the indispensable David Vine. 'Look at *that*!' cried David. 'Oogh! Aagh! Ease coming down the ill!'

The hill he was coming down was at Val d'Isère. The event being the downhill, the emphasis was on speed, courage and danger. David verbally evoked these concepts for the benefit of those of us who were unable to deduce them from the visual information amassed on the screen. 'Augh! You wouldn't! Ease going into the bend . . . Ease gone!' Gallantly providing David with the appropriate provocation to eloquence, a condom-clad competitor got his skis crossed at 100 m.p.h. and rammed the snow with his helmet.

The women go slower than the men but not much. One feels protective when they crash, especially since the protectives they are wearing do not look all that protective. Luckily the British girls, in sharp contrast to their continental counterparts, move at a sedate pace. Valentina Iliffe is our star. She has been canned from the British team for breaking training. 'A lot of talk in the British camp about this,' opined David, as Valentina finished in twenty-seventh position, five seconds behind the leaders. Apparently the rest of our girls are even more stately in their progress, so clearly they are in no peril.

The big sporting occasion of the week was *Sports Review of 1979* (BBC1), during which the British Sportsman of the Year was chosen. For weeks the question had been asked: who can beat Sebastian Coe? (Known to his admirers as Seb, Sebastian is temporarily immortal for holding several world records at once.) The *Radio Times* ran a long article about the programme, asking: who can beat Sebastian Coe? People throughout the sporting world, it was plain, had been forming agitated huddles to ask: who can beat Sebastian Coe? In the event it was no surprise that Sebastian Coe won the trophy. Only Kevin Keegan looked mildly startled, possibly at his own generosity in flying all the way from Germany just to come third.

Awarded during the same programme, the trophy for International Sportsman of the Year went to Bjorn Borg. Borg, Frank Bough reminded us, had won Wimbledon four times. 'Can you make it five?' asked Frank. 'Why not?' Borg replied. Nastase handed Borg the trophy. 'Is a nice trophy, you know?' Borg nodded politely, as if another trophy were just what he wanted.

Borg is always nice, knowing that he will never be resented for his wealth as long as he stays shy. Meanwhile the Scots sprinter Alan Wells is being hounded about his expenses at the Highland Games. Perhaps he fiddled an extra haggis at breakfast. There is something very British about the possibility that Wells might lose his amateur status and thus miss next year's Olympics in the Soviet Union – whose every athlete is a full-time professional.

Appearing in the World Gymnastics Championships at Fort Worth, the Romanian girl gymnasts showed up on *Sportsnight* (BBC1) as unlovely streaks of gristle and sinew. 'Remarkable how slim the Romanian girls are,' mused Ron Pickering and/or Alan Weeks. 'Quite slim indeed.' Poor, grim little darlings, they looked anorexic. Obviously the general idea is to keep mass to a minimum, so that the girls can achieve speed without momentum. The tricks are stunning, but the physical cost is high. Breasts look exactly like shoulder blades. By now Nelli Kim, who won a stack of gold medals for the Soviet Union, is almost an anachronism, being in possession of a detectable bottom.

As well as for sport, it was a big week for Shakespeare. Latest in the Beeb's Bardathon, *Henry IV, Part I* (BBC2) was good, solid, worthy stuff, proceeding staunchly between the lower levels of excitement and the upper strata of tedium. Interiors tended towards straw-on-the-floor naturalism, an effect not much helped by the studio floor-cloth. More straw or less cloth would have taken care of that, but some of the costumes sat with incurable stiffness on the people inside them.

One of the people inside them was Jon Finch, who played the King. The King had a thing going with his gloves. The gloves were grey and the King kept fiddling with them as if to find out whether they were real velvet. The odds are almost overwhelming that they weren't. The trouble with low-budget naturalism is that it never looks natural. Imagination is a better bet, but inevitably it is in short supply.

The exteriors, perforce, had to be scamped a bit, which meant that the cameras had to move in close on the actors and leave the background to suggest itself. As usually happens, the whole affair instantly became more convincing. The night scenes before the battle of Shrewsbury looked particularly fine. The actors wore their colours and metals with a swagger. Hal (David Gwillim) and Hotspur (Tim Pigott-Smith) had at each other loudly. Clive Swift, playing Worcester, scored points by keeping relatively quiet.

Stumbling about the battlefield in a tin hat, Falstaff cut a believably preposterous figure. Anthony Quayle was necessarily competing with Orson Welles's portrayal in *Chimes at Midnight*, but came out of the contest well. He was also competing with George Melly, who fronted the accompanying episode of *Shakespeare in Perspective* (BBC2). Puffing and blowing, with mighty consumption of ale, Melly conjured the great heart and chicken liver of his rotund predecessor. He also quoted the odd Shakespearean line, showing that he could tell a pentameter from a pint pot. Singers are nearly always good at bringing out the rhythm of blank verse.

Actors nearly always aren't. There are notable exceptions, but as a general rule it can be assumed that even the best actor will bring everything out of a blank verse line except its five pulses. Since Shakespeare's blank verse has so much in it anyway, it might seem churlish to want rhythm too, but there is such a thing as being inundated with the superfluous while remaining starved of the necessary. This, I thought, was the central issue of a fascinating *South Bank Show* (LWT) featuring the Royal Shakespeare Company at work on the technique of verse speaking.

The first of two programmes to be devoted to this subject, here was a show you could get your mind into. Trevor Nunn was the man in charge. As thoughtful as he is gifted, Nunn is not a man to disagree with lightly. Backed up by John Barton, who provides the scholarship, Nunn took his actors through speeches and sonnets. Lines were pointed until every drop of double meaning stood out like sweat on a navvy's forehead. Yet in the end Alan Howard's was the voice that thrilled. I have seen him only once in the theatre, playing Coriolanus as an Alternative Miss World. But he has a knack for Shakespeare's rhythm – the rhythm that holds melody together.

16 December, 1979

St Vitus's gospel

'It could be argued,' argued Kenneth Griffith while fronting his programme *A Famous Journey* (Thames), 'that I am out of my mind.' But viewers familiar with Kenneth's mannerisms knew that he was merely being intense.

During the course of his career as a maker of documentaries, this compact but variously gifted Welsh actor has been intense about such figures as Napoleon and Cecil Rhodes. Now he was after even bigger game – Jesus Christ. Retracing the journey of the Magi, Kenneth landed in Iran. Immediately he was thrown out. As usual Kenneth interpreted this rejection as an Establishment plot. Kenneth is convinced that the Establishment, everywhere, is out to get him, stifle his voice, ban his programmes, etc. 'I certainly have automatic high velocity RIFLES!' he shouted sarcastically.

Nothing daunted, Kenneth joined the Magi's trail at another point. Ruins of ancient cities trembled in the heat. A stage Welshman darting abruptly out of doorways, Kenneth blended obtrusively into the scenery. He has a high visibility factor, mainly because he is incapable of either just standing there when he is standing there or just walking when he is walking. Standing there, he drops into a crouch, feet splayed, arms loosely gesticulating, eyes popping, teeth bared in a vulpine snarl. Walking, he makes sudden appearances over the tops of small hills.

Kenneth can ask you the time in a way that makes you wonder how he would play Richard III, so it can be imagined that when discussing Jesus he was seldom guilty of underplaying a scene. 'Jesus', he whimpered, ramming his hands deep into his pockets and staring sideways into the camera, 'was . . . a Jew.' In possession of this and much similar knowledge that the Establishment would like to ban, Kenneth kept moving through the desert, aiming the occasional slow karate chop at a rock. 'Of course all truth', he confided to the camera and a surrounding mountain range, 'is dangerous to all Establishments.' But even while saying this he was positioning himself on top of a particularly inviting mountain.

Kenneth's version of the Sermon on the Mount was delivered to all points of the compass. Spinning, jerking, ducking and weaving, he made you realise just how it was that Jesus attracted so much attention. As the son of a Nazarene carpenter Jesus would have remained unknown. It was by carrying on like a balding Taff actor with St Vitus's dance that he got his message across. 'Blessed are the MEEK!' shrieked Kenneth, climaxing a programme to which I unhesitatingly award, for the second time in the history of this column, that most rarely conferred of all television trophies, the Tin Bum of Rangoon.

The rules for appearing on television are all don'ts. The first thing you don't do is project. A close-up makes the performer's head about the same size as it would be in real life, so he should use no more emphasis and gesture than it takes to make a point across a small living room. As Kenneth Griffith has inadvertently proved, if you talk any louder than that you instantly become inaudible, while every meaningful gesture simply renders your message more meaningless.

On television the spectacular wide shot yields rapidly diminishing returns. The television version of Trevor Nunn's production of *Antony and Cleopatra* was an important event because it concentrated on close-ups and suggested the scenery. In all television productions of classic drama which have since been mounted, good can be divided from bad according to whether or not they learned that lesson. Most of the productions in the BBC's Bardathon have at least half-learned it, and so attained the level, if not of inspiration, then of reasonably satisfactory humdrum. There has so far been no attempt to equal, for instance, the Brian Large production of Verdi's *Macbeth*, an earlier and very strong contender for the Tin Bum.

Henry IV, Part 2 (BBC2) was like the previous week's *Henry IV, Part 1*. It was never worse than dull and at its best gave you a straightforward presentation of the characters in their full complexity, with no tricks of interpretation. In other words, the writing was allowed to do most of the work. The actors delivered it the same way it had been composed, as blank verse. Playing Hal, David Gwillim had the advantage of a face out of a Renaissance portrait, but more importantly he had an ear for rhythm. When Hal becomes the King his words put on gravity as surely as his shoulders put on ermine. Reading out what's there is not the only thing the actor must do, but it's certainly the first thing, and Gwillim did it well. 'How ill white hairs become a fool and jester.' Falstaff (a quietly excellent impersonation by Anthony Quayle) was crushed.

As for the second part of the *South Bank Show* (LWT) devoted to the RSC's technique of verse-speaking, it continued the gripping story unfolded in the first part, but did not always carry conviction. Ian McKellen gave a thoughtful account of how he prepared his rendition of 'Tomorrow and tomorrow and tomorrow' in *Macbeth*. The number and subtlety of the points he set himself to bring out stunned the mind. But the finished product, though worthy of respect, was intelligible as everything except verse.

It was notable, in this respect, that Alan Howard, preparing one of Achilles's speeches in *Troilus and Cressida*, carefully rejected most of the advice he was given and concentrated on picking out the driving impulse of the verse, which thereupon yielded up its meaning of its own accord – the exact effect Shakespeare had in mind when he wrote it that way in the first place.

On *World of Sport* (LWT) American trucks slowly raced while the commentators flogged excitement into the proceedings by saying things like 'Some race!' Variations on this theme were 'Talk about racing! Talk about your wheel to wheel!' and 'Really *driving* those trucks!' The man who won leaned out of his cab to say, 'I just thank the good Lord that we were able to pull this thing off.' Another truck, in which the good Lord was evidently less interested, fell apart.

This year's instalment of the *World Disco Dancing Championship* (Thames) was better value. Not even the zombie commentating of David Hamilton and Pete Gordeno ('How about that!' 'Fantastic!' 'Something else!' etc.) could blunt the excitement. Setsuo Yamakuni, a Hiroshima car-parts salesman with interests in the martial arts, represented Japan. He favoured suicidal dives over his own right shoulder. Lydia Loo from Malaysia was almost as interesting as her name. But Julie Brown of the UK very properly took first prize.

Lynn Seymour was among the judges and must have been patriotically delighted by Julie's inventive energy. Wearing pants sticking out at the side as if she had winged thighs, Julie bounced around doing kill-a-bee kicks in double-time and looking as if she was about to burst with joy. You would have had to be dead not to be thrilled to bits by her.

23 December, 1979

Santa and the Seed

I F Santa was wondering what entertainment he was missing out on as he pursued his annual giant slalom through the television aerials, the answer was that he wasn't missing much. When all you've got to watch on Christmas Eve is *The Tamarind Seed* (Thames) you might as well be driving reindeer.

The Tamarind Seed was ITV's big movie on the magic night, playing opposite *The Go-Between* (BBC1), a Pinter–Losey collaboration of no small merit, but which I had seen already. Presumably Santa had too, but he had something else to do with his time. The rest of us had to settle for Julie Andrews, Omar Sharif, and whatever was signified by the said seed. Very believably playing an English secretary, Julie fell for Omar, who had been cast as a Russian spy because there was no role available as a date-picker.

Every day of the festive season the channels attempted to clobber each other with old movies. It was the viewer who ended up stunned, especially if he had seen them all before. Some of them, especially the Gene Kelly musicals, gained from a second or third viewing. *Cleopatra* (BBC2) was spread over two days, like a small golf tournament. The first half of the film once again revealed itself to be pretty good, mainly because Rex Harrison is highly credible as Julius Caesar and the part is well written. The second half revealed itself to be even worse than one remembered, there being nothing except Richard Burton's concussed Mark Antony to distract your attention from what Elizabeth Taylor gets up to in her doomed attempt to incarnate the title role.

There was more Rome in *Ben-Hur* (Thames), an epic film which people tend to think of as a chariot race wrapped in miles of spare celluloid, but which has in fact a lot to offer the discerning viewer.

Ben-Hur's mother and sister become lepers. Ben himself does time as a galley slave. Eyeing the muscular Ben as he toils at the oar, Quintus Arrius (Jack Hawkins) is plainly boiling with suppressed lust. Is Quint a queer quaestor? Perhaps he is a poofter praetor, soon to become a camp consul. 'Hail Jupider!' cries Stephen Boyd, who is either playing a particularly bad Roman or else playing a Roman particularly badly. Rather than stick around for any more of this, Jesus takes the easy way out.

Richard Burton was back again in *Where Eagles Dare* (BBC1). So were the Romans, although this time they were dressed as SS officers. They had no chance against Richard. Playing a British spy dressed up as a German officer, he added to the confusion by sporting a page-boy hairstyle and giving his usual impersonation of a Welsh rugby forward who has just been told that he has been dropped from the team. Thus disguised, he was able to slip through the German lines, accompanied only by Clint Eastwood, Mary Ure and Miss Ure's hairstylist. This last interloper wasn't actually visible, but must have been there somewhere, since the lady's coiffure remained in tip-top condition even when the Germans, recovering from their amazement at Burton's appearance, started throwing grenades.

Leaving their fair companion at the beauty parlour down in the village, Richard and Clint hailed a passing cable-car and rode up to the castle in which Cleopatra and Ben-Hur were incarcerated. Could they complete their mission before the Germans forced Julie Andrews to tell them the secret of the tamarind seed? Clint shot everyone except Richard with a silenced pistol. Fighting their way back through several divisions of the German Army, our two heroes had the advantage of being equipped with real ammunition, whereas the Germans, apparently, had made the mistake of issuing their men with blanks.

Though at first it might appear to be an ordinary story about a luxury liner turning upside down and killing all its passengers except a handful of actors, *The Poseidon Adventure* (BBC1) has a solid connection with Christmas. The actors climb a Christmas tree in order to reach the floor of the inverted ballroom. I watched the film all over again just to count the number of times that Gene Hackman assisted the girl with the pretty behind by holding her hand, putting a protective arm around her shoulders, firmly gripping her waist, or all three simultaneously. He copped 1,247 separate feels.

Staying natural takes effort. In a way it is to the Beatles' credit that they became less and less bearable on screen. To stay as sweet as they were would have taken a great deal of artifice. Instead they did the honest thing and gave way to the 1960s fashion for self-discovery, ending up with selves no more interesting than anybody else's. The before-and-after effect was cruelly on show during the Christmas season, since the BBC screened all the Beatles films right through to *Let It Be* (BBC2). The first films bubbled with high spirits and good songs. The last was a sullen, portentous compendium dogged by the baleful presence of Yoko Ono.

But not every programme was a movie. *My Fair Lady* (BBC2) should not have stopped the alert viewer watching *The Knowledge* (Thames), a play by Jack Rosenthal about what taxi-drivers have to learn before they get their badge. What they have to learn is London. It drives some of them crazy. I know this because some of them have driven me crazy telling me about it. Nigel Hawthorne did a bravura number as the examiner who quizzed would-be drivers on the Knowledge, testing their nerve by laughing hysterically during their answers, while doing violent calisthenics with an inhaler jammed up his nose. Jonathan Lynn, Maureen Lipman and other members of Rosenthal's salt-beef stock company were also present. Some of the acting was nearly as unsubtle as some of the writing but the thing worked.

Christmas with Eric and Ernie (Thames) was opposite the Beeb's blockbuster Christmas Day movie *The Sting* (BBC1), but it was well worth watching, even though they did little that was new. David Frost interviewed them. Obviously Frost's aim is to speak a language equally unintelligible on both sides of the Atlantic, but for the moment it is possible to understand him, especially if your wits are as quick as Eric's. There was an old ATV clip showing Eric and Ernie in full dance – a laugh a second. Des O'Connor turned up to receive the benefit of his usual million pounds' worth of free publicity. Getting goosed by Eric and Ernie is the best thing that ever happened to him and he is smart enough to be grateful.

On *The Dick Cavett Magic Show* (BBC2) Cavett introduced his voluptuous girl assistant as Retired Rear Admiral Harvey S.

Beeswanger, USN, master of disguise. Interviewed by *Parkinson* (BBC1), Tommy Cooper was still distraught after losing £200 on a horse. (He backed the horse at twenty to one and it came in at twenty past four.)

Cooper also made an appearance on *This Is Your Life* (Thames), helping pay tribute to Eric Sykes. Cooper made an entrance that showed every sign of going on all night. Sykes feigned apprehension while Spike Milligan wept with laughter in the wings. It was a gathering of the giants, among whom Eamonn stood bemused, nervously clutching his book. For a few minutes there was enough good will about to make it feel like Christmas.

30 December, 1979

Scoop it!

I F you are a dog or a dog's owner, you'll already be watching *Training Dogs the Woodhouse Way* (BBC2). But those who are neither of those things shouldn't miss it either.

Barbara Woodhouse trains dogs by breaking the spirit of the owner. 'Get your dog *in*, Mr Bagshaw! Scoop it! HALT!' The expression on Mr Bagshaw's countenance as he weathers this tirade is pitiable to behold. His nose is dry, his eyes are wet and his ears hang sadly beside his shaking jowls. A dozen owners, each with a dog of different size, cower beside their canine escorts and silently give thanks that they are not Bagshaw. Each sweats with terror that he or she might be next.

'You were too *slow*, doctor! You've got to do it – BANG!' Thus addressed, the shattered doctor turns to his labrador for comfort. But there is no time for tears. 'Keep it up, all of you! There's a huge gap there! Forward! SIT!' in the nick of time, the owners remember that this final order is directed, not at themselves, but at their dogs. They push downwards on the rear end of their dogs. For those with tall dogs it is relatively easy, but to be in charge of a corgi at this point means that you must stoop pretty smartly, else Barbara Woodhouse will be snapping at your heels. 'Can you get down and praise your dog, Mrs Williams? FORWARD!'

Man Alive (BBC2) scrapped its scheduled programme and mounted a special debate on the Olympic Games. Since there are at least three tenable points of view on the subject, it was obvious from the start that the argument would tend to drift. Nevertheless the proceedings were illuminating. Marina Voikhanskaya, who knows exactly what happens to dissident opinion in the Soviet Union, described the process of 'cleaning' Moscow in preparation for the games. The reason for moving the children out is that 'children are spontaneous people.' Despite the lying Soviet Press, she said, if the games were withdrawn from Moscow then the people would know it was because of the invasion of Afghanistan.

This was a strong view well put. Lord Exeter, representing 'the Olympic movement', had even stronger views, but you could not say that he put them. He dumped them in your lap and left you to do what you could with them. 'I've spent my life in this movement,' he barked, as if anyone cared about that. 'We've always kept out of politics.' When faced with the argument that by being allotted to Moscow the Games had been involved in politics willy-nilly, Lord Exeter either chose not to get the point or else didn't get the point. He just stuck to his line about the purpose of sport being to 'promote the development of physical and moral qualities', as if it went without question that Brezhnev felt the same way.

So far the pro-boycott argument had the edge, but the athletes restored the balance by pointing out that it was unfair to arrange the most important fixture of their lives and then jeopardise it after they had spent irretrievable years in training. David Bedford rhetorically wondered what other action the British Government was taking.

The commentator, Ron Pickering, showing admirable forensic skill, summed up this side of the argument and carried the debate. Wherever the games were allotted, he said, political objections would always be possible. Even the suggestion that the games be given a permanent home in Greece would be open to the objection that Greece had had a repressive regime in the recent past and might well have one again.

Pickering did himself honour and restored the sound of sanity, which had been missing from this discussion ever since Mrs Thatcher took a hand in it. The Moscow Olympic Games might as well go ahead. Complaints about tainting them with politics are nonsensical, since they became fully saturated with politics from the moment they were awarded to Moscow, and indeed have been reeking with politics ever since the Soviet Union was allowed to compete.

27 January, 1980

Face your dog

SHARP-EYED correspondents have pointed out a sinister new development in that most compulsive of eerie series, *Training Dogs the Woodhouse Way* (BBC2). Some of the dog-owners have been disappearing.

It happens quietly, from one week to the next. Either because they have not come up to scratch, or because they have shown signs of rebellion, the dog-owners in question are discreetly eliminated. The process of liquidation takes place somewhere in the background, while the foreground is being dominated by the Pooch-teacher Extraordinary. 'When I say "Face your dog!" you will turn around and face her. Don't be a leg-clinger.' Not wanting to be a leg-clinger, a poor wimp with large feet wheels awkwardly to face his dog. 'Get your legs *together*!' bellows the Mutt-moulder General, doom in her eye.

Barbara Woodhouse has her commanding personality in common with Servilan, the only reason for watching the otherwise worthless *Blake's Seven* (BBC1). Played by a statuesque knockout called Jacqueline Pearce, Servilan is President and Supreme Commander of the Terran Federation. Being this, or these, she is obliged to spend an unconscionable amount of time pursuing Blake's dreary Seven through fitfully shimmering time-warps and into the awkwardly whirling vortices of low-budget black holes. 'We will attack!' she cries.

For some reason the attack never succeeds, even though Blake's Seven scarcely add up to one brain. On board their space-ship, a tasteless light-fitting known as the Liberator, they shout orders at one another while Servilan closes in. 'Give me a parallax scan of the alien craft!' 'Alien craft eclipsed at half a million spatials!' 'Parabolic orbit exit alpha four!' But even the photonscrambulator is no match for Servilan's bacterial spasm guns. Accompanied by a platoon of her myrmidons, who would look embarrassed in their hastily repainted motorcycle helmets if they were not wearing Second World War gas masks, Servilan teleports aboard.

Once again the ruthless Servilan has only to turn down her immaculately manicured thumb and Blake's rebarbative associates will be transmogrified into seven small piles of dehydrated molecules. Unfortunately Servilan is continually distracted by her irrepressible inner stirrings towards romance. Such tender feelings were meant to have been suppressed by her training as President and Supreme Commander. She zaps planets without a qualm and would gladly feed her own mother to the muff-diving molluscs of Mongo. But what really interests her is men. Why else would she be wearing that slinky white sheath evening gown with the external seams and the wired gauze whatsit erupting on one shoulder? Flaring nonsense from beyond the galaxy.

Barbara Woodhouse and Servilan got where they did by asserting themselves. So did a charming South Korean character called Mr Moon, hero of a cult called *The Moonies* (ATV). By now there are Moonies all over the world. In theory they are all members of something calling itself the Unification Church, but in practice they are simply dedicated to carrying out Moon's wishes. What those wishes might happen to be is not easy to fathom, partly because Moon talks like the leading heavy from an episode of *Batman* made in about 1946. 'Many people will die. Those who go against our movement.'

Fronting the programme, Sue Jay conjured up the gruesome spectacle of Moonies arriving in force on our shores to steal the souls of our children. There can be no doubt that the Moonies are very unpleasant. As with the Scientologists, they offer all the attractions of an organisation that is easy to join but difficult to leave. Such groups have a strong appeal for people who are simultaneously self-obsessed and deficient in real personality. But you can't legislate against inadequacy. People who want that sort of thing will find it one way or another.

The term 'brainwashing' should be reserved for cases in which there are brains to be washed. On the subject of religious cults there is always a body of expert opinion ready to prate about how people have had their brains washed. A less sentimental onlooker might reflect that nothing more elaborate has happened than the filling of a vacuum, and that if it hadn't been filled by one brand of nonsense it would have been filled by another.

There was more of the same in Andrew Carr's play *Instant Enlightenment Including VAT* (BBC1). A hectoring twerp called Max (Simon Callow) brow-beat a group of truth-seekers until they became his creatures. It was convincing but tedious, since the awful truth is that the whole subject is essentially a yawn, even when it ends in catastrophe. After the disaster in Guyana there was a concerted attempt to witter on about the dimensions of the tragedy, etc., but in fact only the children involved met a tragic fate. The adults had already suicided simply by the completeness with which they had handed over their lives to the beloved leader.

10 February, 1980

Ultimately and forever

DID you see *Liberace's Valentine Night Special* (Thames)? It was like being forcibly fed with warm peppermint creams.

Frank Sinatra gave yet another farewell performance. This time is was called *Frank Sinatra – the First Forty Years* (Thames), although really it should have been called 'Frank Sinatra – the First Four Hundred Years', since it must have taken him at least that much time to meet all those people and do all that philanthropy. The people were present to congratulate him on his decades at the top and to remind him of the philanthropy in case he had forgotten it.

The venue was Caesar's Palace in Las Vegas. It was jammed with celebrities, many of them still alive. The death rate during the course of the evening must have been fairly high, because it was obligatory to clap at every mention of Frank's outstanding qualities. During Stalin's speeches to the Praesidium the first delegate to stop clapping was routinely hauled off to be shot, but at Caesar's Palace peer-group pressure was enough to keep everybody clapping indefinitely. Even the comedians were inundated with applause, instead of being greeted with the yell of abuse that their material deserved.

Sadat and Begin both sent representatives. There could be no doubt Frank is a force for peace in the Middle East. Indeed, to hear Orson Welles tell it, Frank is practically the light of the world. Orson was clad in a black barrage balloon cleverly painted to look like a dinner jacket. He was equipped with rhetoric to match. Frank, he averred, manifests 'something of the dangerous glamour of a great bandit chieftain' who 'makes us a present of his great vulnerability'.

A cut-away to the man thus described showed that he was taking all this pretty well. But Orson wasn't finished: '. . . this complex, hugely gifted, multi-faceted human being . . . a power-house, a pussycat . . . and ultimately and forever he is undefeated.' The audience rose to Orson as it would rise to a ton and a half of hickory-roast ham.

Milton Berle confidently announced that Frank thinks of John Wayne every day and prays for him every night. Sammy Davis outdid even Dean Martin in suggesting by his manner that he knew Frank better than anybody else did. The mother of the President of the United States showed no sign of wanting to shut up. Finally only Frank himself stood a chance of saving the evening from a permanent first place in the annals of sentimental banality.

He did it with his sense of rhythm, which remains unimpaired under the hair-transplant. The lyrics came out with all the old bite and swing. He really is a great entertainer, even though all the not-so-great entertainers say he is. Being unusually public-spirited as well, he has every right to bask in glory, even to the extent of saying goodbye more often than Sarah Bernhardt. But really, aren't Americans strange? They are the new Japanese, living a life of ritual, with every evening an occasion and no one allowed to be alone.

Back at the start of the week, *The Enigma* (BBC1), adapted by Malcolm Bradbury from a story by John Fowles, was a play about a rich Tory MP who went missing. This being a work of art instead of an ordinary thriller, the mystery remained unsolved. Instead of casually watching as you might have done if the thing had been a run-of-the-mill whodunnit, you found yourself heavily committed. I, for example, when it became obvious that we were never going to find out exactly what had happened to the missing man, gave a very loud cry of 'Bloody hell!'

But there were compensations. The Special Branch man assigned to the case was granted several interviews with Nigel Hawthorne, brilliantly playing a club bore. Hawthorne was terrific with the menu and at signalling waiters. 'Interesting crowd here. Well, not today.' The MP's awful son had a marvellously intuitive and beautiful mistress, played by Barbara Kellerman. The Special Branch man ended up in bed with her, which was probably some consolation for not being allowed to solve the mystery.

As the titles rolled, we were led to believe that the missing MP might possibly have been in the ornamental lake of his country house. But nobody wanted to look, because of the embarrassment, and because the play would have then become a forgettable armchair thriller, instead of lingering in the mind as an Enigma.

Another alienated man of affairs was the hero of *Very Like a Whale* (ATV), a play by John Osborne. Alan Bates played Sir Jock Mellor, captain of industry. Sir Jock had a strange temperament for a captain of industry. He was just like a playwright. He had built himself up to wealth, a title, a divine-looking secretary/mistress and an equally divine-looking wife, played by Gemma Jones. Yet he was not happy. Something about all this material splendour left his spiritual propensities unfulfilled. Perhaps he should have been a playwright all along.

Frustrated, Sir Jock behaved abominably. He was rude to everyone he met. Among even the most intelligent playwrights, such as Pinter and Osborne, it is always taken as axiomatic that a sensitive man, when suffering from mental turmoil, will behave rudely. This is a dramatically useful convention but is the exact reverse of what happens in real life, where a sensitive man, when suffering from mental turmoil, usually behaves more politely than ever up until the moment when he keels over. In fact Osborne's heroes are less sensitive than histrionic, and Sir Jock was no exception.

Alan Bates did his best. Starring in the plays of Simon Gray has given him plenty of practice at looking sensitive, alienated and superior, like a playwright badgered by the petty concerns of ordinary people who have not studied the critical writings of F. R. Leavis. Gemma Jones was very good at being the bitchy Osborne woman who shouts, 'I haven't finished my *drink*!' I'm bound to say I was wowed by the secretary (Myra Frances). If Sir Jock still felt alienated after having his every need tended by a dish like her, he had a case of alienation that not even becoming the author of *Look Back in Anger* could have cured.

17 February, 1980

Cold gold

IN a proud week for Britain at the Winter Olympics, the BBC sports commentators were admirably restrained. Until quite near the end, of course, they had a lot to be restrained about.

Apart from Robin Cousins nobody at Lake Placid was burdened with the heavy tag of British Hope. There is no reason to be ashamed of this: Britain is a country with few mountains and, as far as I have been able to ascertain by asking around, only one ice-rink, open for training sessions before breakfast on alternate Wednesdays in January. It is something of a miracle that Cousins is up there at all. Everybody else in the British team fell into the category of gallant but doomed. Some of them fell into a lot more than that – the audience, for example. But there was no disgrace.

There was tragedy, of course. 'And that . . . is another tragedy for the British speed skaters.' While these sentiments were being uttered, a British male speed skater could be seen sliding along on his nose. In another tragedy, a British female speed skater forgot to change lanes and scythed down the only Chinese female speed skater in existence. This was also a bit of a tragedy for China, but the BBC commentators did not make much of it. They responded better to the event that really *was* a tragedy, namely the enforced withdrawal of Randy Gardner and Tai Babilonia from the pairs figure skating.

The field was left free for Rodnina and Zaitsev. Skating a bit less like a machine than usual – motherhood, we were assured, has mellowed her – Rodnina collected her umpteenth major title. She now has more gold on her sideboard than most Russians have in their teeth. I found myself admiring her at long last, after years of fretting at her lack of poetry. She is certainly an exceptional skater. But the lyricism which the Protopopovs brought to pairs skating lingers tenaciously in the memory. Whatever it was they had, Babilonia and Gardner have got it too, and I'm bound to say that I can't get enough of it.

Anyway, Gardner came out for the warm-up and fell down. The contest was over before it began. Babilonia very understandably burst into tears. She looks terrific even doing that, but it was small compensation. On the other hand Annemarie Moser-Proell's dreams came true. In the women's downhill she creamed the opposition with an authority that left even David Vine bereft of speech.

So it went on, with the giants winning and everybody else taking part. The women's luge was another tragedy for Britain. 'What a disappointment for Avril Walker!' The luge is pretty tricky any-way, since you have to lie on your back standing to attention with your head pointing up the hill while you are travelling very rapidly down it. Avril made things even harder for herself by falling off her luge. When it popped out from underneath her you got a chance to see what a luge looks like. It looks like an intra-uterine contraceptive device in an early stage of development.

All this time the BBC commentators had been doing their best to stay calm about Robin Cousins. They rarely mentioned him more than a thousand times a night. There were only a few hundred interviews with his parents, while whole hours went by without Robin himself being called to the camera. When he did speak, it was with a noticeable American accent – an indication that his gift has been brought to flower somewhere else than here. Nevertheless he is still one of us.

Finally it was the big night, or in our case the big early morning, since by the time they came out to skate on the East Coast it was time to be making your hot chocolate in London. Cousins went into the free skating considerably behind Jan Hoffmann of East Germany. Hoffmann has a mouth like a mako shark and the kind of top lip which, even after he has shaved it, still looks as if it is adorned with a moustache. Also it has by now become obvious that the only way he will ever get his hands on a good-looking costume is to defect. But he is a demon for technical merit. Cousins, we were constantly reminded, was up against it.

'Now for the most important moments of the 1980 Winter Games for Great Britain!' cried David Coleman, anchoring from London. Far away in Lake Placid, Cousins looked relaxed. 'He's looking really, really loose and relaxed,' said Alan Weeks. A man called Emric said, 'I always was a big fan from Robin Cousins.' At this point Alan spotted Robin's parents. 'His mum and dad are sitting in the front row . . . it must be a terrific thrill for them to see their son perhaps in a position of winning a gold medal.' There was no arguing with that, but by this time the potential champion was on the ice. 'There by the barrier . . . that's where he will set out from in his quest for the gold medal.'

Cousins skated, and for a few minutes sport crossed the uncertain border that it shares with art. Great bullfighters are supposed to link their passes with the cape into a flowing sequence which the appropriately sensitive spectator will experience as a unity, although what the bull thinks of it is another question. Great figure skaters do the same thing. Cousins has something of the melancholy grace once exemplified by Toller Cranston, the unsung hero of men's figure skating in recent times. But more importantly he is the culmination of the long line of artist sportsmen – all of them pupils of Carlo Fassi – which leads back through John Curry to Peggy Fleming, the first skater to make an 'artistic impression' that you went on seeing after you closed your eyes.

Cousins muffed a triple, but otherwise got everything right. Hoffmann came on in a costume that was merely dreary, instead of hideous like the one he had worn in the short programme. (Those readers who have never been to the Soviet Union can get some idea of the prevailing standards of dress from the fact that Muscovites regard East Berlin as a fashion centre.) But Hoffmann knocked off the triples with the awesome precision of a fighter pilot swatting flies. He made the same artistic impression as a fringe theatre company producing a minor play by Brecht in the back room of a pub, yet there was no gainsaying his sheer athleticism. 'Not the flair or the presentation of Robin Cousins,' said Alan Weeks reassuringly, but there was a note of worry.

It was another age before the matter was decided, because other people had to skate and anyway even the computer needed time to think. The commentators trod warily. At 3.30 a.m. our time Cousins was still being referred to as 'possibly the new Olympic champion'. David Coleman was on the rack. 'The whole scene's unbelievable. We *still* don't know who's won.' Four o'clock loomed. 'We feel that Robin Cousins is the man . . . the judges still looking at that electronic machine.' There was doubt right up until the moment when the medal was handed over. Alan Weeks found words to suit the magic. 'And I hope the roar from Bristol won't have sent a tidal wave down the Bristol Channel!'

24 February, 1980

Washed-up cat

ON *Nationwide* (BBC1) there was a lady whose cat had recently survived a complete cycle in the washing machine. 'What sort of condition was he in?' asked Frank Bough. The lady answered without smiling: 'My husband said he looked like a drowned rat.'

The essence of a cliché is that words are not misused, but have gone dead. To describe a wet cat as a drowned rat is to use language from which all life has departed, leaving mechanical lips and a vacant stare. But you couldn't blame the lady. Language was not her speciality.

Any suspicions that washing clothes was not her speciality either were allayed when Frank asked what she had done next. There was the cat, looking like a drowned rat. What had she done with it? It turned out that she had dried it manually, instead of doing what most housewives apparently do when they have inadvertently converted the cat into a drowned rat – i.e., put it in the microwave oven.

Before we get down to the main business of the week, a word for the *Open University* (BBC2), from whose programmes a free education is to be obtained if only you can arrange to be in front of the screen when they are running. Last weekend, as part of a drama course, there was a cheaply mounted but consistently dignified production of *Oedipus Tyrannus*, by Sophocles. Costumes consisted of caftans and plastic masks, decor of practically nothing. But the translation was good and the actors delivered it with great force. It

59

was the best Greek tragedy I have seen on television since Eileen Atkins played Elektra.

Other first-rate recent OU programmes include a study of the Concorde project – in which everyone ever connected with the costly beauty was chased up and interviewed – and a splendid series, still running, about astronomy. The astronomy series is fronted by experts, who do not talk down. Nevertheless the whole thing is as clear as could be. Here is proof that a BBC science programme does not have to be what it usually is in the evenings, with Nigel Calder explaining things in ways that make them less comprehensible than ever, while Dudley Moore pretends to look puzzled or Peter Ustinov imitates Einstein. Even when Open University programmes are made for fourpence, they always look like value for money, mainly because they have not been invaded by any calculations about mass appeal.

Having been given a whole introductory programme in which to expound his economic theory, Milton Friedman faced his critics in the second episode of *Free to Choose* (BBC2). His critics did their best to punch a few holes in his argument, but didn't get very far, since Friedman is an eloquent man with a simple idea, and that's the hardest kind of man to interrupt.

As for the idea, it strikes at least one innumerate but interested spectator as being what the immortal A. J. Liebling used to call a system for betting on the horses. Friedman's theory has the dubious merit of being unfalsifiable. It always fits. A country prospers if its government does not interfere. If a country prospers even when the government *does* interfere, it would have prospered even more if the government had not interfered. Adam Smith was right. The market knows best. The market is 'the invisible hand'.

Friedman makes much of the invisible hand. Eric Heffer snorted his derision, making you wish that he had an invisible face. Lord Kearton, of Courtaulds, wasn't impressed either. Nor was Bob Rowthorne, from Cambridge. Thin-lipped with contempt, Rowthorne wagged his finger in a way I remember from a decade or so ago, when he was busy telling Cambridge students about the necessity to dissent from capitalist society. One look at that stabbing digit was enough to tell you why Friedman has become popular. It is because the Left has become unpopular.

Lord Kearton called Friedman's theory a religion. But it is a very attractive religion to anyone who feels his creativity is being stifled by the modern State. Ten years ago people who felt like that were all on the Left. Somebody in America called them the New Class. Nowadays the New Class tends to be on the Right. I would be surprised if this supposedly seismic realignment were anything more than yet another change of fashion, with the truth remaining hard to get at.

All you can be sure of is that anyone who sounds as if he has all the answers hasn't. Meanwhile Friedman remains a television natural, the first man to make economics entertaining. Those who remember a similar attempt by John Kenneth Galbraith – who also had all the answers, although they were not the same ones – will have particular cause to be grateful for Friedman's elfin charm. What the BBC did to Galbraith was a clear case of bureaucratic interference. This time they are letting the free market operate. Friedman simply does his pixilated number, whereupon you can either take him or leave him. I intend to go on taking him, for a while at least.

In *The Tempest* (BBC2) the island was any old hunk of rock, but Michael Hordern, as Prospero, was magical enough to transfigure his surroundings, the television screen and, eventually, you. I doubt that I will ever hear the part better spoken. You could hear the chasm of Shakespeare's approaching death in every line. Ariel popped his eyes, wore a jock-strap and led with his pelvis, making you glad every time he dematerialised, but the young lovers were suitably enchanting. Caliban looked no more off-putting than the average BBC sports commentator. Give him a pork-pie hat and he could have fronted *Rugby Special*.

Just for Today (ATV) was a clumsy but touching documentary about Jimmy Greaves's eventually successful struggle against the demon rum. Booze stood indicted as a bad thing. *Secret Orchards* (Granada) was a William Trevor play about a man who got away with siring two families at once. After his death the whole deception fell messily apart, thereby proving that adultery is a bad thing. *A Gift from Nessus* (BBC1), by William McIlvanney and Bill Craig, was an excellent play about both these bad things, with particular emphasis on the first. Eddie ended the affair because it was hurting his career as a salesman. The girl killed herself. It was only then that Eddie found out his wife had had an affair with his boss. So he took this cushion and . . . but you had to see it. Summed up, it sounds like melodrama. As acted and directed, it was genuinely tragic.

2 March, 1980

Woodhouse walkies

WEEK after week, the most absorbing series on the air continues to be *Training Dogs the Woodhouse Way* (BBC2). It is no use trying not to watch it, because perfect strangers come up to you in the street and start telling you about it.

In the latest episode Barbara Woodhouse was teaching her team of highly trained dog-owners how to take their dogs for a walk. In the arcane vocabulary of the canine world, going for a walk is known as walkies. If you say this word to the dog it will go for a walk. So would I, by God, but that is a side issue. What matters now is the effect produced by Mrs Woodhouse when she gives instructions to the dog, to its owner, or to both simultaneously. 'Walkies! WALKIES! Go and . . . TALK!'

This last order is directed at the owner, who is thereby exhorted to converse with his four-footed companion as a reward for its having gone walkies. If the owner has succeeded in making his dog go walkies, he is home free, and is faced with nothing beyond the mild embarrassment of being obliged to whisper sweet nothings in its hairy ear. But if the dog has declined to go walkies, the owner is in the cart. 'Your trouble is you're *looking* at her! Do you see? I want you to move a bit more naturally. Go on, move! *Move*! Run! WALKIES!'

The recalcitrant dog who finally agrees to go walkies finds itself the object of as much affection as the one sheep that strayed. Indeed some of the canoodling seems to border on the erotic, but this could be my fevered imagination, what with spring in the air. 'Now love her! Get down on your knees and *love* her! And now a tickle between the legs!' A few more lines like that and I was drinking in Mrs Woodhouse's sturdy good looks as if she were the Kate Nelligan of the canicular cosmos, but it was no use. Her husband turned up. 'Now I'll get my husband Michael to come in because dogs very often hate men. DON'T COME IN TOO FAST!'

A drunkard found salvation at the hands of *Charlie's Angels* (Thames), thereby adding himself to the long list of drunkards, reformed or otherwise, who have been featured in recent television programmes. There was another one in *Change of Direction* (BBC2). What made him different from all the others was that his name was Buzz Aldrin and he had been to the Moon. Having been to the Moon, he found life on Earth relatively unexciting, and so he took to drink. His whole life had been geared to achievement and now there was nothing left to achieve. Buzz is not a very dazzling speaker, as Ludovic Kennedy, who had the task of interviewing him, soon discovered. But he is an honest man and his dilemma made sad listening.

Anybody can stop drinking once he accepts the fact that sobriety is not as much fun as being drunk. Harder drugs are more difficult to deal with. Last weekend I tried to give up *Dallas* (BBC1). I have seen every episode since the beginning, usually at the time of transmission. On those occasions when I have been unable to watch it as it goes out, I have always made two separate sets of arrangements to tape it, in case of mechanical malfunction. I knew things were getting out of hand when I found myself acting out both sides of a recent bedroom exchange between Bobby and Pamela. 'Ahm sorry. Ah guess ahm just a little jumpy.' 'What is it? Every tahm ah touch you you turn arse cold. Now tell me what it is.'

Obviously this couldn't go on, so I tried to quit cold turkey by missing an entire episode outright. I went out to dinner and did my best not to think of the hundred different directions in which Sue Ellen can move her mouth. But everybody at the table had a tape running at home and next day I didn't meet anyone who didn't want to talk about JR's reaction to the news that he is, after all, the father of Sue Ellen's baby. The grim fact is that we live in a *Dallas* culture. If you try to get off it, people will try to get you back on. They sneak up behind you and start seemingly harmless discussions about whether or not Lucy is the world's oldest schoolgirl. Before you know where you are, you're raving.

In *Public School* (BBC2) they were still training boys the Radley way. The emphasis in the latest episode was on rowing. The rowers form an elite within the school, perhaps in part compensation for being shouted at from the river bank. 'Length! Length! Take it up! Going up! Oogh! AAGH!' The Warden took a keen personal interest. We saw him interviewing a prospective rowing coach, billed as the finest oarsman in Britain. The finest oarsman in Britain was taken on as a teacher, despite having no teaching qualifications. With his assistance, Radley is plainly destined to become an even more formidable rowing force than it has been up till now. The boys in the winning eight will have something to remember for the rest of their lives. Perhaps one of them will even become the finest oarsman in Britain, and be asked to come back as a rowing coach, and . . .

The repeat of *The Lost Boys* (BBC2) is now over. It looked an even more convincing achievement the second time. Ian Holm brought J. M. Barrie's neuroses to life with an intensity that made you wish he hadn't. Obviously it was hell being him. But instead of leaping on small children he wrote stories for them. Usually you can envy the kind of artist who channels his personal unhappiness into creativity, but on this evidence there was no envying Barrie. Retrospectively cherishing the wounded personalities of its per-verted artists is one of the things Britain does supremely well. A country is civilised to the extent that it understands human frailty. Everything else is just shouting from the river bank. 'Length! Length! Take it *up*! Move! Run! WALKIES!'

In *Parting Shots From Animals* (BBC2) John Berger, of *Ways of Seeing* fame, spoke on behalf of animals, who are apparently convinced that we humans are indifferent to their fate. Give or take the odd anatomical discrepancy, John Berger affects me exactly like Jane Fonda – i.e., any opinion of mine which I discover he shares I immediately examine to find out what's wrong with it. In *The Brinsworth Tribute Show* (Thames) the ghastly compère and the frantically posturing dancers could not detract from the mighty Lulu. Clad in a Blake's Seven silver space suit with shocking pink epaulettes, she sang a storm. What does she have to do before she gets another big-budget series – impressions?

Merce Cunningham was the subject of an interesting *South Bank Show* (LWT). You had to admire his uncompromising adventur-ousness, especially when all the evidence suggested that he and his dancers come fully to life only when the music is the old, melodic kind. On *What the Papers Say* (Granada) Donald Woods ably analysed Fleet Street's success in getting everything wrong about Mugabe.

9 March, 1980

Tanya talks Russian

IN *Russian – Language and People* (BBC1 and 2) regular viewers have by now progressed far enough to accompany the intrepid team of presenters on a visit to a department store. 'The store', announced the delightful Tanya Feifer, 'was particularly well stocked the day we were there.'

Tanya, who is so pretty she makes you want to burst out cheering, has the kind of Slavic cheek in which it is difficult to tell whether the tongue has been inserted, but I suspect that at this point she might have been slyly hinting, for those with the acumen to catch on, that the Soviet authorities have been not entirely ingenuous in the way they have co-operated.

It was all too easy to imagine a squad of heavies from the KGB's catering division arriving in the store a few hours ahead of the Beeb's camera crew and stocking the shelves with such rare luxuries as meat. The unacknowledged but all-pervading fact about this series is that every foot of film shot on Russian location has been supervised by the Soviet authorities. Sequences incorporating the Kremlin in the background have been cancelled on the spot because prior permission had not been sought to film the Kremlin on that particular day. In other words, the usual fist-brained rigmarole.

Not only has all the location footage been vetted, but everything done here at home has been carefully toned down in order not to offend the tender sensibilities of the host nation. There is no lower price to be paid for filming in the Soviet Union. Total blandness is the bottom line of the deal, into which the BBC went with its eyes open, although doubtless unaware that its hosts would celebrate the launching of the series by invading Afghanistan.

So it may as well be conceded from the outset that *Russian – Language and People* is, as far as it concerns the practical realities of life in the Soviet Union, a work of science fiction. With that question out of the way, one is free to praise the series for the thoroughness with which it gives you the feeling of the Russian language. It is a warm, luxurious feeling, like being hugged by a bear wearing a fur-trimmed brocade dressing-gown.

Tanya Feifer is a great help in this department. She gives those hushy consonants their full sensual value. Indefatigably gathering vox pops in and around Moscow, the Soviet star presenter, Tatyana Vedeneeva, makes less easy listening, mainly because of her apparent determination to say 'Hello' and 'Goodbye' to every citizen of the Soviet Union individually. She rarely has time to say anything else, or perhaps she has not been given permission.

Russian – Language and People comes equipped, on the classic pattern of BBC foreign language programmes, with an embarrassing little serial-within-the-series. This time it is a love story. (In similar series about other languages it has usually been a mystery story, but there are no mysteries in the Soviet Union, where crime is a government monopoly.) Boris and Olga, or whatever their names are, have bumped into each other in the famous Moscow bookshop, the House of Books. 'What a lot of books there are!' exclaims Boris, thereby hoping to attract Olga's attention. Olga looks surprised, as well she might, since Boris has neglected to add: 'Every book except the one you want.' In the House of Books the only books worth having sell out immediately. Queues form for books that have not yet been published. But Boris and Olga are too wrapped up in each other to bother with such questions.

Boris and Olga lose each other in the Metro, but we can be sure that they will meet again. Meanwhile one can press ahead with one's exercises in pronunciation. In Russian the stress is arbitrary and the natives elide like mad, thereby adding an extra element of unintelligibility to a language which is at least as big as ours in vocabulary and even more idiomatic. But it is also wonderfully, wildly beautiful.

The same could be said of Kate Nelligan, currently playing the title role in *Thérèse Raquin* (BBC2). There are several things that can be said about Miss Nelligan, and at the moment the profile writers are knocking themselves out looking for new ways to say them, but the first thing to say is that she has the right kind of nerve to take a hack at a heavy role.

In *The Lady of the Camellias* she did a startling job of not being obliterated by Garbo's memory. As Thérèse Raquin she has another star predecessor to contend with: Simone Signoret played the role on film in 1953. But Signoret, like Garbo, had to do a lot of suggesting in the clinches. Nelligan is allowed to be more explicit. Add that fact to her looks and talent and you have all the reasons why she is able to invest these sex-pot characters with new life.

At present there are still two more episodes to go, so it is a bit early to sum up, but it can safely be said that even in Zola's imagination Paris never looked so tacky. The whole screen is submerged in seaweed soup and liquid sulphur. Somewhere in the middle of the suffocating tedium Thérèse throbs with *besoin*. Finally she manages to be alone with her weedy husband's virile friend. 'Get your clothes off,' she cries, 'and come to bed with me!' Clad fetchingly in well-laundered underwear, she drops on him from the ceiling. Blind passion never looked more believable. Or more fun, either.

I've got to get off Barbara Woodhouse before it's too late. In the last episode of what will undoubtedly be only the first of many series of *Training Dogs the Woodhouse Way* (BBC2) she was to be seen teaching puppies how to poo and pee.

The dog-owners were told that they could give any command they chose, as long as these two activites were clearly differentiated. 'I use "Quickie!" for puddling and "Hurry up!" for the other function.' At least one viewer came close to puddling himself on hearing this, but hysteria quickly gave way to wonder. If 'Hurry up!' is what she says when she wants the dog to perform the other function, what does she say when she wants the dog to hurry up?

Anyway, don't be surprised if, after you have shouted at your child to hurry up, every dog in the district suddenly starts performing the other function. It will only mean that they have been trained the Woodhouse way.

16 March, 1980

Three famous, three high

IN a rich week, *Shadows on our Skin* (BBC1) stood out, mainly because it was that rarest of television events, a play about what is going on in Northern Ireland.

What is going on in Northern Ireland has been going on for a long time, but has lately reached such a pitch of intensity that people can be excused for demanding a more extensive television coverage. This subject, it has been pointed out, ought logically to be inspiring a whole stream of television plays. So why aren't the television companies putting them on? Scarcely anybody has dared to suggest that the reason why there are so few television plays about Northern Ireland is that good playwrights don't want to write them, and that the reason why they don't want to write them is that the subject is not inspiring – merely terrifying, monotonous and grindingly sad.

Nevertheless, *Shadows on our Skin* turned out to be the best television play about Northern Ireland since *I'm a Dreamer, Montreal*. The fact that it was the only television play about Northern Ireland since *I'm a Dreamer, Montreal* was of minor importance. Adapted by the poet Derek Mahon from the novel by Jennifer Johnston, the script economically explored the distorted childhood of a Bogside eleven-year-old boy called Joe, impersonated with admirable precocity by Macrea Clarke.

Nobody except Joe came out of the play particularly well. It was also hard to avoid drawing the conclusion that Joe's own adulthood, when it arrived, would not be very admirable either. Joe's house was loud with hatred and stupidity. Nobody but an Irish playwright would dare to paint his countrymen in such harsh colours – a fact which drastically cuts down the number of possible playwrights at the start. Nor is it much use asking the Irish writers to make clear where they stand. What if there isn't anywhere to stand? The troubles in Ulster aren't the Trojan war. There is nothing stimulating about them. Any good play on the subject is likely to leave you feeling depressed, and doubly depressed for feeling that there isn't anything you can do. The only, small consolation is that a bad play on the subject would leave you feeling all that and cheated as well.

An entertaining instalment of *Omnibus* (BBC1) featured Roger Corman and his low-budget film empire. 'Roger's operation', explained one of his pupils, 'is an exploitation operation on almost every level.' Corman's pupils are glad to be exploited because it gives them an opportunity to make a movie, whereupon they will graduate to the status of alumni and become madly famous like Martin Scorsese and Francis Ford Coppola. Corman's requirements – that the film be shot in five days, use sets left over from *Invasion of the Crab Monsters*, and contain at least twelve head-on collisions between naked go-go dancers riding Hondas – are seen as an invigorating disciplinary framework.

Corman's acolytes are far from dumb. Most of them talked well and all of them were interesting to watch as they went about their frenzied work. There were immensely diverting excerpts from an all-purpose Corman movie called *Hollywood Boulevard*. I never enjoyed an *Omnibus* programme more. Nevertheless somebody should have pointed out that most Roger Corman movies, whether by the master himself or by an exploited tyro, are not just cheap but truly lousy. There is also the consideration that even the most famous Corman alumni, when they run out of real ideas, revert to making Corman movies, only this time they do it on a multi-million dollar budget and stink up the whole world instead of just the local drive-in.

China (Thames) glumly recounted what has been happening to the Peking Ballet Company during thirty years of revolution. The dancers were seen trying to recapture the secrets of *Swan Lake*, which they have not been allowed to perform for the past sixteen years. Instead they have been obliged to concentrate on such masterpieces as *The Red Detachment of Women*. Mrs Mao came in for plenty of vilification from the dancers, as well she might. A ballerina, her hands ruined from eight years' hard labour in the fields, said that what was done to your body would have been less unbearable if they had let your mind alone. 'They would criticise you in front of everyone.' There was a campaign called 'Three famous, three high' in which the three most accomplished people in any area of creativity were reassigned to a decade or so of carting night-soil.

The dancers blamed most of this on the Gang of Four. Apparently it is still not possible to lay the blame where it belongs – i.e., squarely on Mao. 'Mao always believed in the power of art to educate and change people.' Art has large powers to do both those things, but on its own terms. All Mao accomplished was the destruction of art. 'His people, by and large,' said one of the dancers, 'have never stopped loving, even worshipping him.' But where else did the Cultural Revolution come from, if not directly from Mao's great brain? And here were the witnesses to what the Cultural Revolution was actually like. Most of them are still crying at the memory. Shirley MacLaine, a dancer herself, might like to reflect that these people were being driven like cattle at the exact time when she and her gullible friends came back from their visit to China squealing, 'Why do they all look so *happy*?'

Having slagged Frederic Raphael on several occasions, I am duty bound to declare that his episode of *Writers and Places* (BBC2) was excellent. Revisiting Cambridge, he had more to say *in propria persona* than as the author of *The Glittering Prizes*, or anyway he said it better. His epigrams sound more convincing coming from him than from his characters. Perhaps he is his own best character. As Gerry Mulligan played 'Walking Shoes' on the sound-track, Raphael donned his junior intellectual's outfit and sloped off into the past. Billing himself as 'the thinking man's undergraduate of the early Fifties', he once again took up residence in the Whim. 'I sat here on publication day and waited to be famous overnight.' He did a good job of evoking Wittgenstein's cleansingly austere spirit. He did a good job all round, thereby proving once again that nothing beats a talking head for action, if the head talks well.

In the second episode of *Thérèse Raquin* (BBC1) Camille's corpse returned to haunt the guilty lovers. Whether the corpse was played by a gruesomely made-up actor, or by a real corpse of the right size and state of decomposition, was difficult to determine, especially if you had your hands over your eyes and your head under the couch. Camille's remains undoubtedly constituted *le mauvais spectacle de la semaine,* despite strong competition from James Burke, who launched a new series of science waffle called *The Real Thing* (BBC1). 'Look!' cried Burke. 'Watch! See?' There is almost nothing that can't be made uninteresting provided it is approached with sufficient fervour.

23 March, 1980

Your brain's got it wrong

'GOOD evening!' cried James Burke, fronting a trailer for his daft new sci-bull series *The Real Thing* (BBC1). 'Your brain has already made up its mind about which way up I am. And because it doesn't possess the information I have, it's got it wrong.'

What James Burke can't seem to grasp is that I don't care about not possessing the information he has. It is a matter of total indifference whether he is the way he looks – i.e., the right way up and practically exploding with pedagogic enthusiasm – or whether he is upside down, plugged into an electric socket, and all set to eat a live chicken. But there is no way of telling him this, because instead of being an actual presence you can reach out towards and beat repeatedly around the head with a rolled-up newspaper until you get his attention, he is an image on your television screen that goes on and on supplying you with information you don't have. Merely turning the programme off is no good, since the after-image lingers on. You have to kick the set in even to slow him down.

But at least James Burke is doing what suits him. Terry Wogan, on the other hand, had to stand in front of an endless mess called *A Song For Europe* (BBC1). There was a time when this would have suited him down to the ground, but lately he has been cultivating, not entirely without success, a new reputation for spontaneous intelligence. To sustain this new image in the context of the programme under discussion, he would have had, after each number, either to fall to the floor racked with spasms of mocking laughter or else shoot the perpetrator mercifully through the head.

God help Europe. 'This tarm we're on our way' was the theme of every lyric, coupled with assurances that Love still rules. A nondescript group in sagging pink space suits sang 'Love is alive! And it's starting to grow! All over the world! Tell everybody! Have you hurled?' After a few seconds' thought the listener might have reached the conclusion that the last word must have been 'heard' rather than 'hurled', but a few seconds' thought was precisely what was difficult to achieve, owing to severe contractions in the lower bowel.

By sharp contrast, *The Kenny Everett Video Show* (Thames) knows exactly what it is up to image-wise. Tightly controlled by a producer who must have the patience and reflexes to pick up spilled mercury with his bare hands, Kenny has been giving the land of the media one lesson after another in how to keep link-material short, sour and funny. Meanwhile the musical numbers going on up front continue to be the most interesting on television. Unfortunately he has finally allowed his dance group, Hot Gossip, to blot his copybook – not with their alleged eroticism, which is in fact no more attractive than an enema, but with their dim-witted desire to hop about in Nazi uniforms.

In the latest episode the desire was made real. Up until now they have stylised their yearning for the glamour of the Third Reich, but this time they let it all hang down. The black male dancers in the group made a sudden, supposedly dramatic appearance dressed as SS officers. The girls in the group reacted with suitable writhings of submissive lust. I hope it doesn't sound like racism when I say that the black male dancers in Hot Gossip have always been a dead bore, mainly because of their humourless frowns of concentration while making movements with their hips which suggest a doomed, no-hands attempt to scratch their groins against an invisible tree. But boredom is one thing and blasphemy is another.

Hot Gossip are probably hard to talk to either collectively or individually, but Kenny Everett is a bright character, so here goes. The Nazis are a joke all right, but they are not yet a joke to make lightly. They are history's joke on the human race, and will remain so until the last of their victims has gone beyond the reach of being hurt further by a casual insult. It insults not just millions of dead, but a lot of people still living, to employ these images of horror without caring what they really mean. It was perfectly obvious that the Hot Gossip dancers had dressed themselves up as Nazis without having any real idea of the suffering the Nazis caused and the scale on which they caused it. But that's what blasphemy is – to cheapen the central experience of other people's lives.

As for the much-touted question about whether the dance groups are going over the top, it is rapidly answering itself. When the ladies have removed all their clothes there is nothing left to do except start putting them on again. They will put them on even faster once it becomes apparent that the eroticism which the choreographers have been so single-mindedly aiming at has been disappearing along with the cloth. There was never a sexier television dance group than Pan's People at the height of their fame, and that was because they gave you what is known among traditional jazz-men as a flash. You can't have a flash without a skirt.

Back to the Nazis with *World in Action* (Granada). As distinct from the Hot Gossip variety, these were the real thing: white, camera-shy and very, very horrible. Showing admirable tenacity, WIA sent camera-crews after high-ranking mass murderers who are alive and well and living, not in South America, but in the United States. Most of them have done deeds so evil that the mind jibs at the telling. Men who have slain children by the thousand and ripped foetuses out of the bellies of tortured mothers are now shamelessly living out their lives as church dignitaries. Nixon, with typical grace, invited one of these to bless the opening of the Senate.

The FBI goes on being reluctant to turf these people out, mainly because of deals done long ago. They were given sanctuary because they were anti-Communist. Until the advent of President Carter, who has his drawbacks but can tell an ethic from his elbow, every post-war American Administration took it for granted that any enemy of Communism must be a friend of democracy. There is nowadays some hope that the miscarriages of justice brought about by that assumption might be redressed, if independent reporters like the WIA team keep up the pressure.

A play by Stephen Poliakoff, *Bloody Kids* (Thames), was directed by Stephen Frears with his customary nose for the phosphorescent glamour of urban blight. Youths with boiled-potato faces looked even worse for having their features bleached out by lights aimed from the floor. 'I jest remembered sunning,' they mumbled, stabbing each other. A nice boy was tempted into trouble by a nasty boy. Large themes might or might not have been touched upon – it was too dark to tell.

The lights were turned up a bit at the end of *Thérèse Raquin* (BBC1), just in time for the lovers to commit mutual suicide. One quick swig of poison each and they were away from it all. They would never have to look at that decor again.

30 March, 1980

73

Nude bathing in Britain

THE big deal of the week was nude bathing at Brighton. The sky was the colour of washing-up water, the sea was the colour of what floats on top of washing-up water, and the news crews were out in force to immortalise the bravery of anybody who cared to defy the elements with nothing but a birthday suit to stave off death by exposure.

Scarcely anybody did, but by the end of the short, freezing day there were enough takers for the television channels to shoot an item each. From the resulting output you could read off an exact measurement of the inhibitions, or lack of them, obtaining in each organisation. On *News at Ten* (ITN) a naked man came limping and shivering out of the sea to tell the camera what a terrific time he was having. He was visible down to a line drawn about half an inch above what would probably have turned out to be, if we had been allowed to see it, a frost-bitten cashew. On *Newsnight* (BBC2) another man man was to be seen doing the full flash. He was about a mile and half from the camera, but you could tell he had no pants on, unless some manufacturer has recently come up with a line of trunks in subdued shades of potato juice blotched with purple.

Nude bathing, one fears, is destined not to be a British thing. What Britain does best is horses. A case in point was the *Grand National* (BBC1), or '*Sun* Grand National' as it is officially known. 'The Grand National', David Coleman informed us, 'is, of course, sponsored by the *Sun*, as is the next race . . .' The proprietors of a certain newspaper got their money's worth. So, to be fair, did we. It was a tremendous race, with four finishers out of thirty starters, so that by the end there were far more BBC commentators than horses. At the start there were merely a few more.

Before the race the top jockeys relax by talking to David Coleman. They smile to themselves, as one does when one is dressed in a funny hat and then suddenly meets a man dressed in a hat even funnier than one's own. David's special racetrack hat is a great loosener of tension. His opening question is invariably about the horse. 'Hooray Sod is a bit of a family pet at home, isn't he?' 'Yeah, the governor still rides 'im eventin'.' The next question usually focuses on the jockey's recent injuries. 'That bone . . . you've suffered?' 'Yeah. Bit of a boogah.'

The next bit is the race itself. Nothing about it is predictable, except that a lot of horses will crash and that The Pilgarlic will not win. Towards the telephoto lens they all come thundering, as if the course were a terrace of rice paddies. A jockey hits the ground and rolls carefully into the path of every horse available. Far out in front, an American amateur is in the lead, challenged only by a loose horse. A loose horse is any horse sensible enough to get rid of its rider at an early stage and carry on unencumbered.

The American wins and is regaled with the big prize – a long interview with David Coleman. 'It was a thrill. There's nothing like it. Great thrill. Great thrill.' There is modesty to go with the enthusiasm. 'I happened to be a passenger today on the horse that was the best of the day.' The *Sun* Grand National is over for another year. Nude bathing cannot hope to compete, although aggressive sponsorship might help to transform the picture. There could be a prize for what the cold sea does to the lower regions of the average male. The Everest Double Glazing Chilled Acorn Competition. The Birdseye Frozen Foods Jelly-bean Puissance.

Occupying a whole evening on BBC2, Donizetti's *Lucrezia Borgia* was a gas. Short of money, the designer was thrown back on improvisation, with excellent results. Some of the costumes, in particular, looked marvellous. For once Anne Howells was given clothes worthy of her captivating looks. Usually there is a very British conspiracy to weigh down this telegenic mezzo with a load of unlovely schmutter, thus to offset the advantages conferred on her by nature. This time she was allowed to strut dynamically about in highly becoming velvet pants-suits plus Renaissance accessories.

Joan Sutherland was clad monumentally in outfits that fully occupied any part of the set she happened to be parked in. This worked especially well in the climactic scene when the back wall flew up to reveal Lucrezia stashed behind it. The look of the thing matters: with musicians of such high calibre one expects every-thing to sound good, but if it doesn't look good, then the whole thing is a step back, since there is no point in televising an opera performance if the main result is to turn off the punters.

Somewhere in the middle of a marathon Agatha Christie mystery called *Why Didn't They Ask Evans?* (LWT) I had to go to Paris. Arriving in my hotel room just in time to switch on the American Grand Prix live from Long Beach, I watched the cars fall apart while the French equivalent of Murray Walker did his *chose*. But all the time a question was nagging me: Why *didn't* they ask Evans? Back in London, I switched on my new Japanese miracle VCR that watches three channels at once and writes my column. Alas, it had failed to discover why Evans had not been asked. Instead, it had made me a cup of coffee. Obviously I had pushed all the wrong buttons.

After a desperate search I gained access to the relevant cassettes, and settled down to a further two hours of viewing which would surely yield an answer to the question of why Evans had not been consulted. Eventually all was made plain. As with all Agatha Christie's stories, there was no hope of sussing the plot. The old dear cheated like mad.

Why Didn't They Ask Evans? was filled with glaring impossibilities. People imitated each other's voices, etc. But it was all highly enjoyable, once you accepted that the idea was to wallow in what you could not swallow. Nonsense has rarely been so well dressed. The clothes, cars and aeroplanes were all solidly in period and a treat to look at. You could feast your eyes on them while the characters got on with wondering why no inquiries had been directed at Evans.

At the centre of the sumptuosity, Francesca Annis was her radiant self, plus an upper-class accent and a limitless wardrobe of silk suits. Everybody in the cast had a good time, the directing was done with a light touch and only a curmudgeon would have objected that it took so long and cost so much money to find out why Evans had not been subject to interrogation.

6 April, 1980

Moral imagination

EXISTENTIALISTS have to remake their personalities every day. Last week Jean-Paul Sartre finally ran out of chances to remake his.

For someone so clever he was a hard man to like. There is not much point in hating torturers, who are the way they are. But there is good reason to despise a philosopher who, self-proclaimedly free to choose what he shall think, goes on and on providing justification for the sort of regime that employs torture as a matter of course.

It is a moot point whether Sartre went on backing Stalin and Mao because he couldn't see how ruthless they were or because he could and liked it. (Actually the point isn't moot at all, since he was very well informed, but the dead should have the benefit of the doubt.) Perhaps he was taking revenge for his bad eye. In the news programme last week it was usually staring off to camera right while the good eye looked straight at you. The ITN announcer called him Jeanne-Paul Sartre, thereby proving that forgetfulness sets in fast.

What Sartre lacked was a moral imagination. He had everything else, but could never grasp the elementary principle that ends do not justify means. Lionel Goldstein, author of an excellent 'Play for Today' called *The Executioner* (BBC1), would probably not be able to match Sartre's power of abstract thought, but can think rings around him when it comes to the concrete subject of morality. Played with quiet force by Paul Rogers, the Executioner of the title was a one-time officer in the Polish Army who, while travelling through West Germany in 1979, suddenly finds himself under arrest. In January 1945, while serving with the Allied armies of liberation, he had killed a captured German officer. By putting him on trial the German prosecutor (Robert Stephens) hopes to prove the law's impartiality and thereby get the statute of limitations lifted so that he can go on bringing the other kind of war criminal to justice.

Unfortunately, or rather fortunately, the Executioner turns out to have been a Jew all along. The man he killed was an unrepentant

SS officer. Since the Executioner's entire family had been wiped out by just the sort of man he had killed, there is not only little chance of getting a conviction, there is every reason to put him on the next plane back to Britain. But by this time he doesn't want to go. As he explains to his unsympathetic defending counsel (Deborah Norton), Germany must be told. By refusing to acquit himself he puts a whole nation on trial.

The whole chain of thought, deed and consequence was brilliantly worked out, with only the odd spot of cheating to aid the tension. The German authorities would probably have sussed much earlier that the man their computer had helped them pick up was too hot to hold – they seemed strangely reluctant to ask him what had happened to his family, and in the circumstances he seemed even more strangely reluctant to tell them. But that was a blemish rather than a flaw. Otherwise the whole thing clicked.

All the natives spoke proper English without any cheaply atmospheric peppering of German words, although Robert Stephens employed the word 'irregardless' on one occasion. Deborah Norton was her usual stunning self – a bucket of ice who melted for one second, then froze up again. She didn't want her generation indicted for crimes it didn't commit. She was right, but not obviously right. The Executioner was right too. It was a stand-off. Several of the players were also in *Holocaust*: typecasting, but piquant, since it was *Holocaust* that really *did* get the statute of limitations lifted – the most powerful single instance to date of television affecting history.

The Executioner, though more subtle than *Holocaust*, nevertheless had its mechanical aspects. You knew you were being steered through hoops. But the total effect was enough to make you wonder about the amount of hoo-ha generated by the live theatre. How does it happen that a chucklehead like Rolf Hochhuth gets so much coverage when a playwright of Mr Goldstein's quality is largely unknown? They both deal in the moral problems uncovered by political upheaval, but the difference between them is the difference between a light way of being serious and an hysterical way of being frivolous. Still, no doubt some of those glowing theatrical reputations are deserved.

I would like to think that Simon Gray's is, although I might have to take the dizzy step of actually going to the theatre to check up.

Those plays of his which have been on television have impressed me mainly as exercises in mental superiority, in which the hero stands revealed as pretty much bored and insulted by the petty concerns of the ordinary mortals around him, although sometimes he manages to achieve a sort of weary compassion. But *The Rear Column* (BBC1) had a bit more in it. For one thing, there was no playwright-like hero standing around being bored, insulted and/or wearily compassionate.

Instead there was an assorted batch of British officers waiting for Stanley in the Congo. Eventually Stanley, functioning as the kind of *deus ex machina* whose machine has run out of petrol somewhere off stage, would tell them what they had to do. Meanwhile they had to wait, with their native bearers dying messily in the wings. Their commanding officer, played excellently by Barry Foster in his Orde Wingate manner plus a pint of sweat, was clearly bonkers. Others were less clearly bonkers. One of them, the artist, seemed not to be bonkers at all, but turned out in the end to be the most bonkers of the lot. He had been quietly drawing pictures of a cannibal cook-out in which an eleven-year-old girl had been barbecued.

It was possible that Mr Gray was grappling at this point with the problem posed by the man with artistic temperament but no moral sense. If so, it was not a very strenuous grapple. Compared with *The Executioner*, the play was without focus. But it was not without incidental interest, and Harold Pinter, in his first try at directing for television, broke with the tradition established by other famous stage directors who come late to the cameras – he planned his shots with tact, avoided all gimmickry and unassertively ensured that the whole thing moved forward with what inexorability it could muster.

20 April, 1980

All fingers and toes

BAD SIGHT of the week was on *TV Eye* (Thames). Chinese whose fingers had been cut off in industrial accidents were to be seen having them sewn back on or replaced with toes.

During the long operations, which involved micro-surgery of staggering intricacy, the patients stayed awake, presumably so that the visiting round-eyes from *TV Eye* could interview them. Some of the patients had had whole hands or even arms sliced off. These, too, were replaced. The cause of the accident was usually some such piece of machinery as a circular saw. Thousands of Chinese per year have digits or limbs removed in this way. Apparently it is deemed more interesting to explore surgical techniques for replacing the missing appendages than to devise safe machines.

We were introduced to Mrs Ho. 'Four years ago Mrs Ho's forearm was cut off by a milling machine.' She did not offer to shake hands, but otherwise seemed in good shape. Chinese surgeons, it was announced, achieve a 92.3 per cent success rate in finger replacement. By my count that leaves 7.7 per cent of all severed fingers still being buried in separate graves, but not even Chairman Mao's teachings can give you the moon. Gratitude to Chairman Mao was universal, expressing itself in a steady drone which helped lull your senses while you were confronted with a rich display of pulsing arteries and twitching tendons. Dissenting voices could be counted on the toes of one hand.

The Imitation Game (BBC1) was a 'Play for Today' of rare distinction. It counts as Ian McEwan's first television play, since an earlier effort, called *Solid Geometry*, was cleverly scrapped by the BBC as part of a long campaign to injure its own reputation for being a patron of talent. But this time something went wrong and McEwan managed to get his script on the air.

Helping him to realise his searchingly original idea, Richard Eyre directed with an unfailing touch and Harriet Walter brought seemingly limitless reserves of intelligent emotion to the incarnation of the central role. Cathy lived. She could hardly muster the words to say what was on her mind, but you knew exactly what was going on inside her head, even if the men around her noticed nothing.

The time and place were the last war and England. Cathy welcomed the war as something that would break the crushing routine of home, in which her squint-minded father led the conspiracy to keep women in their place. The Second World War, it is generally accepted, provided splendid opportunities for women to get out of their place, but McEwan, like David Hare in *Licking Hitler*, prefers to believe that such notions are wishful hindsight: the old prejudices were not undermined as much as they were reconfirmed. War was a man's game which put women in their place more firmly than ever.

Cathy had a knack for codes and a gift for music. Apparently the two gifts often go together. But nobody was interested in harnessing Cathy's abilities to the war effort. The closest she got to the inner secrets of Bletchley Park was making tea. She had previously been one of the hundreds of girls monitoring German radio transmissions but had lost the job after kneeing a publican who had slapped her face because she wouldn't leave the pub when he wanted to throw her out because she had been sitting there without a man and we all know what an ATS girl is after if she sits alone and . . . And so on. It was an unbroken and unbreakable sequence of stifling repressions, just like home.

Meanwhile, in secret rooms full of ticking equipment, the men were leading the exciting life. A nice young boffin tried to go to bed with her and blamed her for his impotence. One of the play's male reviewers, I notice, has picked on this scene as the play's only flaw: he said it was out of character for the nice young man to turn so nasty. Alas, not so. Nice young men can and do turn nasty in those circumstances. A man's emotional education can take a long time.

One of the many commendable things about Ian McEwan is that his hasn't. He seems to possess the sexual insight of Tiresias, who, it will be remembered, experienced the woman's viewpoint at first hand. A good test of feminist writing is whether it makes men feel guilty. During this play I spent a lot of time feeling apologetic about my own past behaviour and I suspect that there were few male viewers who didn't feel the same. The small patronising remarks were just as effective as the big cruelties in the protracted but eventually successful job of driving Cathy into a corner. She ended up behind bars, but then she had really been behind them all along.

One of the Highlights of My Viewing Year, the *World Professional Snooker Championship* (BBC2), known to its sponsors as the Embassy World Professional Snooker Championship, entered the first of its scheduled two glorious weeks of braincurdling transmission. I would almost rather watch it than watch Wimbledon, which is saying plenty. But perhaps I had better save the unbridled enthusiasm for next time. Enough for now to say that as a curtain-raiser to the fabulous fortnight, the final of *Pot Black* (BBC2) would have been hard to beat. A kill-or-be-killed nailbiter between Ray Reardon and the mighty Eddie Charlton, it featured an incredible range of flukes, in-offs, break-your-cue snookers and outlandishly accomplished positional play.

In *Manon Lescaut* (BBC2) James Levine stood revealed as a great conductor and Placido Domingo as a changed man. He has lost at least two stone, most of it from around the stern. But the voice is bigger and more beautiful than ever, like his eyebrows. *Gates of Eden* (Yorkshire) slipped by so quietly that I forgot to say how good it was at evoking callow sensitivity. Perhaps I have been brutalised by television's heady sensationalism, as exemplified by *World of Sport* (LWT), which last weekend gave full coverage to the World Record High Diving Challenge, direct from the US.

The platform was set 166 feet above the water, which from that height looks like sheet steel. Divers were interviewed on the platform and interviewed again upon surfacing. In between the two interviews they had to accomplish their dive, during which the commentator did all the talking, since no means have yet been discovered of interviewing the diver on his way down. 'Oogh, he's in trouble now . . . AAGH! Rick could be hurt! But he's up! You looked as though you had a moment of uncertainty coming out of that dive.' 'Yeah,' replied Rick weakly, 'I . . . I just . . . ooh.'

But the winning dive, by Dana Kunze, was worth every dime of the $10,000 it earned him. A triple gainer with a lay-out between two of the somersaults, it was beautiful to see. So was Ava Gardner in *Pandora and the Flying Dutchman* (BBC2). So, under the harsh make-up, was Isobel Black, making a welcome return in *The White Bird Passes* (BBC2).

27 April, 1980

Oodnadatta Fats

LETTERS have been pouring in from ex-members of the ATS saying that their war-time experiences were nothing like what was portrayed as happening to Cathy in Ian McEwan's play *The Imitation Game*, which was praised in this column last week. My high opinion of the play remains unshaken, but it is only fair to record the outrage of these ladies. After all, they were there.

Some of them were actually at Bletchley Park or else monitoring German broadcasts at one of the subsidiary centres. None of them remembers feeling either excluded from the action or socially despised. Rather the reverse, apparently, in each case. I'm bound to record that what they say rings true. My own instinct, perhaps based on absorbing too many genteel reminiscences, is that the Second World War actually did produce a hitherto unheard of degree of social cohesion among the British people.

The trouble is that when talented young playwrights like David Hare and Ian McEwan engage on some solid research on the subject, which for them lies in the historic past, they come up with a picture of the same old divisions being perpetuated and even intensified. Perhaps they find what they look for, but if so, why are they looking for it? Is it because the same old divisions are still being perpetuated and intensified? I leave you with these un-answered questions and turn to the main business of the week, namely Eddie Charlton being eliminated from the *World Professional Snooker* (BBC2).

I hope I will not be accused of patriotic immoderation when I say that Eddie Charlton is not only incomparably the world's greatest all-round athlete, he is also a philosopher of rare distinction. No man was ever better equipped to defy the laws of probability. On the other hand, when the odds turn against him he can take what fate hands out. Those deep-set eyes which have stared so long into the far distance are well used to focusing an unblinking gaze on looming doom.

But to be defeated by Kirk Stevens! It must have hurt. Those of us who have seen our man knocked out should speak generously of his opponent, so let me be the first to say that the youngster wields a fair cue and is a demon for the long pot. It could be said that the little mouth-breather looks like a glass of milk in that white suit and has a hair-style like a grass hut. Yet nobody beats Eddie Charlton by accident.

Nobody beats Terry Griffiths that way either. In fact Griffiths usually has to beat himself, being unable to rely on assistance from others. Drawn at ten frames all with Steve Davis – another adolescent from the Kirk Stevens peer group, but differing from Stevens in the ability to close his mouth – Griffiths went for a fine cut instead of a safety shot. The result was a disaster for him and for the cigarette firm sponsoring the tournament, since the Welsh maestro is a formidable consumer of their product. While his opponents were plying the cue, Griffiths was always to be seen sucking an Embassy. He puffed and dragged. He ashed and stubbed. In the Embassy boardroom they must have been cheering with bated breath – not an easy trick, but presumably they have time on their hands.

Eliminated from competition, Griffiths became a voice-over. Presumably he was still inhaling the fumes of his free Embassies, but unfortunately a voice-over makes zero visual impact. His vocal impact, however, was all that could be desired. 'Those slow pinks to the centre pocket across the nap of the cloth', he murmured, 'are never easy.' I nodded wisely at this. When I am playing snooker my cue ball either misses the target by a yard or else follows it into the pocket with dream-like precision, but in my mind I am that most renowned of champions, Oodnadatta Fats.

Hurricane Higgins is another great consumer of free fags. He smokes the way he plays – as if there was not only no tomorrow, but hardly anything left of today. With adrenalin instead of blood and dynamite instead of adrenalin, he sprints around the table, mowing down the referee, and lines up his next shot before the ball stops rolling. Usually these tactics, combined with an irrepressible urge to attempt the impossible, guarantee his exit at an early stage, but this year he could be seen making heroic efforts to rein himself in. He would have scored a 147 break and walked away with £10,000 if his cue had not screwed him. Even without that he stood revealed as a truly great smoker, capable of reducing an Embassy to ashes in a few seconds.

Meanwhile, back in London, a gang of Iranians were threatening to do the same. As far as I can tell from the news programmes, the embassy they have taken over is theirs, but they come from a part of Iran that wants its independence, possibly because the Ayatollah Khomeini's regime is regarded as too rational, Westernised, etc. Anyway, the standard scenario unfolded with tedious rapidity, like a made-for-television movie. The embassy filled up with Iranians who hated each other. More Iranians who hated each other gathered in the surrounding streets. The police, at untold cost to the taxpayer, were obliged to cordon off the whole area, thereby forcing the television news crews to shoot through long lenses from upper windows in the next postal district. It was all very exciting. To put it another way, it was as boring as hell.

4 May, 1980

How do you feel?

WHILE the Special Air Service covered itself with glory, the viewing public gloried in the coverage. Both the BBC and ITN were there in strength throughout the siege – which, for those of you with short memories, occurred at the Iranian Embassy in Knightsbridge.

The BBC gave you the front of the building and ITN gave you the back. All the cameras were plugged in on a semi-permanent basis while their crews settled down to the daunting task of consuming the meals provided for them according to the rigid specifications laid down by their unions. Days went by, then everything happened in a flash, not to mention with a bang.

Unfortunately for the news-gatherers most of it happened inside the building. When the stun grenades went off a certain amount of flame and debris emerged from the windows. You could hear the bop-bop-bop of automatic weapons being fired. Afterwards there were ambulances, fire engines and a press conference.

The next group of terrorists to try this trick will probably have the sense to invite the cameras inside. The news crews, unless the law tells them not to, will probably do their best to accept the invitation. For the terrorists, publicity is half the point. For the media, a siege is just too good a story to pass up. The television news teams were drunk on adrenalin for days afterwards. When Constable Lock got home, he found ITN waiting for him. 'No, no,' said Constable Lock politely. 'Another time maybe, but not now.' 'WHAT ARE YOU GOING TO DO WHEN YOU GET IN-SIDE?' 'Well, I'm going to see my children . . .' 'HOW DO YOU FEEL?' 'No, no. I've got to go now. Later.'

On *Newsnight* (BBC2) the BBC sound technician who had been caught up in the nightmare told his story at length. As a sound technician he is not required to possess the gift of vivid speech, so it would have been foolish to expect that the scenes he had lived through would come alive. That he himself was alive, along with all the other hostages except two, was something to be grateful for. But I think the time has now come to be a bit sceptical about the role of television and the Press in these matters.

While the siege is on, the media give it stature. When it is over, they help prepare the stage for the next one. The ecstatic articles about the SAS currently appearing in the newspapers are a case in point. Next time the rescue might not come off, whereupon the SAS, owing to the expectations of infallibility which have been built up, will be held to have failed.

The cold, dull truth is that when self-loading weapons are fired in confined spaces, even if they are being wielded by trained men firing single, aimed shots, innocent people can very easily get killed. The thing to do is to avoid sieges in the first place, not indulge in wild fantasies about camouflaged supermen licensed to wipe out wogs.

It is only in civilised countries that this kind of terrorism can hope to succeed. To leave the terrorists unpublicised would be to render them ineffective, but the terrorists are able to count on the likelihood that in a civilised country the freedom of information will not be restricted. Yet there are many freedoms which a civilised country must restrict if it is to stay civilised, the classic example being the freedom to shout 'Fire!' in a crowded theatre. The time might now have come for the freedom to report certain terrorist acts to be restricted.

The problem would be one of definition, but need not be insuperable on that account. The present voluntary code of media conduct might, for example, be improved if it could be agreed that the public interest may require certain terrorist acts, involving the seizure of hostages, to be reported only after their release. Normal access to information would be allowed, but its dissemination would be delayed. As things stand, we can expect London to become a vast TV studio with ambitious performers heading towards it from all over the world. Nor will the prospect of being blown away by the SAS prove much of a deterrent. I have hung around television studios long enough to know that there are people perfectly ready to commit suicide in order to star in a show of their own, even when they have nothing to say.

'Such lips would tempt a saint.' In *'Tis Pity She's a Whore* (BBC2) Cherie Lunghi had a mouth to match the line. One could easily imagine her brother falling prey to a forbidden impulse. Updated from the time of John Ford to somewhere about the time of Shelley (whose *The Cenci*, it should be recalled, touched on similar happenings in the time of John Ford), the taboo intrigue took place within a country house lavishly appointed. Settings, costumes and lighting could not have been bettered. In an atmosphere of luxurious decorum, innocent sin fought it out with law-abiding evil.

The piece works if you believe in the lovers. Kenneth Cranham's Giovanni would have got more of my sympathy if I had not been so busy casting myself as his rival. Annabella was enough to bring out the brotherly instincts in any man. Anthony Bate, as the suavely powerful Soranzo, was understandably disappointed to find his attentions rejected. Little did he know that it was because brother and sister had already acquired the habit of collapsing regularly into the cot. Eventually the inevitable happened and Annabella married Soranzo to save the situation. He was displeased to find that she was pregnant. His boy assistant, Vasques – the reliably threatening Tim Piggot-Smith – got the job of finding out who had been responsible.

Vasques was hard to like. For one thing, he had already murdered one of the play's star attractions, namely Hippolita, wonderfully played by Alison Fiske. In fact Alison Fiske was so wonderful that I rather resented seeing the back of her. Vasques saw the back of her too, since that was the angle from which he preferred to slake his fell desires. Then he killed her. Then he killed someone else. Then he killed Giovanni, but not before Giovanni had killed Annabella.

Sex and violence were aspects of each other. The text was played straight, which helped ensure that the comic relief (Rodney Bewes as Bergetto, the thick suitor) was actually comic. Having seen the play twice on stage, I had made my mind up about it too long ago to change. I really think it is not much of a play. But this was a great interpretation.

Nixon popped out of the woodwork again, this time on *The Book Programme* (BBC2). Previously he had been on *Panorama* (BBC1), where he had attempted to flatter his hosts by suggesting that the problem about the hostages in Iran might be solved more quickly if the British were appointed as brokers. On *The Book Programme* he was equally eager to please, but his immediate audience was less receptive.

Nixon was plugging his new book, *The Real War*, which apparently advances the thesis that the Third World War is already on. Nobody else in the studio really concurred with this and indeed Professor Taylor was prepared to say that the whole notion was actively mischievous, but Nixon for some reason carried on as if they were all agreeing with him.

11 May, 1980

Master stroke

A⊤ a time when lovable Irish rogues are harder than ever to love, Frank Cvitanovich, with his film *Murphy's Stroke* (Thames), somehow succeeded in making lovable Irish rogues seem quite lovable.

Led by Tony Murphy, lovably played by Niall Toibin, the lovable rogues staged a caper by which a horse named Gay Future would come in first, instead of, as the world had been led to expect, last or never. They would thereby stand to make a profit of 270 grand. It was a measure of Cvitanovich's psychological subtlety that you quickly found yourself hoping they would get away with it.

But then, all caper movies work on the same principle. The audience must pull for the lovable rogues, or else the entertainment has failed. The challenge resides in winning the audience over. Thus the movie becomes a species of heist in itself. There are two main ways to sucker the punters. First of all the caper, or heist, or in this case the stroke, should be of elaborate ingenuity, so as to stun the groundlings with its brilliance while not being too complicated for them to follow. Second, the villains perpetrating the con should be as adorable as possible.

Murphy's Stroke scored heavily in both these departments and thus rated as a formidable stroke on its own account. But it left even the most successful caper movies behind when it came to the matter of atmospherics. Indeed these proved, in the long run, to be the point. Through a neat twist, the clever Irishmen were let down by an Englishman who behaved like a thick Mick. This made them gloomy, but you were made to see that they would have been that anyway, even if their brainchild had been safely delivered.

Murphy's mob had been wasting their intelligence and energy on a poor cause. Cvitanovich didn't have to hit you over the head with the metaphor: it was there in the desperate laughter. In the bar the pranksters sadly eyed the portraits of the great Irish writers lined up on the wall. Somebody started singing 'The Mountains of Mourne'. Nobody in the gang raised his voice but you could hear the delirium of wounded national identity.

Without touching on any subject more violent than the anger of a hoodwinked bookie, *Murphy's Stroke* succeeded in being one of the more penetrating television accounts of the permanent role Ireland seems destined to play in the affairs of Britain.

Rock Athlete (BBC2) is a new three-part series about people who climb rocks. The director is Sid Perou, who earlier, if my memory serves me right, gave us one or more programmes about people who go down holes. They are the same kind of people in each case, but they point in different directions. The ones who go downwards talk in echoey voices and have to be rescued by the Army. The ones who go upwards are less likely to end up as news items and seem to lead a healthier life generally.

United in possessing finely tuned physiques, the rock climbers are divided in their methodology. Some rock climbers believe that anything goes. They hammer expanding bolts into the virgin rock and link them up with ropes. Given the appropriate budget they would obviously build a marble staircase all the way to the top. A purer breed insists on ordinary pitons as the upper limit of artificial aid. The most pure breed of the lot goes straight up the rock face with no means of attachment except chalk on the fingertips.

Believe me, if you didn't see this last bunch, you should have. They're *evolving*. Their fingers are long and sensitive, like those of Vladimir Horowitz or certain species of climbing frog. Crouching in space, with fluttering fingertips they search the smooth rock for irregularities, like a blind man reading Keats. Sensitive toes propel them upwards. 'Oof! Aangh!' they say quietly. 'Harf! Ungh! Hoof!' Clearly they have left the English language far behind. The commentary, alas, was still stuck with it. Every climber was described as the most unique in creation. 'More than anyone else he has extended the frontiers of the sport.' But this was a programme so brilliantly photographed that not even dull talk could make it boring.

Getting a welcome repeat, *Fred Dibnah, Steeplejack* (BBC1) had all the excitement of rock-climbing plus high-grade chat as well. Fred, in his offhand way, is a natural talker. Since he does a lot of his natural talking 300 feet up a brick chimney on a windy day it will be appreciated that his words carry weight. 'I feel better when I'm doin' it,' explained Fred, meaning that he feels better when he is a long way off the ground and moving on horizontal surfaces so restricted that one false step will entail a quick return to his starting point. 'You're dicing with death with the rotten old top of a chimney,' he said, casually flicking a butt down its gaping maw. 'Been a lot of men died muckin' around with them things. Hah, hah.'

Fred's vocation is to bring down old chimneys by the traditional method. He removes bricks at the base and replaces them with wooden props. Then he builds a fire to burn away the props, whereupon the chimney falls where he wants it. Dynamite does the same job a lot cheaper, with the result that Fred is feeling the pinch. But he fights back by pointing out just how thoroughly dynamite has been known to drop a chimney on the wrong spot. On one occasion, he informed us, the dynamiters dropped a cloud-piercing stack 'straight through the middle of a mill just kitted out for a three-shift system. Hah, hah.'

Fred then showed how it should be done. The fire burned happily until the chimney, as if lulled to sleep by warmth, toppled exactly where Fred wanted it – only a few inches from where he was standing. At least five cameras recorded the event for posterity, which will be a dull stretch of time if it has no room for people like Fred. 'I've got to go and climb up something,' he mused: *per ardua ad astra* in a flat cap.

Brian Moser, of *Disappearing World* fame, has launched a new series called *Frontier* (ATV). The people of the Barrio in Ecuador are not well off. Moser and his team went to live with them in order to find out just how hard poverty can grind. This is better than a tip-and-run raid, but it makes you wonder if the people won't perhaps feel worse off than ever when their new friends go away. While pondering that question you can work on your Spanish, since everything said is fully subtitled. You can also count your material blessings. The people of the Barrio haven't got *any*.

'It's a very special night in Hollywood,' said Olivia Newton-John during the course of introducing her all-star spectacular, *Hollywood Nights* (BBC1), and instantly you knew it wasn't a very special night in Hollywood: it was a very ordinary night in Hollywood, with a lot of averagely famous names you didn't particularly want to hear from loyally pitching in to help Olivia in the doomed task of putting herself across as something more fascinating than a nice girl.

Ageless in the sense that she has never begun to grow, Olivia will always hold the microphone as if it were a lollipop, sing of love as if it were a case of mumps, look sultry as if she were about to sneeze. It is not one of the great ironies of history, only one of the small ones, that the squeaky-clean Olivia should have been chosen to star in *Grease*, a movie of such grubbiness that after seeing it I felt like washing my skull out with soap.

25 May, 1980

Someone shart JR

IN a week which contained a full-scale production of *Hamlet*, the well-known tragedy by William Shakespeare, there could be no question about what was the most important event – the long-delayed episode of *Dallas* (BBC1) in which JR got shot.

The BBC overdid the joke, as the humourless are wont to do. After JR had been plugged there was an item on the *Nine O'Clock News* (BBC1) to tell the world that it had happened, almost as if anyone who hadn't been watching would be interested in hearing about it. Before the episode rolled there was a great deal of preparatory barking from the link-men. 'The long-awaited dramatic climax to the present series of *Dallas* – the shooting of JR!' In the event, all you saw was JR getting mown down. You didn't see who was pulling the trigger. Thus was the way left clear for another long tease-play before the next series arrives to put us out of our supposed misery.

The Beeb should realise, poor soft creature, that the *Dallas* thing is only a gag if you play it straight. After all, that's what the actors are doing. With the possible exception of JR himself, everybody in the cast is working flat out to convey the full range of his or her, usually her, emotional commitment. Sue Ellen, in particular, was a study in passionate outrage when she realised the extent of her husband's perfidy. Her mouth practically took off. You will remember that JR swindled all the other big oilmen in Dallas by selling them his oil wells 'off the coast of South-East Asia' just before the wells were nationalised, presumably by the South-East Asian Government. This behaviour filled Sue Ellen with disgerst, and she reached for her gern.

Sue Ellen keeps her gern in a bottom drawer. Or perhaps it is JR's gern and on this occasion she was only borrowing it. Whatever the truth of that, you were left certain of one thing: that you could not be sure it was Sue Ellen who shot JR. Candidates for the honour were queueing up in the corridor. It is even possible that Miss Ellie shot him, since she has been showing increasing signs of madness, singing her dialogue instead of saying it. Don't be surprised if the sheriff turns up with a wornt for her arrest. There could be a tornt of wornts.

And so to *Hamlet* (BBC2), starring Derek Jacobi in the title role. As writer/presenter of *Shakespeare in Perspective: Hamlet* (BBC2), which was transmitted on the previous day, I am duly grateful to the BBC for the opportunity to say my two cents' worth about the best play in the world. This, however, was only an average production of it. It didn't matter so much that Elsinore was set in a velodrome, although you kept expecting cyclists to streak past on the banking while the Prince was in mid-soliloquy.

How the play is staged certainly matters, but not as much as how the lines are spoken, and in this production it soon became clear that there was a mania on the loose to speak them in the most pointed manner possible, so that the Bard's meaning would be fully brought out. We have the Royal Shakespeare Company to thank for many virtues and this one vice – a way of speaking Shakespeare's blank verse that is almost guaranteed to deprive it of its binding energy, which is not meaning but rhythm. To a large extent the meaning will take care of itself if the rhythm is well attended to, but if the rhythm is broken then no amount of searching emphasis will make up for the loss, and you are left with the spectacle of an actor trying to exhaust the semantic content of William Shakespeare, with about the same chance as a thirsty man trying to drain Lake Windermere through a straw.

Derek Jacobi was an excellent Richard II, but as Hamlet he went out of his way, presumably with the director's encouragement, to give every line an explanatory reading. Enterprises of great pitch and moment, we were informed, with this regard *their* currents turn awry. The implication, presumably, was that enterprises of great pitch and moment don't usually do this, and that it usually happens only to enterprises of lesser pitch and moment. Many a time and oft I was reminded of Robert Stephens's classically over-explanatory first line as Oberon. '*Ill*-met (as opposed to well-met) by *moon*light (as opposed to daylight), *proud* (not humble, like other Titanias Oberon had had the good fortune to meet in his time) *Titania* (not some other well-met fairy of equivalent high rank walking proudly in the moonlight in that particular forest).'

Hamlet's mother and uncle were more inclined to play it straight and thus drew most of my attention, although Claire Bloom could not help but remind you that she was better handled in an earlier production, *Henry VIII*, a well-thought-out occasion to which she rose brilliantly. Ophelia was encouraged to participate in the by now hallowed directorial tradition of fiddling about with Ophelia: she looked as if she were just about to sit her Danish O-levels with small hope of passing. Eric Porter rattled on lovably as Polonius, but that's a hard one to get wrong, since the reactions of all the other principal characters are carefully specified.

Clad in complete steel plus a flying panel of what looked like tulle, Patrick Allen, voice-over in a thousand commercials, was a good ghost, although you would not have been stunned to hear him recommend Danish bacon. One should be grateful, of course, that the ghost was allowed to appear at all. In the latest London stage production, I am told, the ghost is a figment of Hamlet's diseased fancy, an interpretation which involves re-arranging the text so that Horatio and the sentries never see the spook. How drama critics stay sane is beyond me.

As the Japanese Like It (BBC2) engagingly showed the aforesaid Derek Jacobi on tour with the Old Vic *Hamlet* in Japan. The stage version of his performance sounded twice as good as the television version. Presumably some of the Japanese theatre companies learned a lot about how to underplay a scene. Their leading actors, even when engaged in contemplation, show a tendency to stamp around like Toshiro Mifune with piles. The Haiyuza company, however, looked wonderfully accomplished. Their transvestite Rosalind was lyricism incarnate and the whole production around him/her bubbled with inventive life. The same director will be staging *Hamlet* next January. Doubtless he will include plenty of tumbling, juggling and magic sword-fights.

On the *South Bank Show* (LWT) Melvyn Bragg interviewed Polanski, who was fascinating about his craft. It was refreshing to hear someone of his unchallenged technical skill declaring outright that Laurence Olivier is a film director of genius. Polanski has seen Olivier's *Hamlet* twenty-five times. Bragg screened an excerpt from it and there you had it, if you had ever forgotten: the way Shakespeare should look *and* the way he should sound, with Olivier's voice moving as quickly and accurately as his body, so that the meaning of the verse rippled outward in your mind as the stress skipped rhythmically forward like a stone flung across the water.

1 June, 1980

Idi in exile

As if to demonstrate that the tangles democracies get into count as nothing beside the horrors of tyranny, Idi Amin made an appearance on the *Nine O'Clock News* (BBC1). Exclusively interviewed by Brian Barron, Idi spoke from his mysterious hideout, which nobody except everybody knows to be the Sands Hotel, Jeddah. That the BBC agreed with Idi to keep his whereabouts secret bespeaks a certain old-world charm, like the punctiliousness with which, during the Second World War, they are reputed to have paid Hitler's royalties into a Swiss bank account. Idi's phone number at the Sands, incidentally, is Jeddah 692020. Give him a bell in the middle of the night and tell him you're the voice of retribution. God knows he's got it coming.

But Idi looked as innocent as a chocolate Easter egg as he faced up to Brian Barron's exotic vowels. 'Hay,' asked Barron, 'did you get eight of Uganda?' Idi earned some marks for understanding the question, even if his answer left something to be desired in the area of veracity. He called his precipitate flight a Tactical Withdrawal. There was a lot of emphasis on his determination to regroup and stage a comeback. Soon his country would call him. At this point the viewer was assailed by a profound sense of familiarity. Where had we heard it before, this talk of answering the people's summons? Of course! Oswald Mosley!

Idi stood revealed as a black Blackshirt. His rather pleasant dial, however, showed you just how little you can judge by appearances. A sinister buffoon whose idea of a good time is to make innocent people bash each other's heads in with sledgehammers, Idi has all the self-righteousness of the truly dedicated nut. 'I am fresh, strong, and I am concerned with the question in Uganda.' Uganda had better sort itself out pronto before Idi checks out of the Sands and comes back to look after his adoring flock. 'Most of them love me . . . they want me to save them from the chaos situation that is now happening in Uganda.' What made this last utterance particularly horrible was the element of truth in it. Apparently Uganda is now in such a mess that half the population would welcome Idi back just so as to have a maniac they could rely on.

With that degree of unintentional humour available, the intentional kind had little chance of snaring the viewer's allegiance. Nevertheless Victoria Wood's play *Nearly a Happy Ending* (Granada) made its intended impact on the benumbed funny-bone. Written by Victoria Wood and with lyrics by Victoria Wood, the play starred Julie Walters and Victoria Wood. The lady's credits gang up on you in a way that was once reserved for Orson Welles, to whom, in her own self-awarely self-conscious mind, Victoria bears a certain physical resemblance. She's got herself pegged for a fatty. Even the slim version of Victoria Wood thinks like the fat one, with nervously defensive but almost invariably funny results.

In this play Victoria had slimmed down to find love. Unfortunately nobody wanted her body even in its narrow form. She discovered this fact while out on the town with her hopeless friend, engagingly played by Julie Walters. Julie was a scruff with an X-certificate kitchen you couldn't have cleaned with a skip. The exaggerations are Victoria's: she has a knack for them. Her jokes fall into shape as naturally as her figure doesn't. Witness her midnight emergency telephone calls to the Weightwatchers' duty officer. 'I'm on the kitchen extension staring full-face at a Marks & Spencer's Individual Spotted Dick.' Spotting that word 'Individual' as the indispensable comic element is a gift that can't be taught: you've either got it or you haven't, and Victoria's got it. Next time, however, she might care to go deeper.

8 June, 1980

Hrry Crpntr

THE FIRST week of *Wimbledon* (BBC1 and 2 recurring) started Harry Carpenter and his famous Rain Commentary. During the opening days there was hardly any tennis, but there was more than enough rain for Harry to perfect his commentary, if perfecting was what it needed.

It has been years now since Harry began calling Wimbledon Wmbldn. Later on he contracted Wmbldn to Wmln. This year it is back to being Wmbldn, possibly because Harry's lockjaw has been loosened by the amount of rain demanding commentary. 'Covers still on the outside courts. Thousands of people waiting, hoping against hope . . . Not a pretty sight is it?' The cameras zoomed in elegiacally on the canvas covers as the raindrops bounced. 'Still, we're pretty cosy here in the BBC commentary box under the Centre Court, and what's more I've got Ann Jones with me.' Obviously it was a Beatrix Potter scene down there in the burrow.

The downpour lifted long enough for Borg to demolish El Shafei and his own racket, which exploded. To be more accurate, it imploded, since it is strung to a tension of 80 lb. As we saw in *Borg* (LWT), the young champion strings his rackets so tightly that they go 'ping' in the night, thereby waking up his manager. Borg runs a taut ship. He likes his headband tight too, to bring his eyes closer together. He likes them touching. 'Do you think it's going to make any difference to Borg's play, when he gets married?' somebody asked Gerulaitis. 'I hope so,' was the sad reply.

Like a Volvo, Borg is rugged, has good after-sales service, and is very dull. There is no reason to begrudge him his claim to the title of greatest of all time, although it is not only Australians who believe that Rod Laver would have won Wimbledon ten times in a row if the absurd rules against professionalism had not kept him out during the best years of his career. But Borg's role as chief mourner in a Bergman movie becomes positively treasurable if you compare him with Nastase, as it was possible to do when the rain briefly stopped on a later day.

I turned on the set hoping to see more rain, but instead found Nastase on his hands and knees banging his head against the turf. Then he got up and pretended to skate. Then he got back down on his hands and knees and had a lengthy conversation with the electronic eye, a machine which threatens to crab his act, since he will be able to dispute no more line calls. Imagine how exhausting it must be being Nastase, especially during those terrible few minutes in the morning when there is nobody to show off to except his own face in the shaving mirror. You can imagine him drawing moustaches on himself with the foam, sticking the brush in his ear, etc.

'There's a drain down both sides of the court where the water can escape,' Harry explained. 'Brighter weather is apparently on the way. But it's going to be some time . . .' More rain next week.

But now, a word of praise for Jonathan Dimbleby's *In Evidence* (Yorkshire), a double-length programme which set out to investigate the police force. Dimbleby deserves points for his ability to go on asking awkward questions long after the people he is talking to have shown signs of wanting to steer the conversation into a blander channel. Such admirable tenacity should be kept in mind when you are reflecting that he writes with a trowel and expects us to be stunned when he uncovers corruption in South America.

'Yesterday almost a child. Tomorrow an officer of the law,' announced Dimbleby as a new recruit to the police force went through the mill. Prospective bobbies were shown how to talk with choleric citizens. 'It appears to me, sir, that you're a bit irate.' This contrasted nicely with what would presumably have happened in America, where the recruit would have been holding a large gun and the irate citizen would have been spreadeagled against a wall.

That the British police do not as a rule go armed still seems to most of us a healthy tradition. As Chesterton pointed out, tradition and democracy are the same thing. Dimbleby is very properly worried about the Special Patrol Group, but his concern would have been more forceful if he had explained that he objected to it as an innovation. By his relative silence on this point he tacitly aligned himself with those Left-wing wiseacres who believe that in becoming overtly brutal the police are at last revealing their true nature. This approach is neither as true nor as useful as saying that 'saturation policing' is something new and causes more trouble than it is worth.

Dimbleby had no trouble digging up horror stories in the big cities. An entire and clearly law-abiding family had been picked up for no reason and suffered a lot of inexplicable bruising while being run in. The police investigated themselves and found themselves innocent. You don't have to be a member of the Anti-Nazi League to find that unsatisfactory. On the other hand one would have welcomed from Dimbleby a more forthright acknowledgment of the possibility that the British police force does at least as much to hold society together as to pull it apart.

Dimbleby doesn't seem to realise that the police force is the only thing that keeps him from being carved up by people who don't like the way his face is currently arranged. The tip-off came when he explained that the police force attracts people of 'authoritarian' sympathies. Undoubtedly it does, but it also attracts people who simply believe in authority, which is not the same thing as being authoritarian. A fine distinction but a crucial one, which a television reporter should be able to make.

The BBC's *Dance Month* has been more robustly enjoyable than its twee title sequence might have led you to expect. A programme about Nureyev called *I Am A Dancer* (BBC2) dissuaded you from any notion that he might have been a bricklayer, but like many independent productions it suffered badly from sclerosis of the script. 'This routine of training, day in and day out, year in and year out, it never stops. It never stops, this routine of training . . .'

During one modern ballet performed to the sound of what could have been fifty or sixty of Borg's tennis rackets gradually exposed to intense heat, Nureyev and a drowsily sexy ballerina engaged in a long attempt to pull each other's tights off without using fingers, toes or teeth. It sounds difficult, but was fun to watch, although probably not as much fun as it was to do.

No Maps on my Taps (BBC2), an excellent import from American public television, gave you the essence of black tap-dancing. The technique, lovingly fostered during long years of harsh neglect, came up as fresh as paint. There was some attempt to suggest that white tap-dancing was done by numbers rather than from a true rhythmic sense, but this was an understandable case of racism in reverse. As was proved by the miraculous dance numbers in *You'll Never Get Rich* (BBC2), Fred Astaire had as much rhythm as a human being can have. So did Rita Hayworth, who incredibly succeeded in dancing to the standard set by her own beauty.

29 June, 1980

Borg's little bit extra

THE second week of *Wimbledon* (BBC1 and 2) was largely occupied with yet more rain. Between downpours Borg dealt rapidly with Glickstein. 'The reason Borg is the champion that he is,' explained Mark Cox, 'is that he has that little bit extra to pull out, and he certainly has pulled it out in these last four games.'

Thus Borg progressed majestically into the closing rounds, continually pulling out that little bit extra. When McEnroe pulled out his little bit extra, you rather wished that he would tuck it back in. For a long time he did his best to contain his awful personality, tying his shoelaces between games instead of during and merely scowling at the linesmen instead of swearing. When sulking he kicked the ground but raised no divots, nor did his service take more than a quarter of an hour each time. You have to realise that McEnroe is serving around the corner of an imaginary building and that his wind-up must perforce be extra careful. He has a sniper's caution.

Finally the rain got to him. By Thursday he was behaving as badly as ever, thereby confirming the rule that Wimbledon, like alcohol, brings out the essential character. Virginia Wade tried losing to Betsy Nagelsen but couldn't make it, even when she resumed her old habit of throwing the ball out of reach when attempting to serve. 'I must say, Ann,' said Peter West, 'that Virginia's living dangerously.' 'That's self-evident, Peter,' said Ann Jones. In the last set Virginia managed to convert her 5–1 lead into a 5–3 lead by making even more unforced errors than her opponent, but it was too late: defeat had eluded her.

What she needed was an opponent even younger and more inexperienced than Nagelsen. Andrea Jaeger was the ideal candidate. With a smile that looked like a car-crash, Jaeger practically had to be wheeled on in a pram. Her range of gesture was no more prepossessing than McEnroe's, plus the additional feature that she expressed annoyance by driving the edge of her racket into the court, the next best thing to attacking the turf with a mattock. This was just the kind of opposition that Virginia knew how to lose to. Having duly sacrificed herself, our girl was last seen talking to David Vine.

The rain went on. Eventually it got to Harry Carpenter himself. Harry's Rain Commentary continued triumphantly into the second week, but the mark of a true champion is not to be made nervous by success. Like Borg or Nicklaus in their separate fields, a great rain commentator must be single-minded. Above all he must not be rattled by criticism.

As the cameras once again surveyed the system of lakes forming on the court covers, Harry showed signs of cracking. 'These shots will please one or two of our critics in the national press,' he gritted. 'Seem to prefer the rain shots to the tennis, some of them. It's not raining. It's drizzling. The forecast earlier wasn't too optimistic . . . it gave the impression that once the rain started it might hang around for some time . . .' He still had style, but his confidence was gone.

Dan Maskell, on the other hand, never falters. He might say break point when he means set point, or either when he means match point, but his authority only increases with the years, or yers. 'Ooh I *say*! That's as brave a coup as I've seen on the Centre Court in *yers*.' It takes more than a flood to stop Dan, who would wear Scuba gear if he had to, and often sounds as if he is wearing it already. Self-control is everything, as Martina Navratilova proved by losing to Chris Lloyd. Navvy has the talent, but Lloyd has the temperament. A bad call lost Navvy the second set, but the way she brooded on it lost her the match as well. Dan convicted her of a 'somewhat wayward temperament'.

Navvy was lucky to last that long. Only failing energy stopped Billie Jean King from putting her out a round earlier. 'Well, this is an up and downer, Ann, isn't it?' 'You can say that again, Dan.' For a moment I thought Dan might, but he decided not to. It was a thrilling match, but still had nothing on the Olympian struggle between Connors and Tanner, during which the ball was only occasionally visible.

Tanner won the first set in a few minutes. Connors would have done better to take a seat in the stands. Right up until the sixth game in the fifth set they sounded like frantic woodchoppers in a frozen forest. Then Tanner slowed down and Connors broke through. Jimbo is not a particularly attractive personality – although compared with McEnroe he has the charm of Arthur Rubinstein – but we should enjoy him while we can.

Those of us who remember *The Brothers*, the BBC's all-time most absorbing sudser, will accept no substitutes. Nevertheless *Buccaneer* (BBC1) could well do at a pinch. The Brothers, you will remember, were in road transport and thus spent most of their time trucking around. The Buccaneers are in air transport. They run an air freight service called Red Air, represented by a single Britannia which spends most of its time grounded at foreign airports, stranded by sabotage. Meanwhile the company directors of Red

GLUED TO THE BOX

Air devote themselves to intrigue, much of it sexually motivated.

This is a clear case of top-heaviness at boardroom level, since considering the airline's carrying capacity there should be only one part-time executive and no directors at all. But the ladies involved, who include Shirley Anne Field, are fetching enough to prove that somebody at the BBC has at last grasped the principle by which any given episode of a modern soap opera must feature at least three delectable females, one of whom shall not be fully clad. Put a stetson on all that and you've got *Dallas*. Put wings on it and you've got *Buccaneer*. You still haven't got *The Brothers*, but perhaps that era is never coming back. It was all so very British, and all so long ago.

In *The Big Time* (BBC1) an unknown girl called Sheena Easton was given her chance to become a pop star. Since she was pretty and could sing rather well it was no surprise that her dream started to come true, although first she had to endure a lecture from Dorothy Squires. 'I had tomatoes thrown at me, apples thrown at me . . . that's what made me a performer,' gushed Dorothy. 'If you can hold an audience in the palm of your hand, sometimes make them laugh, sometimes make them cry . . .' Sheena sat silent through all this, no doubt resolving to go and do otherwise. She has the temperament to go with the talent and just might make it.

6 July, 1980

Big-time Sue

A MEDICAL reader writes to say that the BBC's preoccupation with *Dallas* (BBC2 recurring) should not be called Dallasitis. Apparently the correct term is Dallasosis, meaning a condition brought about by excess Dallas. Dallasitis merely means that one's Dallas has become inflamed.

But one's Dallas *has* become inflamed. Also it is producing offshoots. One of these is called *Knot's Landing* (BBC1), a series likewise dedicated to recounting the doings of the Ewings, except that these Ewings are the ones who couldn't make it back in the Big D, where the clouds sail through buildings made of mirrors. Now they are somewhere in the dreary north, at Losers' Landing. In the latest episode Gary finally confessed to being an alcoholic – the sum total of his achievements to date. You will remember that in the early episodes of *Dallas* Gary had a drinkin' prarlm.

While *Nationwide* was concerning itself with *Dallas*, *The Big Time* (BBC1) was concerning itself with *Nationwide*. The idea of *The Big Time* is that ordinary people get a chance to fulfil their dreams of becoming pop stars, free-fall parachutists, brain surgeons, etc. But since the programme would be a no-no if the people chosen were complete duds, the pressure is on to find someone with a reasonable chance of making it.

The latest episode featured Sue Peacock, a housewife, who wanted to be a *Nationwide* presenter. She was trained up to have a shot at being a *Nationwide* presenter for a day. To everybody's astonishment, except the viewers', she did quite well, rendering the *Nationwide* regulars awe-stricken at how quickly she had mastered the fundamentals of their supposedly arcane craft.

But it was obvious from the start that Sue simply had what it took, whatever that is. Most people very correctly find that being on television is a madly artificial experience. A few people find it as natural as breathing. Whatever airs these few might tend to give themselves, the fact remains that they have merely been blessed with a knack that ought to be common, but for some reason is quite rare. The best television presenters are those who regard their own ability to keep their heads while talking to camera as rather less than a sufficient qualification for immortality.

Of the people Sue was given the opportunity to meet, Robin Day and Sir Ian Trethowan were the most substantial, principally because they are both something rather more than just talking heads. As a natural corollary, they are also both devoid of an artificial manner. But everyone else, from the narrator on downwards, was all charged up with cheap drama. 'One of the hottest seats on television . . . hard, demanding, ruthless . . . come and meet Frank Bough.'

Catching the mood, Sue kept saying 'I just don't know whether I'll be able to do it.' This was exactly what the professionals wanted to hear her say. The more she went on about her nerves, the more they could indulge themselves in a lot of calmly purposeful moving about.

Finally it was the big night and Sue, having complained duti-
fully about her nerves right up to the last minute, ripped through
her part of the show without a fluff. All concerned showered her
with praise, but only Bob Wellings had the nerve to say that she
was frighteningly good – i.e., that the job isn't really all that hard.
Or to put it another way, being a personality isn't a job. Staying
calm, reading out the words and asking the elementary questions is
merely where you start from.

The substantial television personality has much more than skill.
Indeed David Dimbleby is almost devoid of a sprightly manner,
but in *Panorama* (BBC1) he did an exemplary job of following up his
earlier investigations of South Africa. By now he has made himself
part of the landscape down there, to the extent that he will
probably be invited back when the big change comes. That the big
change will one day come emerged from this latest programme
without having to be stated.

Dimbleby has always made a point of letting the white South
Africans put their case. But the way they go on putting it is enough
to tell you that they will one day lose everything unless they see
reason soon. A white farmer explained that there was nothing
wrong with cramming 120,000 blacks on to a piece of arid land
which had previously been designated as fit for a tenth that
number: if you put six whites in a car they would complain about
overcrowding, but you could put sixteen blacks in and they
wouldn't notice.

By contrast, the black and Coloured leaders were articulate and
widely comprehending. Not that Dimbleby was out to prove that
the white ruling class is congenitally stupid – only that it has a
vested interest in not being able to understand the issues. In South
Africa it takes an unusually perspicacious white to see that if power
is not soon shared then the non-whites will take all of it.

From where we sit, any of us can see it straight away. This makes
it easy for us to be contemptuous, but Dimbleby, to his great credit,
never lapses into a sneer. His manifest objectivity has by now won
him the respect of all the contending parties, with the possible
exception of the police, who at one point threw gas at him. External
reporting will probably not have a direct influence in South Africa,
but it is certainly useful here, where people who should know better
seem constantly to need reminding that it is possible to be objective

and politically committed – indeed that for a television reporter his objectivity *is* his political commitment.

On the first day of the *British Open* (BBC2) I tuned in and found the blond head of Jack Nicklaus barely protruding from the deep rough. Five strokes adrift from the leader, he seemed on the verge of going down the sluice, but a birdie at the 18th kept him alive. He registered disappointment with a slight down-turn of the lower lip. So it was with Don Juan in Baudelaire's great poem: the calm hero leaning on his sword. What Baudelaire left out was the rain, which fell on Muirfield as if Wimbledon had been only a rehearsal.

20 July, 1980

There is no death

PUTTING two weeks of sun and surf between himself and the Olympic Games was the smartest move your reporter ever made. While David Coleman and the rest of our squad were performing strongly in the stadium, I was performing weakly in the surf. Very small waves came in with yours truly standing briefly on top of them.

My surfboard was the size and weight of an armoured car. I could stand up in it like Rommel. Small children dancing in the spume were mown down as I charged the beach. Thousands of beautiful French girls removed much of their clothing as a tribute to the hot sun and the green Atlantic. It occurred to me that in some previous incarnation I had been closely related to Poseidon on my mother's side. The possibility that this suspicion might not be without substance was underlined by one of the first programmes I saw when I got back, a speculative round-up called *I Have Seen Yesterday* (BBC1).

The show was full of people convinced that the life they were currently leading was only one of many lives which had featured their own wonderful personalities as the central attraction. Christmas Humphreys was the most substantial name involved. He was a big noise back in the 1950s, unless I am getting him mixed up with Humphrey Bogart or Father Christmas. Somewhere back around then he wrote a Pelican about Buddha, or it might have been a Buddha about pelicans. On his reckoning he might well have written it at the time of Alfred the Great, or Rameses II, especially the latter. For those Westerners who believe in reincarnation, ancient Egypt exerts a magnetic attraction. Presumably Easterners gravitate towards a more Oriental epicentre, shaded by a small, gnarled tree under which Buddha once sat.

'There is no death.' Flutes, tom-toms. 'For some reason Egypt often occurs in people's memories from the past.' Perhaps it is because they have all seen the same Hammer movies, in which Peter Cushing braves the Curse of the Arab Scarab only to be hounded to his doom by a lurching mummy earning Equity's standard rate for a non-speaking appearance. But one of the programme's star witnesses, a pop flautist, was convinced that his complex being had its roots in the hot sand of long ago. 'You went into the pyramid?' 'I went into the pyramid, yes.'

He went into the pyramid because he had heard there was a 'great sound' in there, meaning that his flute would make an even more bewitching noise than it did in, say, Abbey Road. But inside the vast pointed structure he gradually found himself absorbed by the past. 'You were sitting in there in the dark playing a flute?' 'In a sarcophagus, yes.'

Back in England, the flautist met a Hungarian girl called Karina who was similarly convinced that her own startling psychological make-up could only be explained by reference to the Valley of the Kings. Certainly her eye make-up needed some such justification: either she had been daubing the mince pies with kohl and myrrh or else she had been mugged.

'Karina's interest in the occult led her to investigate her previous lives.' Inspired by Karina, the flautist has incorporated the Egyptian theme into his stage act. While guitarists dressed as mummies twang mysterious Egyptian chords, the flautist shouts appropriate lyrics into a defenceless microphone. 'I am the Lord of Light! Bestowing life on earthly matter solely by my . . . sight!'

Next on was a lady who had once been James IV of Scotland. The vanished monarch had thoughtfully bequeathed her his costume, which featured lace cuffs and some rather fetching velvet sleeves. Presumably the gold nail polish had likewise once formed part of the regal ensemble.

What the past was really like formed the theme of *Montaillou*
(BBC2), the name of a small French town near the Pyrenees.
Nowadays the town's population is being thinned by industrial-
ism. In the old days the town's population was thinned by the
Inquisition, which used to root out heresy by raising its suspected
proponents to high temperatures. The local people, peasant folk in
the main, were oppressed simultaneously by five separate power-
structures: the Count, the King, the Church, the fire brigade and
the VAT inspector. Of all these the Church was the toughest,
torturing people at the drop of a pointed hat, usually because they
had called the Church the instrument of the devil.

The Church disabused them of this notion by toasting them over
a low flame. But first the Bishop extracted confessions. What
makes Montaillou remarkable is that this register of confessions
still exists, providing a sobering record of that Organic Society to
which Dr Leavis, among others, was always so fondly harking
back.

We have it on the Bishop's own authority that one of his own
priests deflowered virgins. A lady called Beatrice mixed cocktails
of menstrual blood and amassed an impressive collection of um-
bilical cords. By the time all these stories had been collated it was
obvious that the only thing to do was adopt a root and branch
attitude to the whole problem.

The few villagers left alive were then successively subjected to
the Black Death and a particularly disgusting invasion by the
English. Today there are only twenty-five people left. Wandering
among these in a nifty cap, Robert Robinson looked chipper but
thoughtful. A clever man, he was obviously pondering the fine
membrane of time that separates us from an age even more
unimaginably violent than the one we live in now.

As if to remind you that the present is no picnic either, that
excellent series *Women of Courage* (Yorkshire) gave us Sigrid Lund,
a Norwegian pacifist who saved Jewish children from the Nazis.
Sigrid met her first Nazis at Bayreuth, long before Hitler came to
power. She immediately identified their race theories as sheer
poison. Later on she got a bunch of children out of Prague and took
them to Norway.

To get there they had to go through Berlin, where grown-up
people spat on the children. When the children asked Sigrid why

this was happening, she said it was because the people had a cold. All the children were billeted with Norwegian families, but after Norway was invaded one of the families turned out to be Nazi. With great regret this family handed their child over to the Gestapo. They had grown to love the child but wanted to do the right thing. The child died in Auschwitz.

Inside Story (BBC2) pronounced itself concerned about prostitution. 'This has been a very difficult film to make,' intoned the director, popping up before the camera to hammer home the subject's unusual significance. 'By its very nature a lot of what goes on goes on in the dark.' Holland, Hamburg and the United States were all visited in search of a solution. Only New York turned out to be worse than Soho, but the dialogue from all sources was cleaned up for our tender ears. 'I think you're a (beep) (beep) you (beep) (beep) (beep), so why don't you (beep) (beep) with a (beep) (beep)?'

An American proprietor of a legal brothel called the Chicken Ranch irrefutably pointed out that the only way to make prostitution benign is to legalise brothels. Since this argument contains the monopoly of common sense on the subject there was nothing else to say except (beep) (beep).

10 August, 1980

You tested the gyroscope?

ANTIBES was the venue for this season's first international heat of *Jeux sans frontières* (BBC1), a television phenomenon which encapsulates the Europe of the present and presages the world of the future. It is omnilingual yet inarticulate, multicoloured yet homogeneous, frantic yet static, contrived yet banal. It is a girl from Urps-am-Gurgl dressed as a duck and it is Eddie Waring.

'And here we are live on the site of an old Roman fort,' cried Stuart Hall. 'Her her her! Har har har! He's gone!' A giant fibreglass goblet had just been knocked off a greased plank and was upside down in the water with a pair of legs sticking out of it. The legs being French, Stuart felt free to expatiate on his theme. 'Hee

hee hee! He really must be a little bit disappointed at his perform-ance! Hoo hoo hoo! A little *distrait*, I think.'

For years I have been following Stuart through heat after heat and final after final of both *It's a Knockout* and *Jeux sans frontières*. He is an intelligent, cultivated man, yet somehow he has managed to embrace his task without recourse to drugs. The question is not how he does it, but how we will do it when our turn comes. 'Doctors and teachers, I ask you what is Hell?' wrote Dostoevsky. 'I submit it is the agony of being unable to love.' Nice try, Fyodor, but the correct answer is very different. Hell will take place on earth, will consist of *It's a Knockout* and *Jeux sans frontières* played every day forever, and nobody will be permitted not to watch.

Here comes the British team dressed as knights in shining armour. They are carrying prop maces. They are riding bicycles. They must ride their bicycles across a greased plank and hit a dangling shield with their maces. The shield goes further up in the air as the game goes on. If they swing and miss the shield they fall into the water. If they swing and hit the shield they still fall into the water. 'With your donger you have to smash the gong!' cries Stuart. 'Come on, Britain! Keep it going! WATCH IT!' But Britain turns out to be no good at hitting shields with dongers while dressed as knights and riding bicycles. Our lads accumulate in the water like the Tour de France in a pond. The German team, on the other hand, looks as if it has been trained specifically for this event since the Spanish Civil War.

'You tested the gyroscope?' Spacemen delivered lines like that to each other in the first episode of *The Martian Chronicles* (BBC1), purportedly a faithful rendering of the Ray Bradbury book, but actually the latest in a long series of undeviatingly tacky science fiction epics which carry the name of Milton Subotsky prominent among the credits. I like Milton Subotsky, who once did me the honour of asking me to write a movie for him. He is under the illusion, however, that if one actor asks another actor whether he has tested the gyroscope, the audience will be convinced that they are both spacemen. Subotsky productions, whatever their budget, are dogged by an ineradicable naivety. The only difference be-tween *The Martian Chronicles* and such hallowed items of Sub-otskiana as *They Came From Beyond Space* is that this time more money has been spent on getting things wrong. In *They Came From*

Beyond Space the female lead was Viviane Ventura in a crash helmet. In *The Martian Chronicles* you get Gayle Hunnicutt to look at – a distinctly more rewarding experience. But the guys in the spacesuits are still asking each other whether the gyroscope has been tested.

Anyway, it is 1999 or thereabouts, and Rock Hudson is in charge of the first NASA mission to Mars. 'The atmosphere on Mars, though thin by our standards,' Rock tells the waiting pressmen, 'is perfectly capable of supporting life.' This suggests that Rock has not been keeping up with the previous quarter-century of research into the subject, and has perhaps stayed on in the job too long. It is important to remember at this point that actors do not write their own dialogue. Rock was a perfectly credible submarine captain in *Ice Station Zebra*, where he had some convincingly technical-sounding things to say. But that was a real movie, whereas this is the pits.

The spacemen, whose attire suggests that in 1999 military uniforms will be very badly tailored, climb into their module and fly up to join their waiting rocket, an order of events which intriguingly reverses the usual procedure, in which the chief function of the rocket is to lift the module. As it staggers through deep space, the rocket has smoke coming out the back. It would look more like a real rocket if it did not have smoke coming out the back, but the people responsible for this series have either never seen any film of what a real rocket looks like or, more likely, have seen it but not taken it in. Their imaginations were formed by *Flash Gordon Conquers the Universe*, in which rockets had smoke coming out the back.

On Mars, a local lady telepathically detects the approach of the Earthlings. She has no ears but otherwise looks like a soubrette from a Paris nightclub circa 1921, an effect reinforced by a hat borrowed from Josephine Baker. Her husband swans epicenely around in a white négligé plus choker. He has no ears either, which leads you to suspect either that these two are freaks huddling together for warmth or that earlessness is a Martian characteristic. The lady telepathically falls for the leader of the mission. Her husband, in a fit of Martian jealousy, wipes out the whole expedition with a gun that looks like a cream nozzle.

The second mission also gets wiped out, having made the

mistake of dining with the inhabitants. 'The chocolate pudding was drugged.' The third mission is led by Rock in person. Having said goodbye to Gayle Hunnicutt and tested the gyroscope, although not necessarily in that order, he leads his men to a rendezvous with the unknown. On the sands of the Red Planet it is suddenly revealed that one of the expedition's members is a drunken psychopath. For some reason this fact eluded the screening process on Earth. There is a Martian city close by. It is composed of cubes, cones and . . . well, balls, actually.

The black member of the crew falls in love with Martian culture, steals the cream nozzle, zaps the psychopath and disappears into the city of balls. At the end of the episode Rock is forced to shoot a mysterious figure in yet another white nylon négligé. I hoped this would turn out to be Gayle Hunnicutt, but it was the black. Gayle was back on Earth, counting the days before she got out of the series.

There have been some good repeats. Bamber Gascoigne's *The Christians* (ATV) survives a second viewing and P. J. Kavanagh's *William Cowper in Olney* (BBC2) is an impeccably composed and delivered little programme. The commercial for Bounty Bars features girls with bodies as beautiful as their faces are dumb. It is into the latter that they cram the Bounty bars, their features contorted as if something wonderful were happening to the former. What times, as Cicero said to Catiline, and what customs.

17 August, 1980

A horse called Sanyo Music Centre

RIDDEN by Harvey Smith, Sanyo Music Centre collected eight faults during the feature event of *Showjumping from Hickstead* (BBC1).

You might have imagined that Harvey was mounted on a piece of stereo equipment, but Sanyo Music Centre, though it has a leg in each corner like certain types of radiogram, is in fact a living creature with no provision for the electronic reproduction of sound.

By now the habit of delivering thinly disguised commercials is well ingrained. The number of BBC programmes involved in flogging products has become something of a wonder, and would by itself constitute a weighty argument for a more realistic system of funding, so that the hucksters could be kept at their proper distance. Sponsoring an event should be enough. When the event itself sprouts bill-boards and trademarks the sound of the cash-register drowns the roar of the crowd. *Match of the Day* (BBC1) has now moved to Sunday with no slackening in its determination to use money for a measure. 'Brown coming in . . . cost £300,000 last year . . .' Does that include spares?

Getting back from Italy last weekend just in time for the last episode of *The Martian Chronicles* (BBC1), I was pleased to see that it lived down to the previous two instalments. Rock Hudson hasn't worn a look of dismay like that since he had his skull drilled in *Seconds*. Raquel Welch, on the other hand, had a good week. *The Legend of Walks Far Woman* (BBC1), despite its awful title, proved to be a far from negligible movie about the Red Man, featuring a brilliant performance by Nick Mancuso as a Red Man called Horse's Ghost. He was a completely believable Red Man who somehow managed to be a very funny straight-faced comedian, like Chevy Chase plus feathers.

The only way you could be sure Raquel was a Red Woman was by her make-up. Not a very good singer or dancer, she is not a very good actress either. But she will take a lot of trouble to set up a serious project and deserves a measure of applause for it. Her chief failing is to introduce an element of *décolletage* into whatever costume she happens to be wearing. This sartorial quirk was particularly inappropriate in *Fantastic Voyage*, where the costume was a pressure suit, but it didn't look quite right for Walks Far Woman either. She looked like Sticks Out Woman.

Raquel also turned up as guest star in the latest episode of *Mork and Mindy* (Anglia), a slick imported American comedy series in which the one-line gags pile up in struggling heaps. Raquel wasn't quite fast enough for the regulars, but she made up for it with her figure. Playing a ruthless invader from space, she was particularly ruthless with the top buttons of her uniform, which had evidently cracked under the strain.

In the first scene of the Elvis Presley movie, *Roustabout* (BBC1), Raquel, then at the start of her career, was briefly visible as a teenage walk-on. She didn't say her line particularly well, but her face registered. The best thing she ever did was her small part in *Bedazzled*, where clever direction made it look as if that extraordinary shape of hers were light on its feet. Actually she has to march into position and set up camp for the night. She is Walks Awkwardly Woman. But there is something nice about her.

Trevor McDonald's night-to-night analysis of the Polish crisis on *News at Ten* (ITN) was consistently the best thing of its kind on television. No doubt the reason for the TUC's silence on the subject is that their leaders and ideologues are preparing a lengthy, ringing endorsement of the Polish workers' demand for free trade unions. The only other possible explanation is that the TUC is run by shambling mediocrities who are an insult to their own heritage.

The bravery of those Polish strikers who talked to our television interviewers simply defies belief. It won't be enough for them to win temporary concessions. If they don't succeed in changing the entire social structure of Poland, they are doomed. 'We must not stop our fighting,' one of them told the BBC, 'it's too late.'

The boys and girls on *Newsnight* (BBC2) did their best with Poland too, but a more typical item was the investigation of Christine Keeler's 'lifestyle' – their word, not hers. After a hard decade and a half at the bottom of the barrel, Christine is apparently now slated to make a come-back. She has just been appointed an editorial adviser to *Men Only*. Imagine where she has been, if working for *Men Only* is a step up. The programme showed Christine in action, giving her expert views to an editorial conference. The assembled brains strove to look impressed while she filled them in on the arcana of her special field, sex.

Christine's outline is as lissom now as it was then, when Government Ministers dished their careers because they couldn't keep their hands off it. Also her natural dress-sense – one of the distinguishing marks of the 1960s was that the hookers looked as good as the socialites – has survived her reduced circumstances. But her face is a bitter expression of the emptiness inherent in the whole idea of love as a commodity.

Christine's reasons for surfacing as an editorial adviser were more negative than positive. 'I might as well,' she told the camera, 'because they won't leave me alone.' She meant the Press, but might well have mentioned *Newsnight* in the same indictment. The programme affected a lofty detachment, but in fact had no thoughts on the subject.

Worst documentary of the decade was *Ladies from Hell* (BBC1), all about the role played by the kilt in the history of the highland regiments. This turned out to be roughly the same as the role played by trousers in the history of the lowland regiments. No questions were asked about what must surely be the kilt's basic drawback, namely the danger to which it exposes the warrior's vulnerable parts when he is hurdling the hardier varieties of heather.

In *Swan Lake* (Thames) Makarova was too good for words. As Odette/Odile, she made Odile look worth losing Odette for. Indeed Odile, at the end of a mind-watering *pas de deux*, threw Siegfried a smile which plainly asked 'Your place or mine?' and would have set his tights alight if he had had his eyes open. Here was proof that sex can go public only as art. Anything else is just the vain attempt to transfer a non-transferable asset, but there is no call to despise the other girls merely because they are not Makarova. If Raquel Welch could move like her and Christine Keeler knew a tenth as much about eroticism it would be better for them but worse for us, since the world would be less various, and there would be no *Miss United Kingdom* (1980) to help remind us that people are not to be despised just because their dreams are cheap.

31 August, 1980

This false peace

I N the latest episode of *Lou Grant* (Thames), Lou was tired. We were meant to assume that he had grown weary from the accumulated pressures of being City Editor of the *Los Angeles Trib*, but it was equally permissible to assume that he was all worn out from carrying Emmies. In Washington on Sunday night I tuned in and saw Lou's programme pick up so many of these awards that there were scarcely any left over.

I was in America as part of a concerted attempt on the *Observer*'s part to anatomise the entire country for your instruction. As you might have gathered from our bill-board advertising, we were all disguised as various sections of Mount Rushmore in order to blend into the scenery.

Back in London, it was a relief to switch on something with a bit of depth to it, even if the depth contained the murky shapes of German terrorists. Part Two of *The Miracle Workers* (BBC1) set out to demonstrate that Germany's Economic Miracle had a sinister underside. As proof, a highly articulate ex-terrorist was encouraged to explain his conduct.

He had a sinister underside and a sinister overside to go with it. Not that there was anything scruffy about him. On the contrary, he looked like a bureaucrat. 'I guess I am a good German,' he mused, 'because I always try to live in coincidence with my Ideas.' The Ideas revealed themselves to be the standard kit of speciously logical abstractions.

'It's hard to see', probed the interviewer, 'why political murder was necessary.' The ex-terrorist, who no longer goes in for that sort of thing but still thinks it was reasonable at the time, had his answer ready. 'We were convinced that our welfare state was only possible by exploitation of the Third World . . . we must disturb this false peace in our country.'

He appeared humble and probably thought himself to be so, but in fact it takes infinite arrogance to assume that you know your own motives for committing murder. How can you be sure that you are not just a murderer? On the subject of Schleyer's death, however, our friend remained confident. 'What we did to him was part of what we are trying to change.' Which practically made it Schleyer's fault, if you thought the thing through: Schleyer hadn't done much about fixing things in the Third World, so he was asking for it.

The ex-terrorist signed off with an eminently quotable version of an Idea basic to the playtime Left. 'We did what we thought was right and found out it was wrong. So we are richer than before.'

In the latest instalment of *Invitation to the Dance* (BBC1), once again hosted by Rudolf Nureyev, we were treated to Béjart's version of *The Firebird*. The dancers were dressed in blue cotton outfits which were presumably meant to evoke the proletarian overalls worn by Chinese ballet companies during the long period when Mao's cultural Ideas were being carried into action.

What made this particular notion not just frivolous, but lethally frivolous, was the fact that during all the time when the Chinese ballet companies were performing such masterpieces as *Taking Tiger Mountain by Strategy*, real creativity was being brutally suppressed. The Gang of Four, who sent the best dancers out into the fields to have their muscles ruined, were merely taking this Idea to its logical conclusion.

It was hard to quell a mental image of what Béjart would look like slaving in a rice paddy, but there was always Rudy's mode of dress to distract you. This time he was wearing a patchwork-quilted bedspread for a horse. The previous week it had been a sweater open right across the shoulders, the better to reveal his superbly articulated bone structure.

In *Cambodia: Year One* (ATV) John Pilger did a follow-up to his famous programme *Cambodia: Year Zero*. There were horrible flashbacks to the first programme in order to remind us of what Pol Pot's regime had been like. 'Meanwhile, in the West,' Pilger complained, 'memories are fading.' If they are, it isn't Pilger's fault, but really I doubt if anybody capable of appreciating the issue has forgotten a thing. If Pol Pot has any historical function at all, it is to show us what happens when an Idea is fully realised. Everyone got the point, and anyone who tries to forget it can only be acting from cynical motives. According to Pilger, the United States is now doing exactly that. The Americans, he says, want Pol Pot back in power – a disgusting prospect. To back up his thesis he showed convincing evidence of how the remnants of the Khmer Rouge are being well looked after. Less convincing were his assurances about the North Vietnamese.

In *Cambodia: Year Zero* Pilger claimed that the North Vietnamese wanted to help the Cambodians but that aid from Western relief agencies was tardy. In my review of the programme I said that there seemed to be a lot of independent evidence to suggest that the Western relief agencies were being denied access to Cambodia by the North Vietnamese. Pilger wrote a letter to the *Observer* calling me a McCarthyite for saying this, but in fact subsequent evidence proved that he had indeed been wrong on this very point.

However well the North Vietnamese are behaving now – and apparently they are behaving so well that Pilger deems it tactless to mention the Boat People – there can no longer be much doubt that they were obstructive then. Yet for some reason Pilger can't bring himself to modify his account of the past. Does this obstinacy spring from pride at being the man on the spot, or is he afraid that a full picture of reality will be too complicated for us to grasp?

14 September, 1980

Bottom of the sea

ONE and a half miles down off the Galapagos Islands, according to *The World About Us* (BBC2), there are hot-air vents on the ocean floor. Around these vents cluster some of the least photogenic life-forms known to man.

Man goes down there by means of a cute little submarine known as Alvin. When man gets there, he searches around for hot-air vents. The vents are caused by the pressure of the earth's molten core blowing holes in its thin crust. When this happens, the temperature of the sea is raised, and life appears where no life had been before. The life includes tube-worms, sea-spiders, weirdo fish of the type that we are always warned we will have to eat when we have finished off the kinds we don't mind looking at, and, inevitably, Alvin.

Crouched in the bowels of Alvin, American scientists gaze out in rapture at the clustered tube-worms. The tube-worms are red-blooded, like scientists. They dwell in lengths of tube. They look like lengths of tube. There is nothing about them which is not tube-like. But look over there! What is that strange, spaghetti-like structure? Is it spaghetti? No, it is more worms. And now a rat-tailed fish noses towards the window, obeying the universal instinct of all creation – to be on television.

As a special edition of *Panorama* (BBC1) inadvertently demonstrated, life around a hot-air vent on the bottom of the sea off the Galapagos Islands has a lot in common with modern China. For example, there is about the same standard of public debate in each case. Reporter Michael Cockerell devoted his investigations chiefly to the Role of the Media in Chinese Society. The *People's Daily* now has the democratic right to say anything it likes about the Gang of Four. This right, however, must not be abused. Nobody is allowed to criticise the Communist Party.

Since the Communist Party, as personified by its all-wise father Chairman Mao, was directly responsible for the Gang of Four coming into existence, you would think that being debarred from mentioning this fact would place a pretty large restriction on political analysis, and you would be right. The *People's Daily* keeps Deng's clichés set up in type so that they can get his latest speech into print without delay. This is merely laughable, but it was pitiable to see and hear the paper's editor trying to think in the same manner.

The editor had been arrested during the Cultural Revolution and tortured for a grand total of seven years. During the daily torture sessions the Red Guards invited him to criticise his own errors. Not much of a one for public displays of emotion, he nevertheless gave way to tears when he remembered this. Yet recently his newspaper congratulated the Party on jailing the dissident Wei for fifteen years. Wei's crime had been to suggest that Deng's famous Four Modernisations would be meaningless without a fifth, namely democracy. Plainly Wei was right, but tube-worms are not allowed to talk like that. All they are allowed to say is glug.

We were shown some dedicated cadres removing Mao's sayings from a wall in Peking. Perhaps some day soon his god-head will be removed too. The problem will then arise of whom to worship next. I suppose it will be Deng, but a better choice would be Wei, who is a true hero. Wei, when you think of it, is the hope not just of China but of the whole world. As a teenager he was a Red Guard, which meant that he spent his days making life miserable for his elders and betters. But when he grew up he realised that it had all been a mistake: that the Party was not infallible after all, and that there was such a thing as individual conscience. Wei figured this out all by himself even when the whole pressure of the State was coming down on top of him. One's conclusion – small consolation, but some – is that human society can never be *quite* like the bottom of the sea.

21 September, 1980

Bouquet of barbed haggis

HAVING missed the first episode, I am still catching up with whatever is going on in *Mackenzie* (BBC1). Developments happen faster than the mind can sort them out.

It was an error, I can now see, to assume that the series was set in Scotland. In fact Mackenzie, though of Glaswegian origin, has now settled in London, where he is attempting to make it big as a builder. In Glasgow the chances of expressing his building talent to the full were necessarily limited. In London he will be able to build what is in him – a whole row of bungalows, for example. There is creative fire in his eyes, dispelling your suspicions that his thickness of accent might be accompanied by an equal density of mind.

It was also a blunder on my part not to spot that the series is set in 1958. The way that old Ford Consul keeps turning up should have tipped me off. Also Mackenzie's mistress, the classy model Diana, wears outfits that might have been created by Norman Hartnell, although only during a black-out. All these clues should have been enough to establish the period, but I was led astray by Mackenzie's haircut. I assumed him to be a fairly ordinary-looking builder from about now. It never crossed my mind that he might be a daringly advanced builder from the 1950s who signals his rebellion by wearing his thatch at a challenging length.

Andrea Newman's great strength as a writer is that she sees the drama and passion in the lives of ordinary people. Her housewives carry on like Maria Callas. Her builders are driven men. Mackenzie himself is the Lermontov of his profession. He might die in a duel. His sons might stab him. But there is nothing he can do to avert his fate, for his mistress has bewitched him. 'You've got magic hands,' she breathes, 'along with a few other magic bits and pieces.' You can see why Mackenzie has thrown caution to the winds – he has never heard a woman speak so poetically before.

Mackenzie's wife, a wan nurse known as Jean, appears to have no chance against this kind of competition. 'I'm an all-or-nothing kind of person,' she pipes, but there is no denying that the beauteous Diana has the breeding to go with the polish. 'Her mother', someone explains, 'was Caroline Venables, the great society beauty.' But Diana is no layabout. She must work hard to keep up the payments on her hideous furniture. The furniture is distributed thinly around a dwelling which was created by Mackenzie. That, I have at last realised, was how they met. She was standing there in a pill-box hat with one foot in front of the other when along came Mackenzie and built a house around her.

Jean has a friend called Ruth. Married to a weed, Ruth finds solace in the arms of Diana's father, a wise old Hungarian whose name, if I have caught it accurately, is Applecrumb. Ruth would like to tell Jean all about that but can't. 'I feel we're all in terrible danger,' she tells Applecrumb when they are in bed together (not all of them at once, just her and Applecrumb), 'She's your daughter and my friend. He's my friend too.' Ruth is putting it mildly, since at one stage Mackenzie was more than her friend. She, too, has run her loving hands over the boiled-potato skin of the priapic builder's capable back.

'If Jean has it out with Diana,' muses Ruth, 'I'm so afraid that David might with me about you.' David is Ruth's feeble husband. He lacks Mackenzie's creative imagination. Mackenzie keeps on getting richer, but it has no effect on his manners or wallpaper. He goes on wearing his vest under his pyjamas as of old. By this time, however, the distraught Jean is beyond noticing her surroundings. She has called in the priest. To him she pours out her troubles, undeterred by the fact that he is wearing his hair long enough to invite instant defrocking. But if virtue is not rewarded, vice is certainly punished. Diana is bearing Mackenzie's child. Another little builder is on the way.

Diana's first instinct is to have an abortion, so as not to interrupt her career as a model, although the clothes she models are so badly cut that she could go on wearing them until she was in labour and nobody would ever know. Her mother has arranged abortions for her before. 'Is it that builder person?' But that builder person is outraged when he hears of the plot to kill his child. 'It's my child,' he brogues thickly. 'I want it.' Diana looks appalled. Her mother looks intrigued. Her father looks drunk. 'I could have eaten your Arp,' he smiles fondly, meaning that he could have eaten her up, not that he could have consumed some surrealist work of art in her possession.

That is as far as my critical analysis has reached, but the series is growing faster than one's ability to deal with it, like a home-grown yoghurt. Some general comments, however, might not be out of place at this point. That Andrea Newman's barbed wire entanglements should prove so wildly popular is no great surprise. She has the energy of the true primitive. Her characters aren't even cardboard but you care what happens to them. My own prediction is that Mackenzie, while engaged in constructing some revolutionary block of purpose-built maisonettes, will fall off a ladder and be nursed back to health by Jean. Diana's affair with her own father will end in his death and her suicide or vice versa. Diana's mother will seduce the priest and the wimpy David will get off with Caroline Venables, leaving Ruth free to pursue her career as a dramatist. One day as she is passing Mackenzie's abandoned building site she will see a bouquet of barbed wire . . .

I don't know what the Greeks did to deserve *The Greeks* (BBC2). This truly awful series is narrated by its producer, Christopher Burstall, who, I am afraid, has developed a bad case of feeling obliged to give us Something of Himself. 'Some time ago,' he told us in the introductory episode, 'I suggested making four films . . .' In later episodes he has shown even greater reluctance to fade into the background. One respects his late-flowering enthusiasm for the Greeks but wonders if enthusiasm is quite enough. Some indication of a willingness to learn Greek, for example, would have been an advantage. It is a difficult language to acquire late in life but not impossible, and there is nothing like some acquaintance, however slight, with the original writings to dissuade you from the notion that the Greek philosophers carried on like ham actors lurching around in frocks.

Denis Healey was the first one of three guests in *Parkinson* (BBC1) last weekend. He was there to plug his book but also managed the odd bout of political exposition. 'The most important thing', he explained, 'is to get this Government out.' This explanation left him no time, unfortunately, for a further explanation, the one about how the Labour Party is to make itself believable again.

28 September, 1980

Thank you, wow

DOUBTLESS the handicapped children benefited materially from the abundant funds raised overnight by the *Telethon* (Thames), but one wonders if even they thought it was worth the spiritual cost. Here was a sample of what the Americanisation of television will do to our collective consciousness if we let it happen. There are less painful ways of committing national suicide.

For example, we could all run a bath and stick our heads in it at a prearranged signal. Threatening to be the first of many, this Telethon was confined to the London area. People living in other areas might like to have some hint of what went on. A full description would take as long as the Telethon itself – i.e., a couple of days – but briefly, what occurred was this. A lot of famous people, some of them more famous than others, were asked to donate their services. The resulting shambles took place in the Wembley Conference Centre and was compèred by Jimmy Young, Joan Shenton and Rolf Harris.

Scores of minor celebrities answered telephone calls from members of the public pledging money. A running total was flashed up so that we could all see how fast the target of a million pounds was being reached. Since there was obviously no way of stopping the Telethon except by reaching the target, it was not surprising that the lines were soon jammed. 'Wo-ho-wo-ho-wo-ho-way,' sang Leo Sayer, 'I love you more than I can say.' If you wanted to hear less of things like that, you had to fork out. An alternative was to switch off the set, but the Telethon had the hypnotic fascination of a rattlesnake.

Joan Shenton talked of 'projects that make the quality of our lives better in the community'. All unaware that she was engaged in a project guaranteed to make the quality of our lives in the community appreciably worse, she struggled bravely to supply spontaneous link material. So did Jimmy and Rolf. The show needed a lot of linking, because the majority of the turns had no clear start or finish, but consisted of bad comedians trying to make other bad comedians laugh, or people playing darts. Occasionally a star came on. Petula Clark was one of these. 'God bless the child who can stand up and sing,' she sang.

This was hardly appropriate in the circumstances, but then Petula was the girl who once climaxed a feminist gala by singing 'I Don't Know How To Love Him'. When the applause died down, Petula had some patter ready. 'Thank you, wow. What an atmosphere here. I just hope the people at home can feel the excitement we feel here, know what I mean?' Rolf Harris said, 'Your blood's worth bottling.' He said that all the time. Then he said, 'Let's see how the darts are going.' He said that all the time too.

Paul Daniels, a magician who is often quite a funny improviser, did some unfunny improvising with a member of the audience. 'O.K., Sandra. You've got a lovely leg. What a pity about the other one.' This, too, was perhaps not entirely appropriate in the circumstances, but by now the Telethon had a momentum of its own, like a glacier on the rampage.

The only certain beneficiaries of a telethon are the corporations who secure cheap advertising time by putting up prizes or making tax-deductible donations. The audience gets little to enjoy beyond the unintentional humour generated by technical cock-ups. As for the handicapped children, they gain some of the means of life – but life in what kind of world? To do what? To watch Bernie Winters host a darts competition? There has to be another way.

After only two episodes, *The Shock of the New* (BBC2), fronted by Robert Hughes, is plainly destined to be one of the more considerable series about the visual arts. Hughes has gone a long way towards restoring to television the combination of wide knowledge and natural eloquence that has not been seen and heard on this subject since Lord Clark retired from the screen.

Not that the opening episode was without faults. Hughes popped up all over the world in different suits, a sequence of transmogrifications made more glaring by the fact that they all occurred while he was uttering a single sentence. This was no doubt planned but it was a bad plan. On the other hand the subject was tackled coherently from the start. You were given a clear idea of why the great talents did what they did.

Hughes has a highly developed historical sense. In the cemeteries of the First World War he scanned the lists of names and reminded us of the different art that might have happened if the slaughter had not. Always one of the most vividly inventive prose writers of his generation, Hughes brings more verbal talent to the task than the task needs. But that has always been the secret of doing this kind of television well – to have something in reserve.

Subtle direction wins little glory. You could make a long list of prizes which Derek Bailey's programme on *Rex Whistler* (BBC2) will not win. Yet anyone with half a clear eye could tell that Whistler's ebullient talent as an illustrator had here found its ideal appreciator. Whistler was a dandy with fashionable friends, but his creations were genuinely inventive: he had fantasy raised to the level of imagination. There was a tragic vision behind his humour. The tragedy fulfilled itself when he died as a war hero. The script, which faced every issue except the one about his sexuality, sensibly took it for granted that he was an important artist.

The President's Son of a Bitch (Granada) was an instructive documentary about a man who tried to stop his government wasting a billion dollars and was persecuted for being right. *Battlestar Galactica* (Thames), though glaringly a cheap *Star Wars* rip-off, looks better on the small screen than in the cinema. The best comic-strip science fiction on television at the moment, however, is *Buck Rogers in the 25th Century* (LWT). The hardware looks good and Wilma Deering looks simply sensational, like Wonderwoman with brains.

For what Wonderwoman looks like without them, there was the dire *Lynda Carter Encore* (BBC1), in which Lynda capped a series of pitiable 'impressions' by attempting to impersonate Bette Midler, the very girl whose inspired naturalness discredited Lynda's brand of lip-gloss glamour beyond redemption.

5 October, 1980

Fast maggots

BAD sight of the week was in an episode of *Horizon* (BBC2) dealing with high-speed and time-lapse photography. Speeded up several hundred times, a gang of maggots devoured a dead mouse.

Before time-lapse photography was invented, it was always assumed that maggots, though they travelled in packs, did their actual eating on an individual basis. But time-lapse photography reveals that they dine as a group. 'They are swimming in one another's juices,' explained the voice-over. First they were all over the mouse's head like a cloche hat. Then they were around its neck like a feather boa fluttering in the wind. Then they were around its waist like a grass skirt worn by a particularly active hula dancer. Then they were sliding down past its hips like a dress being rapidly removed by an impatient lover. By this stage you had to remind yourself of the necessity to breathe.

But if time-lapse photography can tell you fascinating things about maggots, high-speed photography can tell you even more fascinating things about cuttlefish. High-speed photography slows cuttlefish down by roughly the same amount that time-lapse photography speeds maggots up. You are then able to see how two cuttlefish combine to deceive a crab. One cuttlefish creates a diversion while the other gets into position for a stern attack. Then – zap! Or, as interpreted by high-speed photography, zzzzaaaapppp. Exit the crab. Leonardo da Vinci never saw anything like that. He had the fastest eyes in Christendom but they couldn't quite stop a galloping horse, although they could slow it down enough for him to draw it better than anyone had drawn a galloping horse before.

On *News Headlines* (BBC2, with subtitles for the hard of hearing) Kenneth Kendall referred to punk rock star Johnny Rotten as just plain 'Rotten'. Rotten, it was revealed, had assaulted a pub-owner who had refused him a drink. There was a photograph of Rotten to help you understand why an otherwise tolerant man might be reluctant to supply him with intoxicating beverages. Rotten got three months.

Everybody who grew up with rock and roll in the 1950s has his own story about how the music eventually went sour on him. My own story turns on the personality of Rotten. About twenty years after my psyche was first liberated by Bill Haley and the Comets, I encountered the Sex Pistols in a television studio. It was the first television show that the Sex Pistols, headed by the aforesaid Rotten, ever did. I could see the point of their anger. I even thought that their music had a certain vigour. But they had set out to be repellent and in my case they achieved their aim instantly. Rotten himself was a cuttlefish in human form, snapping in every direction at a speed which benumbed the eye. It would have taken high-speed photography to show just how nasty he actually was.

And yet it all started with innocence, as the old films and videotapes dredged up by the BBC's 'Rock Week' unanimously proved. It was particularly moving to take another look at *Rock Around the Clock* (BBC1), a film which even on its first release had the symmetrical beauty of an old shoe. The term 'exploitation movie' in those days meant what it said. The budget barely stretched to retakes. Twelve extras represented a crowded dance-hall, and turned up again half a reel later to represent a crowded night-club. But the music sounded like a miracle at the time and I'm bound to say that to me it still does. Haley, already a veteran when the film was made, had barely launched into the opening bars of the title song before I was out of my chair and leaping about in the style which once had my fellow dancers standing back in admiration, or at any rate fear.

Heroes of Rock 'n' Roll (BBC2) was a long and absorbing compilation of rock clips clumsily linked by an actor. 'Hi. I'm Jeff Bridges.' But the bad chat was no great drawback, since right from the beginning the music had always been accompanied by cheap link material and dumb voice-overs. In *Rock Around the Clock* you couldn't have Fats Domino or the Platters without a few badly chosen words from Alan Freed to introduce the act.

Clips from Elvis Presley's old TV shows showed him for what he was – rhythm incarnate. In short order the television producers were told by their executives to shoot Elvis only from the waist up, but before that happened there was a brief, glorious period in which his entire range of movement was made visible to the waiting world. Standing on his toes, he could wag his knees so far to one side that his behind touched the floor. I once almost got a hernia in my ear trying that. As a dancer Elvis was always at his best when choreographing himself, as he did in *Jailhouse Rock* (BBC1), whose Leiber/Stoller songs still come up as fresh as paint.

But the rarest of the many entrancing things in *Heroes of Rock 'n' Roll* was the sight it afforded of Phil Spector engaged in the actual creation of the Wall of Sound. Even today I still play my Crystals and Ronettes albums on those occasions when my spirits need lifting and soothing at the same time. Spector had the gift of cool excitement. Nobody growing up with popular music now could possibly imagine how *witty* rock and roll used to be.

Still, the young must have their music. That was how rock and roll started in the first place – that your parents couldn't stand the sight or sound of it was the whole idea. If one were able to keep in touch with what is happening now then what is happening now wouldn't really be happening. Nevertheless *Kate Bush in Concert* (BBC2) sort of made you wonder. I thought 'Wuthering Heights' was a terrific single: the lyrics were patent drivel but the melodic line passed the old grey whistle test with flying colours and one found oneself turning up the volume in order to catch the last bars of that exultant guitar solo at the end. Kate has talent to burn.

But she is also a weirdo. For her opening number she appeared in a luminous leotard with Superman trunks, a hairstyle like an exploding armchair, and bare feet. Thus got up, she groped around in the gloom, perhaps looking for her band, who were making a hell of a noise somewhere back there behind the dry-ice fumes. At this point I went away and had a little lie-down. When I came back she was dressed as a white hunter and pointing a rifle at the camera-man. It was all a long way from the Crystals or even from Joni Mitchell, who in *Shadows of Light* (BBC2) was to be heard trilling some latterday additions to the repertoire that seemed the last word in sophistication ten years ago, but nowadays sounds more than a little twee.

Making 'The Shining' (BBC2) was a small programme by Vivian Kubrick about her father's big new movie. All concerned con-spired to worship Stanley – including, alas, Stanley. Jack Nichol-son told of how Stanley had pushed him into an acting style beyond naturalism. Clips of Jack in action proved that there is no acting style beyond naturalism except ham.

12 October, 1980

Donor kebab

SEX CHANGES and organ transplants dominated the week. I gave the sex changes a miss, on the grounds that what's right for some of us leaves others of us crossing and uncrossing our legs while whistling nervously. Organ transplants, however, are of vital interest to all.

You never know when you might need a new heart. The question arises, however, of how the doctors know that the donor is dead. In *Panorama* (BBC1) we were shown the tests that the donor is given when he is wheeled into the hospital. Iced water is dripped into his ear. Does he flinch? A wisp of cotton wool is brushed against his eyeball. Does he blink? If six of these tests all come up with a zero reaction, the donor is considered dead and is immediately raided for his kidneys, his heart, or whatever is required by the patient currently scheduled to be granted a new lease of life.

As a layman I was hugely impressed by the fastidiousness of the doctors concerned. My only doubts arose from the fact that I once knew a girl who would have shown no reaction to any of those six tests or another six like them. Her name was Kerry Mills and I suppose that she is now Australia's Federal Minister for Education or something like that, but at the time I am talking about she was twelve years old and had volunteered as a guinea-pig for a clinical case study I was compiling as part of my psychology course at Sydney University. Everything I did to her produced no result whatever. When I tapped her knee there was no reflex. Nothing.

'The donor's heart has finally stopped,' said the voice-over. 'If he wasn't dead when he was wheeled into the theatre, he certainly is now.' This part went without saying, since they had already taken some bits out of him. But what if he *had* been alive when they wheeled him into the theatre and he hadn't been able to tell them? I stress that this is a personal worry. People related to donors past and present are right to have confidence in medical opinion. When one makes ill-timed jokes about Donor's Club cards and donor kebab, one is well aware that a nagging insecurity is finding verbal expression.

Goodbye Gutenberg (BBC2) deserved its repeat. Here was a vision of the fully computerised future, when all the electronic machines in the world will be linked up and our bodies will consist entirely of transplants. There is nothing more thought-provoking than the spectacle of a Japanese engineer and a Japanese computer having a long conversation in Japanese. The Japanese are able to give their machines voices only because the Japanese language, though fiendishly complicated when written down, consists of a relatively simple set of sounds when spoken. English has thousands of sounds and so will be much more difficult to render digitally. This particularly applies to Brian Walden, presenter of the redoubtable *Weekend World* (LWT), which last weekend illuminatingly analysed the economy. Nor would Eddie Waring be an easy subject.

On *World of Sport* (LWT) there was motorcycle jumping. The venue was Exhibition Stadium in Toronto. As a venue for motor-cycle jumping, Exhibition Stadium is perhaps not ideal. There is no room for a take-off run, so a track has to be laid up the tiers of seats all the way to the high rim of the stadium. This enables the motorcyclist to rush downwards at terrific speed and leap into the air. Unfortunately there is very little room for him to stop in after a successful landing. A few straw bales were provided to soften the potential resistance of what looked like a large toilet.

As has become common with trash sports, there was a welter of expert commentary. 'If you're going too fast,' one commentator explained, 'you're gonna overjump the ramp.' He didn't need to add that if you're going too slow you're gonna break every bone in your body. Another commentator interviewed the star jumper, whose name was Gary. This, too, has now become a trash-sport basic: the pre-interview, usually complemented by a post-interview conducted either on the victory dais or in the ambulance. 'Gary, the wind's gusting 25 m.p.h. How's it gonna *fectya*?' Gary politely declined to point out that the wind wasn't gonna *fect* him half as much as the prospect of taking a nose dive into a toilet while riding a motorcycle.

Gary having by some miracle survived the jump, the next man at the top of the track was Karel Soucek, described as 'a latterday knight who travels the world seeking adventure – a strange and solitary man'. Karel hurtled down the track, up the ramp and into space. His front wheel was too high. 'He's in trouble.' Karel's front wheel was by now directly above the back wheel, so there was nothing he could do except let go and land on his behind at 80 m.p.h. 'He's up! He's walking away from that crash. Ken, I can't *believe* he's walking away from the crash.' But with professional motorcycle jumpers at this level only one thing counts – making it to the post-interview. 'I'm glad', grunted Karel, 'I din hurt myself.'

Gary was trying to break his world record of 176 feet, but the wind and the proximity of the toilet put him off. The commentators later revealed, however, that during a subsequent engagement at Caesar's Palace in Las Vegas Gary succeeded in breaking both his legs while attempting to jump the fountains. 'We can only wish him a speedy recovery.'

Naked armpits were the most arresting sartorial feature at this year's *U.K. Disco Championships* (Thames). Even those dancers whose costumes had sleeves still contrived to leave their armpits bare. Why they should have done this was a mystery, but an even bigger mystery was how the satin trousers stood the strain. If there were some give in the trousers their survival would be easier to explain. But there isn't room for a flea in there.

The most inventive dancer was Clive Smith from Bristol, who does a death-defying routine which he climaxes by grabbing one of his own feet and flinging it at the roof. The inevitable result is that he strikes the floor violently with his head, but by some strange method of self-discipline he seems to be prepared for this, and comes up dancing.

Elton John was the first subject in a new series called *Best of British* (BBC1) which after this can only go up. Paul Gambaccini interviewed Elton at his palatial home. Elton explained that tunes just come to him at dizzy speed and that if he hasn't written the song in twenty minutes he shelves it. Not even Bernie Taupin's lyrics, we were told, always inspired him. Paul tried Elton out on what was described as a poem by John Donne. Actually it was a fragment of a sermon by John Donne, but neither of them noticed. Elton found a tune for it instantly. 'No man is an island,' he wailed.

Kate Nelligan didn't get to bed with the German POW in the first episode of *Forgive Our Foolish Ways* (BBC1). Presumably she will in the second episode. Her missing husband will turn up alive in the third episode and there will be hell to pay in the fourth episode. There is a certain predictability about the enterprise, but perhaps it will stun us yet.

19 October, 1980

Very lovely salver

D EREK HOBSON was the amiable host of *Britain's Strongest Man* (ATV), billed as 'a contest for the British Meat Trophy compèred by Derek Hobson'. Men in leotards towed trucks, bent iron bars with their teeth, etc.

Promising, with explanatory gestures, 'a very extraordinary hour of feats of strength', Derek showed off the British Meat Trophy, which he described as 'a very lovely salver'. Derek, you felt, was at home. So was Robin Day, once again chairing the consistently excellent *Question Time* (BBC1). It would be pointless for Derek to ape Robin's manner, or Robin Derek's. Robin would not be comfortable introducing Mary Kaldor in the terms she would surely inspire from Derek. 'Mary's the daughter of a famous economist. Nothing *economical* about her figure though, eh chaps?'

Of Robin's four panellists in the latest edition of the programme, only Mary could be described as a treat for the eye, since the others were Denis Healey, Peter Thorneycroft and Conor Cruise O'Brien. Mary probably doesn't enjoy being described in sexist terms, but I am trying to draw attention away from her slight case of the Higher Inarticulacy. She has a First in PPE from Oxford and a head full of facts, but for some reason her arguments did not flow easily.

One of Mary's beliefs, as far as I could make out, is that British Leyland's strategy is all wrong: it would be better to build small buses for a rational public transport system than to hope that production-line workers will co-operate in turning out a supposedly world-beating small car. There is something to this belief, and there was a production-line worker in the audience who was ready to back it up by pointing out the salient fact about working on a production line, which is that the work is so monotonous it can't be compensated for by high earnings. Unfortunately what should have been a persuasive argument never got a hearing. Mary probably went away blaming television, but really the fault lay in her approach. She knew so much about it all that she could never say the simple thing first.

When Mary tried for a demotic utterance, she came out with such phrases as 'a completely new ball game'. This girl, you thought, has to be brighter than she sounds. Peter Thorneycroft had incomparably less of interest to say, but managed to get it said. Denis Healey knew exactly how to say what he meant, and to not say what he also meant but found it politically expedient to suppress. As for Conor Cruise O'Brien, if he were not my Editor in Chief I would be able to do a more elaborate job of praising his ability to talk naturally on television without falsifying the issues.

Mary was outnumbered three to one. It was almost enough to make you believe that television is a medium in which even the brightest woman is best advised to sit back and look as pretty as possible. Yet on *Newsnight* (BBC2) Elizabeth Drew of the *Washington Post* fed Charles Wheeler a brilliantly argued summary of American politics. I would have liked to hear more from her but *Newsnight* knows what to switch to when an item gets too interesting – football.

Michael Foot's new haircut proclaims him a serious candidate for the leadership of the Labour Party. The haircut made its first appearance on *Weekend World* (LWT). If Foot's hair had always been short, there would be nothing to object to. Similarly if Foot's hair were still long there would be nothing to object to either. But he can't have it both lengths. Clearly his hair plays a symbolic role. When it was long it symbolised rebellion. Now that it is short it symbolises responsibility. Should a great political party even consider being led by a man with a thespian thatch? I am often criticised for placing, in this column, too much emphasis on male hairstyles, but it has long been my belief that a man declares himself by the way he arranges his wisps.

'Poor old World,' said Billy in Dennis Potter's *Rain on the Roof* (LWT). 'It was a lovely garden once, you know.' Escaped from the asylum, Billy (Ewan Stewart) had come to visit Janet and John, played respectively by Cheryl Campbell and Malcolm Stoddart. Billy was either mentally defective or holy. Perhaps he was both. Seduced by Janet under a quilt, he murdered John with a knife of glass. Yes, he had certainly transformed their middle-class lives. It is a cardinal principle with Dennis Potter that all middle-class people except certain playwrights need to have their lives shaken up. The Italian film-maker Pasolini used to have the same idea. In fact his film *Teorema* was a bit of a forerunner to *Rain on the Roof*. But what *Rain on the Roof* was really like was Jerome K. Jerome's *The Passing of the Third Floor Back*, in which a houseful of people had their lives transformed by a holy stranger. It's a perennial plot – a format, in fact.

2 November, 1980

Good lug

As was revealed on *Newsnight* (BBC2), Madame Tussaud's must have been all set for a Reagan victory. Within minutes of the announcement an effigy that looked nothing like him was being lifted into position, while the effigy that had looked nothing like Carter was taken away to be given a new haircut and labelled as someone else – Gary Cooper, perhaps.

Indefatigable as ever on your behalf, I wangled an invitation to the American Embassy on the big night. The embassy was receiving satellite transmissions from the American networks. As things turned out I might as well have stayed at home, because the promised all-night nailbiter had fizzled out by the time our own ITN coverage went off the air at three in the morning. 'The map is turning blue for Reagan' was the cry of the television pitchpersons on both sides of the Atlantic. NBC's John Chancellor is an authoritative broadcaster, but he is no more riveting than any of our own people when all he has to announce is 'a very substantial victory'.

David Dimbleby was in charge at the BBC and had his usual tussle with the technology. Linked up by satellite with a commentator in the US, David suddenly announced: 'We appear to be talking on radio instead of television, so we'll get back to you.' The commentator, who had been in vision all the time, looked understandably nonplussed. Meanwhile Anna Ford was ruling the roost at ITN. Among those roosting were Edward Heath, Roy Hattersley, Jo Grimond and the knowledgeable American Lloyd Cutler. All concerned seemed ready to agree that Reagan would not blow up the world immediately. 'It's an awesome task, isn't it?' mused Heath. Anna, who had done a lot of interrupting, handed back to Alastair Burnet. 'There you are, Alastair, people coming round to President Reagan already.'

Anna had made her presence felt. She is not just a pretty face. Barbara Walters, who is not just one of those either, takes home a million-dollars-a-year salary and has a hair-stylist in attendance twenty-four hours a day, paid for by the network. The size of her pay-slip confers prestige. The prestige confers clout. The clout confers courage. She asked Kissinger how close he was to Reagan. 'I know many members of his endourage . . .' Kissinger wouldn't say what he had discussed with Reagan. 'I'd love to know', piped Barbara, 'what you *did* discuss.' 'I jusd wished him good lug.'

Next day Reagan dominated all channels in his new role as President-elect of the United States. Of the many factors which had contributed to his landing the part, not the least, surely, had been his mastery of television – an accomplishment springing directly from the decades he had spent delivering bad dialogue in the movies. 'Some of you stay here and guard the girl. The rest of you come with me. We'll head 'em off at the pass.' Obliged to utter miles of stuff like that, Reagan cultivated an inner stillness. That's the reason why he looks so natural on television now. He isn't acting.

Carter was an amateur and therefore fell prey to the delusion that on television it is necessary to ham it up. That reference to his daughter Amy probably lost him the debate, and losing the debate probably lost him the Presidency. One or more of Carter's advisers must have thought it a good idea for the President to mention that his daughter Amy was concerned about nuclear arms control. If Reagan had been given a similar line he would have crossed it out, not because it was untrue, but because it was corny. Reagan knows all there is to know about lousy dialogue. One of the reasons he has come so far is to get away from it.

Reagan is unlikely to burn a world in which he has just become the single most influential man. What we can look forward to is not universal destruction, but the agony of little nations. The phrase is

Churchill's and should be resurrected. Under Carter the US largely gave up the practice of helping right-wing regimes to make war on their own liberals. Under Reagan, especially if Kissinger makes a comeback, that sordid brand of *Realpolitik* might well be resumed.

Fronting *In Evidence – The Bomb* (Yorkshire) Jonathan Dimbleby overwhelmingly proved that nuclear weapons were a bad thing. Anybody still harbouring the belief that they were a species of Christmas decoration would have found the programme a rude shock. The point that MAD – mutual assured destruction – was the *only* possible result of a nuclear war was convincingly brought out by a series of experts. To show how convinced he himself personally was, Jonathan included a lot of reaction shots in which he could be seen nodding, holding his chin thoughtfully, etc. As one who admires Jonathan's investigative tenacity I feel justified in suggesting to him that he might care to underpin his conclusions with a bit more evidence that he has thought the subject through. Just how good, for example, is E. P. Thompson's argument in favour of unilateral nuclear disarmament?

Oppenheimer (BBC2) continues, with the dreaded General Groves emerging as a highly engaging heavy. A super-patriot straight out of the worst nightmares of Jonathan Dimbleby and E. P. Thompson, Groves would have been easy to caricature, but the part is reasonably well written and, by Manning Redwood, brilliantly well acted. Unfortunately what I predicted last week has come to pass: the physics have been left out. This leaves more room for the politics, which will doubtless be a revelation to those younger viewers who have no idea just how silly the American witch-hunt was, but the physics could have been made fascinating to everybody if described in the right words. 'Do you think you could *explain* it to me?' Groves pleaded. 'Sure,' said Oppenheimer, 'what would you like to know?' And then they *still* didn't show you.

Gavin Millar made an impressive directorial debut with *Cream in my Coffee* (LWT), a play by Dennis Potter which reputedly spent a large amount of the company's money. Lionel Jeffries and Dame Peggy Ashcroft lavished their combined talents on the task of making Potter's dialogue sound probable. Back they went to the seaside hotel in which they had long ago spent their prenuptial honeymoon. He was now a senile bully, she a wincing target for his invective. Erstwhiles it had all been different. He conked out on the very dance-floor where the spotlight had once caught them kissing. Thus the circle of time was closed. What you missed was any sense that the two of them had been in any way involved during the intervening period.

9 November, 1980

I am a tropical fish

B RINGING *The Shock of the New* (BBC2) to an end, Robert Hughes put a metaphorical foot through that notorious pile of bricks in the Tate. 'Anyone *except* a child can make such things.' From the visual aspect the series was a bit of a scrap-heap, but Hughes's script was of welcomely high quality.

The new job of art, said Hughes, is 'to sit on the wall and get more expensive'. Its traditional job was and is something more exalted. 'To close the gap between you and everything that is not you, and thus pass from feeling to meaning.' The only reason I tear these pearls from context is to illustrate that television need not necessarily be a slaughterhouse for the English language. On the contrary, there is every reason to think that well-chosen words will receive a better hearing on television than through any other medium. The reason why so much of the language you hear on television sounds like ducks talking is that the people doing the talking are, from the aspect of linguistic sensitivity and accomplishment, ducks.

None of this applies, of course, to *Miss World* (ITV), which has now changed channels as if to prove, where no further proof was needed, that tackiness is an international language understandable anywhere. In the BBC version there used to be national dress, evening dress, swimming costume, interview, guest star, decision. On ITV the same format was pursued to the last detail, even down to the master of ceremonies, Peter Marshall, who showed all the signs of having been passed through that famous BBC processing-room where front-men go to be deprived of charisma.

The Albert Hall was once again the venue. Out came the girls in national dress. Miss Bahamas wore a somewhat ill-judged hat, twenty feet across and twelve feet high, composed mainly of fruit and vegetables. Miss Australia was 'a student in communications' and Miss Somewhere Else was 'a student of human relations'. Miss Hong Kong looked like a fan dancer, but turned out to be a cop. The one before Miss Mexico forgot her own name.

Miss Uruguay also forgot everything, but after a protracted struggle managed to recall where she had come from. Miss Singapore had her speech down word-perfect, but there was something wrong with the punctuation. 'I am a tropical fish. Import-export agent.' All of this was so recognisable it was soporific. The only original note was struck by Anthony Newley, but he was electrifying. Singing a medley of his own songs, he gave the most brilliant impersonation of an egomaniac I have ever seen. Only an ice-cool professional brain could have produced such a natural impression of a man in chaos.

Wrinkling his forehead and pouting in mock self-adoration, he unfalteringly kept up the hilarious pretence that his songs were immortal and that he had a divine mission to sing them. Alternately roaring and mumbling, he threw sweets at Bruce Forsyth and a lot of other people, some of whom threw them back with what seemed uncalled-for violence. Stunned, the judges crowned Miss Germany the winner. Miss Germany looked aghast, as if a mistake had been made. It had: a few days later she abdicated.

Making his directorial debut, Jonathan Lewis did a good job with Tim Rose Price's *Rabbit Pie Day* (BBC2), a brief but rich dramatic treatment of a topic whose moral implications most of our more famous playwrights – especially those younger ones who are supposed to be up on politics – would have been guaranteed to miss. The Second World War was coming to an end and Britain was faced with the question of what to do with the Russians it had liberated from the Germans. Stalin wanted them back. Eventually, despite much evidence that to repatriate a Russian was the same as sending him to his death, they were all sent home.

As the play brought out, Russians were already suiciding in the British camps at the mere prospect. Barry Foster played a grey British officer in charge of a camp. At first, cut off by the language barrier and his own understandable conviction that guarding a mob of vagrants was not the most vital contribution to the war effort, he was ready to believe that the politicians had everything in hand. A messy suicide induced doubt.

Gradually it became clear to him that by doing his duty he would be conniving at mass murder. But the orders were coming down from the highest level. (They were coming down, in fact, from Sir Anthony Eden, but the play tactfully refrained from pointing the finger.) In the end, complicity seemed the only possible course. In a peaceful-looking scene which we had come to understand was really an act of violence, the Russians were lured into the trucks and packed off to Liverpool.

Obeying the elementary moral rule that we should be hard on ourselves and as understanding as possible about everyone else, it is wise to assume that we would have behaved no better. As it happened, there were several cases of British service personnel who refused to co-operate. But to write about one of them would have been to write about a hero. As Mr Price deduced, it was more interesting to write about an ordinary man, the better to bring out the magnitude of the tragedy.

Rabbit Pie Day was not particularly strong on dialogue, but it was still a script of high distinction. I labour the issue only because I have lately been so often forced to point out that some of our more famous playwrights have no clothes. Letters come in which tell me that I have no time for television drama. But if playwrights are cried up year after year and year after year it turns out that what they have to say is mainly wind, somebody must be serious enough to take them lightly.

In being thus dismissive, it helps if there is some solid work to point to. The solid work is there, but nearly always it is too quiet to be obvious. Elaine Morgan's adaptations, for example, are miles more interesting than almost anything produced by the name playwrights, whose alleged originality is so often the merest clamour.

16 November, 1980

Not psychic myself

ROD STEWART and his wife, Alana, talked to *Russell Harty* (BBC1). Although obviously still employing a hair preparation based mainly on epoxy resin, Rod evinced a new maturity.

He let only some of it hang down. Probed by Russell, Rod shyly recounted details of the *coup de foudre* that had left him united with Alana in an alliance which already bade fair to tame the tiger in his soul. He and Alana had met in the house of the agent 'Swifty' Lazar. Then they had gone on to dinner at Robert Stigwood's. Somewhere about this time Alana had detected the sensitivity underlying Rod's apparent brashness. He, on the other hand, had at last discovered a woman neither awed by his charisma nor envious of the love borne him by the general people.

Apparently the marriage has gone on being happy week after week. Indeed they are still discovering each other. Rod has discovered that Alana has a natural affinity with the occult. At first Rod 'was very cynical' about Alana's spiritualist proclivities, but by now his native inclination to impatient scorn has been overwhelmed by the sheer weight of evidence. 'I'm very much a believer in clairvoyancy and psychic phenomena,' said Alana, but modestly disclaimed any special powers as a seer. 'I'm not psychic myself.'

The interview – which Russell conducted with a patently genuine sense of inquiry, as one who might ask a child what its latest creation in paints or crayons is meant to represent – was climaxed by a stage performance from Rod. Wearing very tight striped pants, he looked like a bifurcated marrow. He spread his plump legs wide apart and swung the microphone stand like a mace. He hopped along like a pensionable cherub. He sneered and pouted. His career is bigger now than it ever was. He knows all there is to know about being a rock star. The only thing he has left to learn is that although cake might conceivably be both had and eaten, secrets can't be both given away and kept.

Français, si vous saviez (BBC2) was yet another of those blockbuster documentaries – you will recall *Le Chagrin et la Pitié* – calculated to stir the conscience of Frenchmen on the subject of their recent past. This time the specific topic was the career of de Gaulle. Colonel Antoine Argoud was qualified to speak, albeit with some bitterness, on every phase of the General's progress to immortality. Argoud was one of the young officers whose longed-for baptism of fire turned out to be the humiliating debacle of the capitulation. Later on he dutifully tortured and shot people in Algeria. After de Gaulle ratted on his promises to the French Algerians, Argoud was prominent in the Secret Army. He had run the whole course, all the way to criminal status, and all in the name of France.

The original French programme was much longer. The material that was missing from the abridgement presumably included some account of what the Resistance actually achieved at home while de Gaulle was striding around being symbolic in London. You had to take it for granted that de Gaulle's dismissal of the Resistance-fighters' hopes for a different society was an act of gross cynicism. With his part of the war allowed to dominate the screen, it became easier than ever to entertain the suspicion that he was merely being realistic when he brushed aside all those *gauchiste* hopes.

The programme, though quick to seize on de Gaulle's notion that the French people were unworthy of France, was slow to notice that it felt pretty much the same way itself. If the French people are really as easily manipulated as the makers of these programmes sày they are, de Gaulle would have been very foolish to place any faith in their capacity to bring a new society into being, wouldn't he?

International Tennis (BBC2) was otherwise known as the Benson and Hedges Championships. The Benson and Hedges Trophy was prominent in the opening titles. Frequent mentions of the munificence shown by Benson and Hedges were also made in the commentary. The cup was won in characteristic style by John McEnroe. With his hair slightly shorter – an innovation which has the unfortunate side-effect of revealing more of his head – he was as charming as always, which means that he was as charming as a dead mouse in a loaf of bread. His petulance touched even Dan Maskell with sorrow, although it needed to be remembered that Dan was already all worn out from mentioning Benson and Hedges. 'The ladies who serve Benson and Hedges . . . the Director of Special Events for Benson and Hedges . . .'

The Director of Special Events, or one of his retinue, managed to award the runner's-up prize to the wrong man. 'The runner-up – Sandy Mayer! *Gene* Mayer! Ladies and gentlemen, my apologies to Gene Mayer.' From the Benson and Hedges angle this was the only screw-up in an otherwise blissfully smooth occasion. A million pounds'-worth of publicity had been racked up for a nugatory outlay, and nobody at any stage had even hinted at the fact that if John McEnroe smoked as many Benson and Hedges cigarettes per day as Benson and Hedges would like the average viewer to, his name would be Sandy Mayer. *Gene* Mayer.

In Margaret Drabble's *The Waterfall* (BBC2) the plot is now gradually clarifying itself. Jane married Malcolm the lute-plucker. She drove Malcolm away. Then she fell in love with James. 'I could not tell if it was a moment of true corruption that united us, or a moment of true love.' Narrating her own story, she is given to saying could not instead of couldn't. In character, she permits herself to gush. 'I think I'm going to die. I want you and I can't have you . . . I'm wicked and I'm mad.'

But now we must go back – back to Malcolm and his lute. Plunk. 'I know that the fault was partly Malcolm's.' He wanted his shirts washed, poor fool. Whether all or any of this would sound especially or even remotely human if it were not so well acted is perhaps not a point begging to be raised, since I would gladly watch Lisa Harrow and Caroline Mortimer playing anything, including soccer.

For reasons best known to psychiatrists, the BBC has joined the tabloid press in the doomed endeavour to catch Lady Diana Spencer off guard. The only thing that can be said for such ill-advised expenditure of the licence-holders' money is that Lady Diana's unwilling participation makes for a gentle moment in otherwise brain-curdling news programmes. A typical news item last week was about young Belgian terrorists who kidnapped some school children. 'Their demands', said an official spokesman, 'were neither clear nor easily met.' One of the terrorists was President of the local Elvis Presley Fan Club.

At least the Belgian children got out alive. ITN had an even more horrible story about a reckless driver who killed two children and was awarded a three months' sentence plus two years' suspension from driving. Two years' suspension from a gallows would have been the sentence imposed by at least one watching parent, so perhaps it is lucky that he is only a television critic. The reckless driver had been racing another driver when he left the road and wiped out the children who had been feeding some farm animals and . . . forget it. Forget it if you can.

23 November, 1980

Back in showbiz

M RS MAO, up for trial in China, was looking well pleased with herself on all channels. She was back in show-business.

It's no wonder that the Chinese are going mad about their first imported television soap opera, *Man from Atlantis*. The whole country is a soap opera already. Meanwhile, back amongst the capitalist squalor, *Dallas* and *Mackenzie* (both BBC1) were showing signs of convergence. The leading man in each series spent the latest episode in a wheelchair. Some semioticist has probably already worked out a formula to explain this phenomenon. After a certain number of episodes of any given soap opera, the hero will be on wheels. Let f be the number of his love-affairs, n be the frequency with which he goes bankrupt, and p be the snapping-point of the viewer's credulity. When f times n equals p, the leading man will be rolling instead of walking.

JR was in a wheelchair because, as you may have gathered, somebody shot him. Fanned by the BBC news outlets in this country, and by similar organisations throughout the world, the whole planet was supposed to be on tenterhooks to find out who did it. Actually to anyone in possession of the appropriate semiotic formulae it was always transparently obvious who did it – Miss Ellie. The writers, however, worked a switch at the last minute. Having led absolutely nobody down the garden path by focusing suspicion on Sue Ellen for a few months, they finally sprang the news that the mysterious assailant had been Kristin all along.

It won't wash. Kristin couldn't have done it for the same reason Sue Ellen couldn't have done it. Nobody who moves her mouth like that can possibly shoot straight. Miss Ellie tried to frame Sue Ellen and is now trying to do the same thing to Kristin. Alert viewers will have spotted how Miss Ellie did everything she could to help the blotto Sue Ellen convict herself. 'I keep hoping for a miracle. Some proof of your innocence.' Helping Sue Ellen to strap herself into the electric chair was, as you might have expected, the ever-irascible Jock, leaping to the wrong conclusion as usual.

The latest episode of *Mackenzie* was also, alas, the last. Several instalments having already gone by since f times n equalled p, Mac was tardy in acquiring his vehicular sedentary device, but once tucked in he lost no time in setting about doing what he always did best – making large, emphatic gestures with his hands. Mac had crashed a car while driving with his eyes full of blood because his son Jamie had hit him. You could tell Mac was twenty years older than his son Jamie because Mac had a moustache and some white powder streaked into his hair.

Jamie was still obsessed with Mac's wife, who had once been his, Jamie's, fiancée. 'There is something you can do for my father. Hold his hand when he finds out his new daughter is really his grandchild.' Diana, the classy mistress, suicided in order to get out of speaking any more dialogue. She took what Mac's wife described as a novadose. The whole series was a novadose, but millions of viewers will miss it.

In *Oppenheimer* (BBC2) the first atomic bomb went off. The excitement of the scientists was easy for the viewer to share – a measure of the success the series has had in avoiding the standard thoughts about nuclear weapons being a very bad thing. They *are* a very bad thing, but so is a hand-grenade rolled into a restaurant, and anybody who can't find an indiscriminate weapon morally outrageous unless it yields an explosion the equivalent of 20,000 tons of TNT or above is not to be trusted as a student of political reality, although of course he might be handy to have around if you are organising a petition to stop somebody selling thermonuclear warheads to Idi Amin.

But that's as may be. None of the scientists at Los Alamos seriously doubted that the atomic bomb had to be built. The ethical problems arose with the question of how to use it. Oppenheimer was shown giving the reasons why it was better to destroy a real target than stage a demonstration. For young people watching the series, this scene probably enrolled Oppenheimer among the warmongers, but in fact the reasons were convincing at the time and remain so even to hindsight.

When he bent his majestic intellect to the problem, Oppenheimer came up with the same answer as General Groves. In a brilliant performance – one of the best I have ever seen on television – Manning Redwood turned Groves into a sympathetic character without distracting you from the necessary conclusion that wars are bad things to get involved in if you need men like him to help win them for you. The series has made drama out of moral issues – which it had to do, there being no other kind of drama. A pity it fudged the physics.

Shoestring (BBC1), from a near-nothing start, has become must viewing for the millions. The millions include me, for reasons I can't quite analyse. The mysteries Eddie solves are small beer. The big plus, apart from the hero's undoubted charm, is probably the fact that the minor characters are satisfyingly filled out. The same might be said of Pamela Stephenson in *Not the Nine O'Clock News* (BBC2), but she has an uncanny ear to go with the rest of her. In a recent show she impersonated Sue Lawley hostessing a typically shambolic edition of *Nationwide*. It takes somebody with Pamela's dish-aerial aural receptors to pick up the weirdo Doppler and wow effects of Sue's voice.

30 November, 1980

Yes sir, that's my foetus

DAVID ATTENBOROUGH narrated *An Everyday Miracle* (BBC2), featuring a baby in the womb. A very small cameraman climbed into the womb along with the baby and watched it grow. Attenborough was so stunned with the resulting visuals that one of his participles prolapsed. 'When bathed in this fluid, we can see that the tube ends in a mass of delicate folds.'

An ultrasound scan showed the foetus sitting upright in there like a little van-driver. Eventually it turned over like an astronaut and positioned its head against the escape hatch. Perhaps it was tired of having its picture taken. If so, it was heading in the wrong direction, since its father was waiting outside with a stills camera.

Both mother and father seemed extremely nice, but you couldn't help wondering if their concept of private life was not perhaps a trifle attenuated. Lying in his crib, the baby was photographed every few seconds, a process which will presumably continue until adulthood, when the recipient of all this attention might have opinions of his own about the desirability of having his life turned into an archive.

Back came *Ski Sunday* (BBC2) bringing David Vine with it. 'Just watch the way this man has the rhythm through the gates . . . ooh and he's gone! Stenmark has gone!' By now even David must be falling prey to the suspicion that he has the evil eye. All he has to do is start praising a skier for his rhythm and you know the stretcher-bearers are already moving in. I missed *Ski Sunday* in Australia, where the cricket commentators are mainly ex-cricketers who know all about cricket. The commentary thus blends into the action, instead of setting up a fruitful tension with it.

A live broadcast from Covent Garden, *The Tales of Hoffmann* (BBC2), starred Placido Domingo, who was in radiant voice. He was also in radiant trousers, thereby conforming to the tradition by which Hoffmann adopts shining threads in order to signify that he is acting out his dreams. The crotch looked a bit low-slung, but that might have been Placido, who, although very tall, is longer in the body than in the leg. But I carp. He's got the lot: the pipes, the looks and the energy. Production was by John Schlesinger, who has been this way before, having played various small roles in the Powell-Pressburger *Tales of Hoffmann* movie of 1951.

Schlesinger searched for a style to suit the work and ended up with a muted version of the same style everybody else finds – confectionery. Doubtless it would have all looked more ebullient if one had actually been there. The television camera-script tended to pick the decor apart. The Venice act looked a pretty sedate kind of orgy, with the possible exception of what a faun was getting up to with one of the female extras.

But the foreground faded into the background when Agnes Baltsa came on as the courtesan Giulietta. One of those marvellous new lady singers who look the part as well as sound it, she glided around in a believably seductive manner preparatory to nerving Hoffmann up for a duet. Tilting her fair visage towards Placido's bovine orbs, Agnes gave him phrase for phrase. For once Offenbach trembled on the brink of seriousness. It was an uncanny long-distance forecast of one of those great Richard Strauss duets, like the one in the last pages of *Ariadne auf Naxos*. Sometimes you get an awful lot for your licence fee.

Another rich brew was *All's Well that Ends Well* (BBC2), directed by Elijah Moshinsky under the aegis of Jonathan Miller, whose aegis looks like being just the aegis this series needs. Moshinsky echoed his mentor in making the production look like a suite of rooms in an art gallery. Miller's *Lear* was full of French paintings. Moshinsky's *All's Well* was full of Dutch ones. You could have fun sorting out the Vermeers from the de Hoochs. The appropriateness of this to the play's French setting was not entirely clear, but at least a certain visual unity had been provided, and anyway how far is Holland from France? A couple of hours by fast coach.

Sitting at the virginals as if posing for the master of Delft, Angela Down, playing Helena, looked as pretty as – well, as a picture, really. Most of her hair was up, with a few wisps left drifting so that the soft golden light could shine through them. Skin like amber, eyes like liquid silver: the lighting was a treat. Doubtless feeling pampered by the care that was being taken, Angela played a blinder. You couldn't ask to hear the words better spoken. Bertram (Ian Charleson) was definitely a fool to spurn her, there could be no doubt about that. What did the twit think he was up to?

On came Parolles with the sub-plot. Played by Peter Jeffrey as an Osric with bells on, he too spoke beautifully. So did Celia Johnson and Michael Hordern as the Countess and Lafeu respectively. Only Donald Sinden bunged on the fruity voice, but since he was the king, and the king was dying of a fistula, perhaps this was forgivable. Angela cured him and got Bertram. She also got a passionate kiss from the king, which was not in the script.

It is a tough script to speak, since the verse, which hovers on the verge of Shakespeare's later manner, has all of its knottily unified imagery with little of the vividness. 'There can be no kernel in this light nut,' says Lafeu of Parolles, 'The soul of this man is his clothes.' But not much is as quotable as that. The lines have to be played accurately for small returns. They were, and the piece succeeded, except for that kiss, which made the heroine frivolous. She isn't: that's the point.

The History Man (BBC2) got off to a suitably repellent start, with Malcolm Bradbury's arch academic villain arriving at centre stage like a rat out of a trap. As Howard Kirk, Anthony Sher has found a way of making the word 'sociology' into a visual experience. His moustache and sideburns preach well-barbered rebellion. His woolly tank-top worn with nothing underneath proves that he is a man with his armpits bared to experience. He chews gum, talks tripe, and goes through every available female student and faculty wife within the blast-area of his personality.

The university lucky enough to have Kirk as its chief adornment is one of those pre-stressed concrete jobs characterised by Bradbury in an earlier play as having been designed by Piet van der Krank. I laughed aloud at that joke and laughed aloud again several times here. The party thrown by Kirk and his desperately understanding wife was accurate in all respects, right down to the man vomiting resignedly into the kitchen sink. The director, Robert Knights, gave the bacchanal an authentic air of doom.

It is perhaps a little unfair on sociologists that their profession has been all but totally discredited by the advent of Kirk. In fact most faculties in whatever university feature at least one operator just like him. The price of academic freedom is that behaviour which wouldn't be tolerated for a week in any other profession is not just winked at, but actually rewarded.

Don't miss *Triangle* (BBC1), a thrilling new series about 'life on an international passenger ferry'. The international passenger ferry goes from Folkestone to Amsterdam. Kate O'Mara is the mystery presence on board. Sunbaking on the quarter-deck, she threatens the equilibrium of the crew. They are unused to seeing scantily clad women lying down on a cold steel deck while being lashed by a freezing wind. Look forward to innumerable future episodes of a series that does for international passenger ferries what *Sink the Bismarck!* did for the *Bismarck*.

11 January, 1981

While the music lasts

AMONG the few survivors of the Nazi extermination camps, there are apparently some who have never had a decent night's sleep since. They can repress the nightmare during the day, but at night it comes back. *Playing for Time* (ITV) gave you a hint of what it must be like to live like that.

Written by Arthur Miller and directed by Daniel Mann, the film was clearly superior at most points to the famous series *Holocaust*, although it will probably have nothing like the same direct effect. The screening of *Holocaust* in West Germany was instrumental in staving off a proposed statute of limitations on Nazi war crimes, and thereby helped ensure at least the possibility that a few more doddering old killers might be brought to book.

One doesn't have to believe in vengeance, merely in the rights of man, to see that the effect of *Holocaust* was thus a salutary one and something to be grateful for. Nevertheless the series, even when you allowed for the fact that historical memories have to be simplified in order to be transmitted at all, was something of a cartoon. *Playing for Time* was a more complicated piece of work altogether.

Vanessa Redgrave played Fania Fénelon, a half-Jewish French cabaret star who was sent to Auschwitz and escaped the ovens by being selected to play in the camp orchestra. One of the orchestra's tasks was to play up-tempo music while people were being worked to death. Another duty was to provide the SS officers in the camp with their culture ration.

The orchestra was part of the obscenity, like one of those harps in Hieronymus Bosch which have human beings threaded on the strings. And yet for those in the orchestra there were two hopes. One was to preserve some fragment of creative sanity for themselves and anyone else capable of appreciating it. The other was to live.

As presented by Miller's script, Fania embodied the psychic torment of a decent human being who had been placed in the hideous moral fix of being allowed to choose life while other, equally innocent people were being wiped out by the thousand. Redgrave played the role with the passionate commitment you might have expected and with a range of nuance that reminded you, when you could draw breath, that she really is some kind of great actress.

Mentally, Fania reached the only possible conclusion, which was that the Nazis were the guilty ones and that any squalid choices the victims were forced to could not be regarded as their fault, even if the obligation to choose as well as possible remained. Unfortunately, as the look on her face well demonstrated, it is one thing to reach this sane conclusion and another thing to forgive yourself for it.

Another brilliant performance was by Jane Alexander as Alma Rose, the conductor of the orchestra. She was shown to believe, perfectly credibly, that if musical standards were not maintained, then Dr Mengele, who prided himself on his taste, would feed the entire orchestra to the waiting ovens. She therefore kept the orchestra members hard at rehearsal, even when they were swaying in their chairs from hunger. Every concert was like an audition, with the flames waiting if you failed.

At the moment there is an argument going on in the Press about just what Alma Rose's strictness amounted to. A survivor of the orchestra claims that Alma saved all their lives and that it traduces her memory to show the orchestra members turning to Fania for a moral example. If what the survivor says is accurate – and it would be a very presumptuous onlooker who assumed that it was anything else – then to portray Alma as a harsh taskmaster and a fantasist would have been a criminally serious distortion of the historical record. But I'm bound to say that at least one viewer didn't see Alma that way. She looked to me to embody decency just as Fania did, with the additional burden of embodying responsibility as well.

Most of the brutality happened just off screen. The main characters winced at it, and you guessed what it must be like because you knew them. The Nazis were portrayed as being like what they almost certainly were – recognisably ordinary types that anyone who has not led a sheltered life must have lived beside in his own street while growing up.

Most of us know someone with a bee in his bonnet about racial superiority and someone else who would plainly relish the chance of throwing an old lady into a cesspool. The most penetrating thing ever said about the Nazis was said by the writer Jakov Lind, who said that there were no Nazis – by which he meant that a similar aberration is likely to break out at any time, anywhere, the moment that the appropriate social conditions obtain.

There were screams in the night. The electrified fence zapped intermittently in the distance as yet another despairing soul took the only clean way out. Neither the writing nor the production poured it on. Instead, they poured it off. You had to deduce what

Mengele got up to from the way the orchestra members strove so frantically to say the right thing in his presence.

This was a wise understatement, since any attempt at recounting the full horror of Mengele's activities would have doomed itself and the whole film to failure. So ghastly a memory can't be fully retained even in the mind of someone it happened to. Only Mengele could think of it and not go mad, since he had the advantage of having started off being mad already. If Paraguayan television takes the programme, he will be able to see himself.

Good art compresses the coal of truth into diamonds. Vanessa Redgrave's performance in this superior film easily outweighs her political activities, but before glibly dismissing those I had better say why her position with regard to the Middle East has been so well worth despising.

She has backed the Palestinian cause at times when the declared policy of some of its most prominent leaders has been to destroy the State of Israel entirely. Since this could hardly be done without staging the Holocaust all over again, there has always been good reason to regard any outsider aligning himself with such a proposition as incurably frivolous, especially if you happen to believe that the Palestinian cause has a lot to it. Vanessa thinks life is like drama. But just when you think you have got her number, she brings drama to life.

18 January, 1981

Snow job

All the time that Max von Sydow was chasing Liv Ullmann with an axe in *The Night Visitor* (Thames), ITN was putting up captions telling you to stay tuned for the hostages, who would be presented live shortly after midnight, in a satellite hook-up fronted from London by Jon Snow.

Max having dispatched Liv, the screen was cleared for Jon Snow and a man billed as the Archbishop's representative. At some stage the Archbishop's representative had been to Iran and actually seen the hostages, which made him an expert. Jon, as far as I could gather, had never met the hostages, but had been to Iran, which made him an expert too. They were thus able to have an expert discussion while waiting for the action to develop in Algeria, where the Boeing 727 carrying the hostages would shortly land. The Archbishop's representative was asked to predict what condition the hostages would be in. He agreed with Jon that the hostages would be exhausted.

Jon then introduced a film-clip résumé of the whole hostage business from day one. This was followed by a run-through of the year's major events, in order to underline the fact that the hostages had not been around to witness these, on account of being incarcerated. Any hopes that you might at least see some pictures of the incoming plane circling the airport in Algeria were dashed when Jon admitted that the satellite link had conked out. 'But at least our correspondent can see what's happening. What's happening down there, Sam?'

'We . . . we've just seen a plane land,' said Sam from Algeria. 'We're not absolutely sure it's the plane with the hostages aboard . . . if it *is* the plane, then surely the hostages are exhausted . . .' Jon felt it incumbent upon him to break the news to Sam that there were no pictures. 'Sam, let me butt in here . . . we ought to explain that there has been a technical failure . . . Sam, can you see the plane from where you are?' There was a still photograph of Sam holding a telephone in the alert manner of a foreign correspondent. 'Irony for the hostage families,' mused Jon. 'Let's leave Algiers, and let's hope that they can repair that satellite before you can say knife . . . and let's return to the Archbishop's representative.'

The Archbishop's rep once again reached the conclusion that the hostages would be exhausted. Jon tried tuning into Algeria by sheer will-power. 'Let's now . . . let's hope . . . those pictures . . . tragic irony . . . airport full of things we want to see, people we want to see, and we can't see it.' The next best bet was to run some film about Wiesbaden, whither the hostages would be flown after arriving exhausted in Algeria.

There were pictures of wide streets in Wiesbaden with not much happening. 'Their first chance to experience free space', Jon explained, 'will come on the open streets of Wiesbaden.' There was some footage of Wiesbaden's opera house. 'The opera house, which sports lavish German performances nightly.' Yes, Wiesbaden would certainly be the place for the hostages to get back in touch with German opera performances. So much for Wiesbaden. 'Well, I think there's still no chance of getting those pictures back . . . so, Sam, what now?'

'Well, as you say, Jon, the plane, we *think* it's the plane, but so far the hostages, if they are on it, have not come off it . . . all we can do at the moment is wait.' Jon gave the Archbish's rep a brief rest and wheeled on another expert. 'Let's look at the wider implications. I have with me Dr Treverton, of the Institute of Strategic Studies.' But then a flash on the monitor caught Jon's eagle eye. 'They've got the pictures, and THERE'S THE PLANE!' Sam, who can tell a 747 from a 727, cooled him down. 'That is in fact *not* the plane, Jon.' But Jon had spotted another plane landing. Now it was following a little truck. Jon got terrifically excited about the little truck. 'The pilot follows it . . . he stays in his plane of course.'

Stuck in Algeria, Sam was badly placed to hold Jon's hand, but he did his best. 'I think, Jon, that is *not* the plane with the hostages . . .' But another plane was coming in. Surely this one must be it. As if in confirmation, the satellite link conked out again. 'If you're still wondering what's happened to those old pictures,' said Jon for the benefit of any children who might have been watching at half past one in the morning, 'we've got problems up in those mountains and . . .'

It was a bad quarter of an hour in Jon's life, no question. For all he knew, the plane with the hostages on board had been hijacked to Cuba. Luckily he had an ace up his sleeve. 'Watching here with me . . . is the Archbishop of Canterbury's representative . . . what sort of emotions do you think will be going through their minds as they step off the plane?'

The pictures came back. There was a 727 standing on the tarmac. The question remained of whether it was the right 727, but meanwhile there was time to speculate about what, if it was the right 727, might be going on inside it. 'An extraordinary confusion of emotions must be locked behind that door,' ventured Jon. The extraordinary confusion of emotions stayed locked behind that door for a long time.

Sam's voice: 'One wonders what the hostages are going through . . . any second now . . . there is the door opening . . .' But nobody came out except a few diplomats. There were diplo faces everywhere. Maybe it was the wrong plane after all. Maybe the right one was already in Havana. Glimpse of a steward in the doorway. Jon's voice: 'Certainly you can see a steward . . . let us be certain this is the hostage plane . . . bear with us while we sort this out.' More diplo faces in the VIP lounge. Back to the plane. Still no action. Then, suddenly, there they were, waving. 'There they are, waving!' shouted Jon, superfluous to the last.

Every year, by strict rotation, a BBC television crew gets the chance to make a mystery series somewhere around the Mediterranean. This year's perk is called *The Treachery Game* (BBC1). The setting is the Dordogne, which is not strictly the Mediterranean, but at least isn't Southend, and with budgets running so thin who's complaining? The plot is either intricate or hopelessly confused, it is difficult to tell. Mark is a British spy accused of working for the KGB. A scientist called Aird has been killed. Who cared about Aird enough to kill him? It could have been Baird. There are at least three different sets of heavies, many of them with bad shaves. Will Karl kill Arle before Gale nails Kael? The flesh is sad, alas, and I have read all the books.

The *Nine O'Clock News* (BBC1) featured a gung-ho American officer talking of 'the capability to project Marines ashore in a hostile environment as the case may be'. His name was Colonel Looney. On *Nationwide* (BBC1), Frank Bough interviewed the man who pulls the ugliest faces in Britain. His name was Ron Looney. I merely present these facts, without comment. Introducing a re-run of an old episode of *Ironside,* a BBC link-man blew his only line of the day. He asked us to look forward to a story 'revolving round the wheel-bound-chair . . . the wheel-chair-bound Los Angeles police chief.' It's moments those like that make job my while worth.

On *Did You See . . .?* (BBC2), hosted by Ludovic Kennedy, Trevor Phillips of LWT's *Skin* programme said several penetrating things about *Wolcott* (ATV). He said it was badly observed and that the leading character employed three different West Indian accents in one episode. What he forgot to say was that the whole series looked as if it had been financed by the National Front for the specific purpose of demonstrating that blacks glaze over when asked to talk.

Proof that this contention is not necessarily true was variously available in *Babylon* (LWT), which fielded some highly articulate black activists, and *Parkinson* (BBC1), starring Muhammad Ali, who once again demonstrated that he has a way with words, even after having taken one punch too many to his clever head. Freddie Starr was on the same show, on his way through to the asylum.

25 January, 1981

Mass in the crevasse

A PRIEST who got lost in the Andes turned up on *Nationwide* (BBC1) to tell the watching faithful that there is no need to worry about the communion wine freezing at high altitude. It does, but it liquefies when the time comes to say Mass.

'I don't think I was ever near death,' he explained patiently, 'except when I fell down a crevasse on one occasion . . . and also an occasion when I started to gather speed.' His interlocutor, Sue Cook, had a lot of trouble pronouncing Aconcagua. She tried Acancogua. She had a go with Acaconguong. It was that holy smile of his that was throwing her. It threw me too, but it was a nice change from the weekend's *Labour Party Conference* (BBC2), which spilled right through the week like a burst tub of stale molasses, owing to the fact that a split in the party had been heralded and everybody wanted to talk about it.

The conference itself took place at Wembley and consisted mainly of votes being taken, but before votes could be taken there first had to be speeches. Most of these were tedious beyond description, as if to be boring were a declaration of faith. David Dimbleby did the linking while the delegates droned on. Occasionally he cut away to a small studio in which Robin Day sat with Ian Mikardo among others. When the others were making too much noise, Robin barked: 'Let Ian Mikardo have a say. He's a very old gentleman.' Mikardo took a certain amount of umbrage at this. Bill Rodgers was one of the others. As a member of the Gang of Three he was about to undergo a sudden logarithmic increase in news value, since even as he sat there the unions' block votes were assembling like vast phantom armies.

The vote having gone thunderously against the social democrats, the Gang of Three expanded overnight into the Council for Social Democracy. Somebody tried to re-title this latter body the Limehouse Pinks, as a witty variation of the famous dance number 'Limehouse Blues', but the famous dance number was not famous enough for the idea to stick, and anyway the Council for Social Democracy is quite a glamorous title in itself, like the Congress for Cultural Freedom or the Wigwam for a Goose's Bridle. Down to Limehouse raced all the camera crews, in a daring raid that had about the same result as chasing Lady Diana, but at least you got a chance to see Roy Jenkins rubbing his hands. Either Roy has never heard of Uriah Heep or else it is cold down there in Limehouse.

Foot was given a whole-show interview on *Weekend World* (LWT) the day after the vote, but there was no missing the fact that he had suddenly ceased to be sexy. He kept bringing out his little mid-sentence laugh that says 'what I am about to say is so obvious that I wouldn't dream of stating it unless in reply to a question so foolishly misleading as the one you have just asked'. His authority, however, had evaporated. From that day forth the Gang of Three, the Council for Social Democracy and the Liberal Party racked up all the TV time going. Shirley Williams was on *Panorama* (BBC1). She was in Limehouse. She made dramatic dashes from mysterious front doors to dark cars. To demonstrate her social-democratic mixture of dynamism and compassion she wore clothes created by various blind British designers. It's going to be like this all the way to the next General Election.

Ongoingly off-putting to the last, *The History Man* (BBC2) came to a regretted end. 'I think we all owe Howard a debt of gratitude for coming up with the solution to all our difficulties,' said one of Kirk's colleagues. Kirk took it as his due and nodded, ignoring Miss Beniform's accurate observation that all the difficulties had been created by him. The assembled academics had all just tunnelled through the service area under the student picket lines which had been brought into being by Kirk and had surfaced in a conference room to deal with problems which had been fomented by Kirk and had finally got around to passing resolutions in conformity with the wishes of Kirk. He got everything he wanted, including, alas, the divine Annie Callendar. She had his number exactly, but took him on anyway. How could such a thing be?

Perhaps, though transparently a reptile, Kirk was the only real male available. Nevertheless here was a Kirk conquest that the viewer found hard to take. In the book, Malcolm Bradbury gave his terrible hero a certain relaxed appeal: women felt at ease with him. In Christopher Hampton's television script Kirk had no winning ways at all. Given the role of his dreams, Anthony Sher joyfully seized the opportunity to be as horrible as possible. It was fun, but it fudged the subject. If the Howard Kirks were so obviously fraudulent they would do less damage, and if they were so completely unattractive then nobody except duds would be sucked in. The series offered a false reassurance. It said that snakes can't have charm. But of course they can: cobras are famous for it.

Exit Kirk, leaving the question unanswered of whether he should have been allowed to nuzzle Miss Beniform's bosom in sight of all. Since the bosom belonged to the inspiringly lovely Isla Blair I won't pretend that I was sorry to see it exposed. She has a face that makes thoughtful men glad to be alive, so it was no hardship to find out that she has a figure to match. But quite apart from the revulsion aroused by seeing her shapely poitrine being absorbed into the hairy maw of the omnivorous Kirk – a Leda and the Swine tableau that will live long in the memory – there was also the fear that a good actress had been bamboozled by talk of artistic integrity into giving the slavering male public more than it has any right to receive. An element of suggestion might have been even more attention-getting and would have left her with something in reserve to show close friends. But perhaps she is an independent woman and needed no persuasion to disrobe.

Independent women are all over the screen at the moment. They get divorced in order to find themselves. Good luck to them, but one sincerely trusts that the new self they find will be some detectable advance on the old one. There is not much point if they cease to be cute, frilly and fluttery wives, only to become cute, frilly and fluttery independent women. The Beeb's independent woman appears in *Solo* (BBC1) and is played by Felicity Kendall, who has such a knack for arousing the protective male instinct that you would not be surprised to find her house surrounded by a Roman legion, the Coldstream Guards and the Afrika Korps. Her name is Gemma. God only knows what she will have to do to stop men patronising her: shoot a few, perhaps.

Gemma is not really an ex-wife. She is an ex-mistress. The

rejected lover is an ingratiating louse called Danny, played by Stephen Moore in a manner which rejected lovers might well recognise with a twinge of shame. But at least Danny shows signs of life. ITV's independent woman, played by Susannah York in *Second Chance* (Yorkshire), is haunted by an ex-husband of such deliquescence that his newly acquired bachelor flat is practically guaranteed to collapse from wet rot.

Grace Kennedy (BBC2) is just what multi-racial Britain needs after a downer like *Wolcott*. She looks sparky, has good taste in songs and arrangements, deploys a big voice that pours into a phrase like cream into a spoon, and can dance like mad without losing her poise. After giving *Russell Harty* (BBC2) a thoughtful interview, Edna O'Brien, still looking like the head prefect of a private school for the daughters of rich romantic poets, was rewarded by the sudden irruption into the studio of the Dagenham Girl Pipers. As the skirling girls marched and countermarched, Edna eyed them with a lack of appreciation that warmed the heart.

In *World About Us* (BBC2) it was revealed that male butterflies after mating plant an anti-aphrodisiac stink-bomb in the female so that nobody else will want her. Feminist butterflies face a long haul.

1 February, 1981

Ferry funny

B Y now *Triangle* (BBC1), a series about the glamorous life led on an international passenger ferry, has become generally accepted as the long-awaited successor to *The Brothers*, the series about the glamorous life led by the owners of a trucking firm. Regular viewers will already be aware that the international passenger ferry plies between Folkestone and the far-flung exotic port of Amsterdam, where the surf glitters in the pink sunset and they serve drinks in decapitated pineapples. The international passenger ferry is crewed almost entirely by vampy females. A vampy soubrette sings 'I Get a Kick Out of You' while the international passengers dance. There is a vampy international jewel thief, who in the latest episode was arrested and slung into the brig by the vampy purser, played by Kate O'Mara in full war-paint.

The international passenger ferry is actually steered along through the water by a few men, who hide on the bridge to get away from the vamps. One of the officers is violently attracted to the purser, but is such a yob that he can express his affection only through aggressive display. They have misunderstandings on the wind-blown deck. They have misunderstandings in the companionways, on the shuffle-board court, on top of the lifebelt locker and under the compass.

Michael Craig, the captain, is more up-market. He has a Scandinavian wife who talks vid an accent. She drives him to drink. 'Nothing a woman does will ever surprise me . . . women are a different species . . . just a word of warning, my friend . . . nothing is too low for a woman . . . you never can tell what they're going to do next.' And so the international passenger ferry ploughs on, towards the distant rattle of maracas that has always meant Amsterdam.

The towering presence of Alan Howard merely serves to confirm that *Cover* (Thames) is the last gasp of the spy-series format. Philip Mackie is a competent enough writer, but there is so little left to say on the subject that all the dialogue fits templates in the viewer's head. 'She's an agent for the CIA . . . suppose she was deliberately misleading me . . . extreme prejudice . . . how are you going to find out . . . CIA . . .' By this time most of the old spy series production teams have packed up and moved out, like television companies who have lost their franchise. For the actors it is a long, hard slog to get shot of their spy type-casting and get type-cast as something else.

There are several ex-spies in *Partners* (BBC1), an otherwise nothing comedy series which might just keep your attention if you respond to the challenge of trying to figure out which of the frantically gabbling leading players used to be the grim-visaged head of MI6 or the virtually inaudible agent for DI5. Paul Daneman, for example, was a very big cheese in *Spy Trap*, a series I adored. But the old order changeth, giving way to an inexorable plethora of series about marriages breaking up.

Winter sports continue to be must viewing. On *Ski Sunday*

(BBC1) the stellar attractions are commentator David Vine and Britain's lone downhill skier Konrad Bartelski. Barely surviving one brave attempt after another, Konrad is invariably referred to by David as 'Britain's sole representative, the man with the Union Jack on his helmet, Konrad Bartelski'. At the downhill before last, held on some ferocious slope with a name like the Knackenschnitt, Konrad's helmet was for a long time the only part of his equipment in contact with the snow. Yet Konrad always manages, after he regains consciousness, to join David in the commentary box for an exchange of informed views about what the other skiers are doing wrong.

In both *Sportsnight* (BBC1) and special programmes devoted to the subject, the European Iceskating Championships at Innsbruck were well supervised by Alan Weeks, whose commentary is really much more informed than I have sometimes had fun making out. It will take the World Championships, however, to tell us the true standard of pairs-skating at the moment. In the Worlds you get Tai Babilonia and Randy Gardner. In the Europeans you mainly get the Russians, who are at a low ebb, with no athletes to match Rodnina and Zaitsev and no artists to match the Protopopovs.

The true successors to the Protopopovs are undoubtedly Babilonia and Gardner. Until we see those two skate again, the best we can do is watch the way the Russian girls accelerate in the turns. It's spectacular stuff, like a Bolshoi ballet, but there is no pathos in it. There was plenty of pathos in the Taiwan two-man bob, however. Making its first visit to Innsbruck, it went down upside-down the whole way and everybody assumed it was empty until the two guys crawled out with their hands up looking for somebody to surrender to.

8 February, 1981

Paint it yellow

A MAN from the GPO, or is it British Telecom, appeared on *Nationwide* (BBC1) to explain that the underlying motive for the current proposal to paint all the telephone booths yellow was to find out if people really and truly wanted them left red. 'We're very pleased at the reaction,' he confided.

He went on to put the minds of the watching millions at rest. 'We have certainly not got huge stocks of yellow paint.' This was probably only because the yellow paint manufacturers had been temporarily delayed by industrial action, but it left time for *Nationwide* to play its part in deciding the question of whether telephone booths should be left the colour they are or repainted a different colour at heartbreaking expense.

As I switched off to go and have a lie down, the *Nationwide* presenters were telling the watching multitude how to set about casting their votes. This is your country, not mine, but I can perhaps be permitted to say that if you keep this sort of thing up I might as well go home. After all, what with Rupert Murdoch taking over *The Times*, everything I left Australia to get away from has by now come here.

1,263,357 readers have written in to point out that the international passenger ferry in *Triangle* (BBC1, recurring) leaves from Felixstowe, not Folkestone. Sorry, felix. I mean sorry, folks. There's something about the script that numbs the senses. While we're on the subject, did you notice that in the latest episode the inevitable but long delayed romance between the Captain (Michael Craig) and the torchy purser (Kate O'Mara) has at last started to unfold its luxuriant bud? Stuck half-way up a binnacle with a ringing hangover after yet another bout of non-communication vid his Scandinavian vife, the Captain looked pretty creased. The purser stood bravely below with the exotic breeze of Folkst . . . of Felixstowe tugging at her heavily lacquered coiffure. 'You shouldn't miss dinner,' she husked, 'it's not good for you.' If that isn't love, what is it? Answers on a postcard to *Nationwide*.

Edward Teller, variously known as the Father of the H-bomb and the prototype for Dr Strangelove, had a *Horizon* (BBC2) all of his own. Only the loudly billed fact that this was the man himself stopped you thinking that he was being impersonated by a ham actor with glued-on bushy eyebrows. The charm came through, however. You could see why so many brilliant people found him difficult to hate, even when he was carrying on like a mad bomber. At Los Alamos he wanted to go straight for a fusion bomb without bothering to develop a fission bomb first, even though it was universally accepted that a workable fission bomb would be needed to set the fusion bomb off. What Teller was after was a really apocalyptic bang, not merely a huge one. They put up with him because he was brilliant as well as batso.

He finally dished himself with his peers by giving evidence to discredit Oppenheimer, whose General Advisory Committee was against the H-bomb. 'I managed to retain a few frents and ackvire some new ones.' At this point Teller snared the sympathy of at least one viewer. Or, to put it the way the script would have put it, at this point Teller snares the sympathy of at least one viewer. The whole lengthy voice-over was written in the historical present. 'Virtually oblivious to the surrounding political chaos, Teller enjoys the company of the leading physicists of the time.' A certain cheap immediacy can be gained from writing like that, but there is a price to be paid in temporal confusion. 'Robert Oppenheimer . . . will lead the effort.' But he won't be leading the effort, will he? No, because he *led* the effort.

Despite the tangles the script kept getting itself into, the programme could not avoid being a subtle and disturbing probe. Teller's power of argument, not to mention his forceful command of the piano, reminded you that the mad bomber is a highly cultivated European intelligence whose early life gave him good reason to believe that the United States has a right to defend itself by any means. By the end of the show he had started to look positively cuddlesome. What are those eyebrows, after all, but the nests of a pair of rather messy sucking doves? Warming to him as he growled and purred, one sometimes found it hard to remember that here was a man whose idea of a sane defence policy includes not just bigger and bigger bombs to throw, but deeper and deeper holes to hide in.

If the same firm advertised bombs and shelters you would smell a rat. Rats of this nature were assembled for the smelling in a 'Play for Today' called *Beloved Enemy* (BBC1), written by Charles Levinson and David Leland. The plot, which could trace its ancestry to Milo Minderbinder in *Catch-22* and to various novels by Richard Condon, dealt with an exchange deal by which the Russians ended up with our missile-killing laser cannon while we got rich from their cheap tyres.

I'm bound to say that all this seemed pretty standard stuff, but we were told to be frightened because this time it was based on truth. 'Nothing, absolutely nothing, must be allowed to interfere with the flow of those credits . . . word is that in another six months' time there's going to be mayhem in another little corner of South East Asia . . .' So went the dialogue. It all depended on whether you could believe in Britain's capacity to develop a missile-killing laser cannon without somebody wanting to paint it yellow.

Britain's economic dilemma was cruelly exposed in an excellent episode of *Man Alive* (BBC2) presented by Peter Bazalgette. The scene was the Liverpool docks, where Jack Jones arranged that a lot of men should be given Jobs for Life in return for allowing machines to replace them. As a card-carrying Luddite I can see nothing wrong with this: if somebody dreamed up a machine to replace me – and I understand that Hitachi is already working on it – my own price for standing quietly aside would likewise be a Job for Life, if I had the clout to swing it. Unfortunately a lot of men standing around with slung hooks add up to an expensive item, so that several of the Liverpool stevedoring firms have gone broke as a consequence. The costs can't be absorbed because the total volume of cargo is down. The total volume of cargo is down because the economy is depressed. The economy is depressed because . . .

Joe Gormley (the miners) and Sir Derek Ezra (management) squared off against each other in *TV Eye* (Thames). Sir Derek regretted the possibility of redundancies consequent upon pit closures. Joe regretted the possibility of a miners' strike with a general strike to follow. The viewer regretted that the two of them couldn't swap jobs for a while, since it was touchingly apparent that Joe's scope of comprehension was not only at least as large as Sir Derek's, but was accompanied by a better memory. Joe remembers, for example, that the miners were asked for increased productivity. This they gave, with the result that there is now so much coal in stock that there is no room to pile up any more. Nevertheless the Government allows coal imports to continue, since foreign coal is cheaper. Foreign coal is cheaper because . . .

Seals swimming under a roof of ice in *Wildlife on One* (BBC1) provided the visual thrill of the week. *The Winter's Tale* (BBC2) was worthily done, but one gets uncomfortable for the actors when they

are surrounded by cubes and cones. You can't quell the fear that if
one of them sits on a cone instead of a cube the blank verse will
suffer. Bill Haley was the first rock star to die of old age. I can
remember when he was young. I can remember when I was young.
In a while, crocodile.

15 February, 1981

The Colonels are nuts

T<small>HE</small> dingbats were really swarming in a *World About Us* (BBC2)
about the Confederate Air Force, a Texas outfit that preserves
old aircraft and is obviously ready to fly them into action at the
drop of a Stetson.

Ian Wooldridge was the narrator. All he had to do was stand
there while the headcases raced towards him, often at the controls
of a Second World War fighter aircraft in impeccable working
order. 'This country', one Colonel averred grimly, 'is goan down
the drink towards Socialism a damn sight too fast.' All the other
Colonels agreed. Everybody who has taken out a subscription to
the Confederate Air Force automatically attains the rank of Col-
onel. Female Colonels are called Angels. The Colonels wear a
Confederate uniform adapted for flying and salute while taking the
oath, which happens every few minutes. Meanwhile the aircraft
are going by in a constant stream and usually at very low level. An
Angel is not allowed to salute. What she must do is put one hand on
her heart.

While the Angels quelled their leaping hearts and several
thousand Colonels saluted, the planes of the Confederate Air Force
blackened the sky. Wooldridge was not too hot on naming the
various types. Small boys eager to achieve the rank of Colonel
would have been able to tell him that some of those Confederate
planes are a lot rarer than hen's teeth, especially that Twin
Mustang. One slip was enough to prove that Wooldridge lacked
the required background in air recognition: if a Second World War
bomber pilot made a mistake over Germany, the aircraft he saw
last would have been unlikely to be a Heinkel III. But this is

perilously close to the way the Colonels talk over a thick shake.

Bweeeeooowww! Japanese fighter-bombers with rising suns like hot tomato pizzas on their sides came racing at nought feet towards the assembled audience while planted bombs erupted in a fair reproduction of what Pearl Harbor would have looked like if everybody on the receiving end had just been promoted to the rank of Colonel. The Angels suddenly needed two hands to hold their hearts. It was Air Show day – the day the Confederate Air Force shows its power. The power includes, incredibly enough, a fully operational B-29 flown by the man who dropped the first atomic bomb on Hiroshima.

For any Japanese among the prospective Colonels it must have been a stirring sight when B-29-*san* came pounding towards them like a silver dream from the past. The Confederate Air Force do not actually own their own atomic bomb yet but no doubt they have plans in that direction. After all, as one Colonel confided, they are 'tryin' to do a jarb the guvmint hasn't dern'. Some of the Colonels get dressed up as Kamikaze pilots, which made you a bit nervous about their possible next move. Stanford Tuck and Adolf Galland, old enemies from the fighting over Britain, came to pay a call and be awarded the honorary rank of Colonel. Adolf was reassuring about the German youth of today. 'I am convinced they would do zair duty às we haff done, whizzout wondering who gave the order.'

What stayed in the memory, however, was not the pious vapourings of the super-patriots but the sheer loveliness of a P-51 Mustang stunting in a clear sky. It gets harder to blame people for having silly dreams when what inspires them has so much glamour. To have flown those beautiful machines in the great air battles can't help but seem, in retrospect, a lot more exciting than life today. At the time, however, the thrill was somewhat tempered by the prospect of getting killed. Nor do the Colonels seem willing to entertain the possibility that it is not the aimlessness of today's youth they are so incensed about, but the emptiness of their own lives.

Of the four judges who each read 35,000 poems entered in the great Arvon/*Observer* poetry competition, three were brought on stretchers to the *South Bank Show* (LWT) and placed in the sitting position by Melvyn Bragg. One of them, Charles Causley, was able to maintain an upright posture but could say nothing, presumably because the verbalising areas of his cerebral cortex had been reduced to the neural equivalent of wood shavings. The field of judges was thus effectively thinned down to only two runners, Seamus Heaney (bogs, eels) and Ted Hughes (crows, violence).

Both Seamus and Ted are telegenic to such a high degree that they make you worry for the future of poetry, which has traditionally been written to sustain itself, and not to be put over by a charismatic author. It isn't Seamus's fault that he looks such a woolly cuddle and sounds smoother than a pint of Guinness going down a dry throat. Nor is it on Ted's head that his craggy features look as if they should be stuck at an angle in Easter Island. Both poets explained that the task of reading 35,000 poems by other poets had turned their own wells of inspiration into pits of alkali ringed by bleached bones, or words to that effect.

Here was proof that a studio discussion need not be balanced between two conflicting opinions. People who broadly agree with each other can still be illuminating, if they are as bright as Seamus and Ted. One interesting divergence was on the subject of the great modern Russians. Heaney suggested that the efflorescence of Akhmatova and Mandelstam was proof that poetry could flourish in troubled times. Hughes pointed out, surely correctly, that the troubled times were exactly what did them in. A gripping argument could have developed here, but it would probably have been necessary to feed Charles Causley intravenously.

Andrew Motion read the poem for which he had just been awarded the five thousand greenies. He, too, it transpired, was telegenic enough to take over a leading role in *Starsky and Hutch*. It would have all boded ill for the future of poetry as a contemplative medium if it had not been for the inspired absence of the fourth judge, Philip Larkin. The top man wasn't there. Presumably he was exercising his usual judicious reticence, although there was always the possibility that the 35,000 poems had had an even more devastating effect on him than they had had on Charles Causley, and that he had been sent back to Hull in a plastic bag.

I would have liked to hear more of the second prize winner, perhaps because I like long poems in technically demanding stanzas and think that short, suggestive lyrics tend to flatter the reader. It was amusing to note, incidentally, that one of the minor prizewinners was B. Wongar. The famous Australian aboriginal poet B. Wongar has the same corporeal existence as Kilroy, but no doubt he can still use a hundred quid.

The Zeroes were back again in *The Kamikaze Ground Staff Reunion Dinner* (BBC1), a play by Stewart Parker which was first presented on radio, where it instantly attracted wide attention, if only because of possessing the best title of any dramatic work since *Mourning Becomes Electra*. The television production revealed the piece to be pretty thin. It was fun to watch British character actors playing Japanese without bunging on oriental accents, but the gags made you smile rather than laugh. Not many tricks were missed with Japanese detail, although Osaka should be stressed on the first syllable rather than the second and Nakajima on the second rather than the third. I know these things only because it was in Osaka that I met a Japanese taxi-driver who had flown Nakajima torpedo-planes at Midway. This curriculum vitae would have made him an ideal candidate for a full colonelcy in the Confederate Air Force but I think he figured that he'd already done all that.

22 February, 1981

Wedding announcement

Purple Tuesday was the most stunning event in the history of the British monarchy since King Harold got hit in the eye with an arrow. By the time the sirens had stopped howling, all the television channels were at action stations and pumping out special programmes like a pom-pom barrage.

Frank Bough was in charge at *Nationwide* (BBC1). Large photographs of Prince Charles and Lady Diana were behind him. Around him were some plants. Casually but neatly attired, he had the air of one who knows how to stay calm when the crisis bursts. 'So at last the long wait is over . . . we'll be telling you more . . . start by going over to Hugh Scully, standing in front of the building which has been at the heart of today's events.' Frank meant Buckingham Palace, in front of which Hugh Scully was now discovered to be standing, accompanied by several hundred sight-seers and some falling snow.

It was cold and dark, but Hugh was undaunted. 'People waiting to catch a glimpse . . . that hasn't happened . . . we can't actually see . . . the floodlights have not actually been switched *on*.' The bits of Hugh that were inside his sheepskin-lined car-coat were prob-ably quite cosy, but his face was stiffening while you watched. Nevertheless he managed to prise a vox pop out of a nearby woman, who explained how she planned to stay warm during what promised to be an all-night vigil. 'I put two of everything on . . . stay up overnight.' 'Is it worth it?' croaked Hugh. 'Oh yes. Television's not the *same* . . . wonderful, very nice girl.' 'It is quite *cold*, isn't it?' asked Hugh at random, like someone reciting poetry while freezing to death on Everest.

Back to Frank in the nice comfy studio, where he had a theory about why Charles and Diana had not appeared on the balcony. 'I think they're both inside cracking a bottle of champagne . . . highly significant day in the history of the British monarchy.' Sue Cook appeared, with three little ducks flying up the shoulder of her pullover. 'It was while he was at Cambridge', Sue told us, 'that Charles really first discovered girls for the first time.' There followed a comprehensive survey of the girls, culminating in the one who 'could literally be the girl next door'. This last assurance was accompanied by a photograph of next door. There was also a picture of Barbara Cartland, perhaps to galvanise anybody in the audience who had been tending to nod off.

'Amongst our guests tonight', Frank announced, 'is Harry Herbert, a lifelong friend of Lady Diana. What's she really like?' 'She's terrific . . . leads the outdoor life . . . lot of sport . . .' 'She's had some good friends in these past few months,' ventured Frank, meaning those flatmates who had fought off the media. 'Does she have the kind of personality that can withstand that glare . . . pressure . . . publicity?' Tina Brown, editor of the *Tatler*, was there to agree that Lady Diana had what it took to ward off the intrusive Press. 'She's absolutely trained for it. And so are her friends.'

Sue Cook reviewed the activities of 'some of the world's most highly trained newshounds'. Prominent among these was the exceptionally highly trained James Whitaker of the *Daily Star*. Whitaker has been on the Charles trail for yonks, but has not grown cynical. Quite the reverse. Plainly he is besotted by Lady Diana. 'I think she likes me . . . I have been very intrusive now for five or six years.' Whitaker said all this while wearing binoculars and standing in a phone booth, presumably to demonstrate his outstandingly high state of training.

It was made clear that the British Press, however highly trained its news-hounds might be, was a model of discretion compared to the foreign Press. Sandro Paternostro and his very thin moustache were adduced as representatives of Italian television. 'They are like fairy tales,' trilled Sandro, adding something about 'psychological escape from the gloomy of everyday's life'. You could see why Frank fancies himself to be a cut above that sort of thing. 'I bet she's glad to be well rid of *that* lot,' he scoffed, obviously never contemplating the possibility that she might be offering up prayers to be well rid of him too.

'Let's join Hugh Scully,' Frank suggested, 'and of course he's still standing outside Buckingham Palace.' By now Hugh was frozen into position like Shackleton's ship in the pack ice. 'It's now snowing quite heavily . . . hoping for a glimpse . . . snow . . . cold.' An Australian lady standing in the drift next to him was more ebullient. 'I'm so glad I'm here for this occasion. It's been the highlight of my trip.' Back to Frank. '*Marvellous* people down there at the Palace this evening,' he crooned snugly, settling further back in his soft leather chair. It wasn't snowing where Frank was. The North West plugged in. 'She seems a noice enough gurrul, you know,' said a rude mechanical from Dufton, but obviously the Prince's absenteeism had given rise to a certain lack of gruntle in the locals. 'Do you think you'll see a lot of them?' 'Well, if we don't see more of him than we do we won't see much.'

An expert on royalty called Audrey suggested it might be a quiet wedding. 'Very swish wedding?' asked Frank. 'What?' 'Swish.' 'Oh yes, very swish.' Someone going under the name of Hugh Montgomery-Massingberd dazzled Frank with a lot of science about genealogy. 'All four grandparents . . . links with godparents.' 'You've just about lost me,' frowned Frank, but perked up when the bride's father appeared and immediately established himself as a hit act. 'He asked my permission, which was rather sweet of him. Wonder what he would have said if I'd said no.'

The Earl belted on as if P. G. Wodehouse had invented him.

'Diana's life has been very difficult. No protection at all. Very grateful for those girls in her flat. Incidentally, when she was a baby she was a superb physical specimen.' The Earl was hastily supplanted by a filmed interview with none other than the magic couple, so there was an opportunity to check up straight away on the current state of the superb physical specimen. She looked just fine. They were asked what they had in common. 'What a difficult question,' mused the Prince. 'Sport . . . love of the outdoors.'

At about this time a Thames Special started up on the commercial channel, with Peter Sissons in charge. The show began with the same interview, so you got two chances to watch the happy couple. 'We sort of met in a ploughed field,' said Lady Diana, and in the background you could hear the roar of accelerating Land Rovers as the highly trained news-hounds headed up-country to get pictures of the ploughed field. In the foreground was a close-up of the Prince scratching Lady Diana's hand. Or else it was his own hand – it was hard to figure out which fingers were whose, a conundrum which only added to the charm.

'Can you find the words to sum up how you feel today?' the digitally entwined twain were asked. 'Difficult. Delighted . . . happy.' 'And, I suppose, in love?' The Prince looked as if he had just found Sandro Paternostro hiding under his bed, but did his best to find an answer. Cut to Keith Hatfield outside Buckingham Palace. Spattered by those few flakes of snow which had not already accumulated on Hugh Scully, Keith tried to snatch an interview from the bride's parents as they left. 'Don't talk about it,' the Earl instructed his wife. 'We've just done it. Just talked to the BBC and ITN about it.' The Countess found a more gracious way of fobbing Keith off. 'So many imponderables,' she said evasively.

Meanwhile *Nationwide* was winding up. 'Almost all,' said Sue Cook, 'but first back to Hugh Scully in front of Buckingham Palace.' Lit by a sun-gun in the chill darkness, Hugh looked like Scott of the Antarctic several weeks after making the last entry in his diary. 'Crowds outside the Palace now beginning to disperse as it becomes clear that they are unlikely to get a glimpse . . . cold . . . and happy day.'

1 March, 1981

Bovis and Basil

To follow up their monstrously successful *Dad's Army*, Jimmy Perry and David Croft gave forth *It Ain't 'alf 'ot, Mum*, which pulled just as big an audience minus one. But now they have followed up the follow-up with *Hi-De-Hi!* (BBC1) and have immediately climbed back to their former viewing figures. The series is all about the great days at Butlin's, here called Maplin's for purposes of disguise. Simon Cadell plays Jeffrey Fairbrother, a don who shyly embraces a new life as Maplin's entertainments manager. His character is a very useful structural device, because all the other people at the camp must perforce queue up and explain what their work involves.

But the massive, well-greased hub of the action is the master of ceremonies, Ted Bovis, brilliantly played by Paul Shane. The marvellous thing about him is that he could very well *be* a holiday camp comic, except that no holiday camp comic would have such resources as an actor. With his hair arranged in a messily glistening Tony Curtis cut that looks as if a duck has just taken off from an oil-slick, he fills the lower half of the close-up with serried chins while his trained eyes search for campers who need jollifying and his mouth unreels an unbroken ticker-tape of triple-tested patter. Young would-be comedians are no doubt already tuned in and copy-catting furiously, but what they should watch out for is the ability to be outrageous with power in reserve.

The repeat run of *Fawlty Towers* (BBC2) drew bigger audiences than ever and deservedly so. Statistical surveys reveal that only the television critic of the *Spectator* is incapable of seeing the joke, which is that Basil Fawlty has the wrong temperament to be a hotel proprietor, just as some other people have the wrong temperament to be television critics. By putting the wrong man in the right spot, John Cleese and Connie Booth hit on the deep secret of successful farce. But of course it is not enough to hit on it: you have to work it up into a consistent script.

As you watched the episodes coming round again, the fact that you knew roughly what was going to happen gave you time to appreciate how the comic structure had been assembled. Basil didn't just put his soot-covered hand on the Australian girl's breast. He went up a staircase, along a corridor, into a cupboard, out through a window, up a ladder, back through another window, in and out of the same cupboard again, and *then* put his hand on the Australian girl's breast, just in time for Mrs Fawlty to walk in and incinerate him with a look. The fearful symmetry of each episode's grand design was reflected in the attention paid to the smallest detail, right down to Basil's terrible tank-top with zip.

Any programme-controller would give his eye-teeth for a new series of *Fawlty Towers* every season. Unfortunately eye-teeth are not hard currency, and hard currency won't do the trick either. There isn't enough of it in the world to buy more inspiration than exists, and since Cleese and Booth have managed to create at least half a dozen farces each at least as funny as *Hotel Paradiso* it would be unreasonable to expect anything more from them along quite those lines in this lifetime.

There are just some things money can't buy, although from the latest *Man Alive* (BBC2) you wouldn't have thought so. Devoting itself to Britain's rich, the programme pretended to be worried about how the rich get richer even during a recession. What it was really interested in, needless to say, was how they do it. Godfrey Bonsack gets rich by flogging gold bathrooms to people even richer. 'What you do is enjoy yourself in my barse.'

A drone called Rupert Dean does it by checking up on his investments by telephone for twenty minutes each morning, before climbing into his barse as a preparation for lunch, which leads into an afternoon's leisure during which he nerves himself up for a hard evening at Wedgie's. 'January I'm still shooting, basically, because it's too cold to go skiing.' The programme was deeply shocked by Rupert's disinclination to do a hand's turn, although how the economy might benefit from a less leisurely Rupert was not made clear.

8 March, 1981

Whacky world of weather

IN New York last week I was up early each morning in order not to miss the true star of NBC's *Today* show, namely Willard the Weatherman. The way Willard has turned weather into an all-absorbing issue is a lesson to everyone in the land of the media.

British weathermen are confined to small booths elsewhere in the building and often on the other side of the city – their connection with the main news studio is purely electronic. Recently they have tended to break out in checked sports coats and blow-dry hair-styles, but there is a limit to how far they can assert their personalities.

Willard is right in there with the main presenters, sitting at a desk alongside them and often standing in front of them. He is large – somewhere between Eddie Waring and Cyril Smith. He is loud. There is something artificial about his hair, a fact he readily admits, because the admission (he calls his toupee a 'toop') gives him more air-time. His avowed concern is with what he calls 'the Whacky World of Weather'.

Willard talks about the Whacky World of Weather as if the Whacky World of Weather governed your entire life. If nothing much is happening that morning in the Whacky World of Weather, Willard will still refer to the Whacky World of Weather. 'This morning there's nothing too unusual to report from the Whacky World of Weather.'

The main presenters turn to Willard if some such issue as the deployment of cruise missiles or a further downturn in the automobile industry might have something to do with the weather. Willard rises from his desk and crosses to a chart. Occasionally he crosses to another desk and starts selling cat-food.

This last, of course, is, for the visitor, the most riveting Willardian activity of all. It would be impossible to imagine in Britain and is hard to take even in America, where the sheer intensity of the sales-pitch has left very few areas of the media free from the clamour of hucksters barking their wares. But until the advent of Willard his fellow-Americans had some right to expect that the weatherman would not try selling food to their cats.

I was in the *Today* studio myself towards the end of the week and took the opportunity to check out Willard's bowl of cat-food where it stood temporarily unattended on its special desk. It didn't smell very real but perhaps it had been injected with something in order to withstand the hot lights.

Malcolm Muggeridge was already reminiscing when I left Heathrow and was still at it when I got back. The series is called *Muggeridge Ancient and Modern* (BBC2) and is the television equivalent of an unputdownable book. From all serious angles Muggeridge is hard to admire, but he somehow ends up cherishable, like an old boiler that doesn't heat the water, but wins your heart by the way it goes boink-boink in the night.

The latest episode covered the years 1945–56 and was headed by an excellent Trog cartoon in which Muggeridge was to be seen recoiling in fastidious horror from a television image of himself. Thus was neatly encapsulated the theme of the programme and indeed of Muggeridge's whole life – that he has spent most of his life reprehending the very pursuits to which he has been most actively devoted.

These have included, by his own admission, fornication, journalism and television. Nobody but a gossip would dream of mocking Muggeridge with his own lust if he had not made such a heavy point, in his later years, of warning the rest of mankind about the futility of carnal desire. Similarly his fulminations about the despicability of political journalism lose some of their fire when you consider, as you had ample opportunity to do during this programme, that he spent some of his best years engaged in manufacturing the very product he was inveighing against, and not a very exalted form of it either. As for going on television to insist that going on television is not worthwhile, all it can do is remind you of the Cretan who said all Cretans were liars.

With those caveats entered, it can still be admitted that it was good to have the ugly Mugg dredged up again. The present Muggeridge was reverently interviewed on the subject of the past Muggeridge, whereupon the past Muggeridge would appear in his own person, by dint of resurrected BBC television programmes which preserve him in atmospheric black and white.

The past version, it became clear, was no more scrupulous a writer than the present one. He got his reputation by bending a cliché just far enough to convince the gullible that they were listening to vivid language. 'They also serve who only sit and sleep.' 'In the beginning was the news.' 'Give us this day our daily story.' In a context where nobody else could write at all, writing like this might have sounded like good writing, but in retrospect you can't help wondering why he didn't try harder. The real mystery of Muggeridge's life is that he must *know* that most of what he is saying is tripe, yet he says it anyway.

Nevertheless the personality shone through. He was one of the first television performers to demonstrate that all you have to do on television is be yourself, always provided that you have a self to be. It was fun to see him giving Bertrand Russell a bad time, and more fun still to hear about the floor-manager who held up a card saying 'Be controversial'. Muggeridge's ebullience, which seems to have grown no less with age, is enough by itself to take the sting out of his message that the world is getting worse.

The world is too complicated a thing to get worse in any appreciable way except by blowing up, but one doesn't have to be Malcolm Muggeridge to admit that in certain specific aspects human life might not necessarily be beer and skittles. *Open Secret* (BBC1) dealt with child abuse. Granted that we all harbour these impulses, it follows that in the right – i.e., the wrong – circumstances they would come out, with shattering consequences for nearby children. Tots who die of cruelty are commemorated by booklets enshrining official reports on what went wrong. The child's name is on the front. CARLY TAYLOR. There is a little picture.

Newsnight (BBC2) had a story on the Atlanta killings and *TV Eye* (Thames) gave a whole programme to the same dreadful subject. *Newsnight* had the little pictures. CURTIS WALKER. Curtis was thirteen years old. DARRON GLASS. Ten years old. 4 ft 9 in. 75 lb. *TV Eye* had the analysis: Atlanta's official leadership is predominantly black and there is thus a good chance that the town will be able to take it if it turns out that the killers are white. Perhaps because so many blacks have been elected, unelected vigilantes are not wanted. The Guardian Angels were shown being turned away. There was footage of the Ku Klux Klan engaged in military training with modern automatic weapons. Everybody

talked about racial hatred and nobody mentioned the inadvisabil-
ity of making machine guns available to nutters.

22 March, 1981

Beastly to everybody

BACK at the start of the viewing week, *Unity* (BBC2) made a sort
of half impact, like one side of a bomb going off. Dramatised by
John Mortimer from the book by David Pryce-Jones, it told the
story of the Mitford sister who fell for Hitler. Other Mitford sisters
fell, at various angles, for Stalin, Sir Oswald Mosley and the Duke of
Devonshire. In the eye of history it turned out that Unity drew the
short straw, but this was by no means apparent at the time, when
certain sections of the British aristocracy thought Hitler admir-
able. Pryce-Jones's book caused its furore largely because of its
explicit doubts about whether the nobs concerned should be
allowed to forgive themselves for this. Sir Oswald himself turned
up in London to assure the television audience that Unity had been
nothing more than a stagestruck gel and that he objected to the
issue being raised.

A lot of other top-drawer people objected right along with him.
Most of them had never been Nazi sympathisers, but they all
shared what Lord Annan has usefully defined as the aristocratic
theory of politics, by which people's social acceptability can be
held to excuse their political views. Actually the play would have
done a better job of rebutting that theory if it had made Unity
nicer. What it made her was very nasty indeed. Lesley-Anne Down
made her look suitably beautiful but she sounded like a raving
bitch at all times, which rather blunted the point when she was
shown being beastly to the Jews. She was beastly to everyone and
everything, with the possible exception of the beasts. Large dogs
lolled everywhere, so that the Nazis could fondle them, prod them
with the toe of a jackboot, etc.

Hitler spent a lot of time prodding his wolf-hound. For just a
moment he looked believable. Also he had the correct voice – a
slightly husky rich purr, it could obviously have filled a stadium at

the swell of a lung. But in all other respects he just wasn't the man. His incipient dementia was conveyed by pop eyes. Since he chewed the carpet in real life, there are difficulties in the way of making him credible, but there is no point in trying to dodge the fact that he had real charisma. He made a genuine appeal to the dark places in human nature. If he could have been shown doing that, there would have been something both plausible and instructive about Unity's multiple orgasm of *Sieg heil!*

Sieg means victory. Unity thought she was on to a winner. Other golden products of her generation put their money on an alternative brand of totalitarianism, but what united them all was power-worship. They were a minority even within their class. On the whole the British upper crust has traditionally remained impervious to big ideas, although it is a nice question whether this can be put down to good sense or philistinism. Anyway, the British aristocracy is in no danger of being thought dispensable. The inspiration it provides for television drama series would alone be sufficient reason to keep it going, just as the upper middle class is vital in providing material for the spy series which have contributed so heavily to the balance of payments.

29 March, 1981

Actual flow

'EACH school will have to raise the cost of their computer,' announced Sarah Cullen on *News at Ten* (ITN). Each channel will have to clean up their grammar: this are getting ridiculous.

By now not even the editorial writers at *The Times* can tell the difference between 'credence' and 'credibility'. They just bung down the one that sounds posh. The English language will probably survive somehow. Its corruptibility has always been one of its main strengths. Almost everyone in the world feels about English the way Dr Johnson felt about Greek – that you should have as much of it as you can get. On the other hand scarcely anybody feels the same way about Norwegian. These twin facts should be taken into consideration when viewing the *Eurovision Song Contest*

(BBC1), in which an English-speaking song, even if sung by Sweden, often wins, whereas Norway, gamely sticking to its own lingo, invariably finishes last.

This year's contest, staged last weekend in Dublin, ran true to type. Britain won and Norway got no votes at all. Count them: none. To the objective viewer it was hard to tell why Norway should be singled out for opprobrium, since most of the other songs, including the winner, seemed not notably less unexciting than their entry. (I use the plural pronoun 'their' in connection with the singular noun 'Norway' because in this context the singular noun has a plural sense, so put down your pen, Sarah.) Terry Wogan showed signs of scepticism, especially when reading aloud from the press-kits of the more obscure performers. 'A born artist,' the man from Spain was billed as, 'who swells when faced with a difficult task.'

Finland's was a typical entry. Sung by Riki Sorsa, or it could have been Saucer, it was called something like 'Bef norka wumple gorst Reggae OK' and had the same connection with reggae as a dead budgerigar has with a live eagle. If you had leaned two corpses together the resulting dance would have reflected the rhythm exactly. Backed by a red-hot band featuring an accordion, Riki looked like a contemporary of Bertrand Russell and was clad in a pink sloppy joe plus patchwork pants. One got the sense that the only boutique in Finland had been in on the sponsoring. 'You can't say you aren't getting a variety of costume here,' said Terry vaguely.

The only other international language apart from English is French. I think it was Switzerland who featured a Frenchman singing a dreary little something called *'C'est peut-être pas l'Amérique'*, which sounded like the complaint of someone who had arrived at the wrong airport. In the pre-song filmette he wore a bomber jacket *avec* dark glasses and carried on like Yves Montand's older brother in order to indicate weather-beaten creativity. For the song itself he donned a white tuxedo. His name was Jean-Claude Pascal if it was not Claude-Jean Pascal or Pascal-Jean Claude: it is perhaps not important.

And so they droned on. Buck's Fizz from Britain did a hotted-up hokey-cokey which ought to have been no more impressive than the sound emitted by Ireland's Sheba, except that the three Sheba girls retained their upswept-collar Blake's Seven silver glitter frocks until the end of the song, whereas the two girls in the Buck's Fizz line-up were divested of their skirts by the two boys at the point where interest might otherwise have flagged, or at any rate where lack of interest might have turned to torpor.

Then came the scoring, featuring the usual nonsense from the scoreboard ('It gets very hairy', intoned Terry, 'at the old electronic scoreboard'), the inevitable communications breakdown with Yugoslavia ('I am calling Dublin. Do you hear me? Are you there? Here are the results. Dublin, do you hear?'), and the routine embarrassment for poor doomed Norway, whose song 'Aldri I Livit' really hadn't been all that terrible, especially if you translated it into a language, that you, Sarah Cullen and the editorial writer of *The Times* could understand. 'Never in my life, my friend. Not until I join with the wind.'

Two other events occurring on the same day and the same channel were the Boat Race and the Grand National, but there is no need to spend much time on them, since the result was perfectly predictable in each case: the Boat Race was won by Oxford and the Grand National was won by a horse. You could tell from Harry Carpenter's voice that Cambridge were dead ducks before their shell was even in the water. 'Having safely got the boat afloat, back to get the blades. And they really have got a monumental task ahead of them.' Cambridge had the monumental task and Oxford had the monumental crew. The only occupant of the Oxford boat smaller than a house was the coxette. 'Sue Brown, 22 years old,' enthused our Harry, 'who really has stirred up a lot of interest.'

Weighing about as much as the stroke's left thigh, Sue sat looking at her enormous colleagues while her enormous colleagues sat looking at Cambridge, rapidly disappearing astern. Meanwhile the Cambridge cox, Chris Wigglesworth, sat looking at Oxford and the Cambridge crew sat looking at nothing. 'Cambridge not looking very happy,' intoned Harry. 'Not covering the water,' said an expert called Penny, who gave a good commentary, rich in technical terms such as 'fast water' and 'actual flow'.

This helped distract your attention from the actual flow of Harry, who tended to rave on about Sue Brown. 'The young lady having no problems at all with this powerful crew in front of her.' Clearly she had aroused his protective instinct, but really there was no call for him to worry. As long as the boys were rowing flat out their hands were fully occupied – which is more than you could say for a man in one of the stake-boats, who had spent an unconscionable time helping Sue get set. 'I think you can see there the rhythm,' Penny explained, 'the feel of the length, which Oxford have got.'

'Cambridge did their best,' gritted Harry, adding weirdly, 'They won the toss, which was no mean achievement.' Back at the Grand National, David had the feel of the length. Attired in his usual ghastly hat, he gave an admirably detailed run-down on the field as a helicopter went over the jumps at nought feet, thereby making you wonder why any horse should agree to race at all. Film and videotape from past Grand Nationals showed horses nose-diving over Becher's and jockeys turning mid-air somersaults at Valentine's. The actual event fully lived up to its heritage. To the long lens the course looked like a terrace of rice-paddies in which a battle staged by Kurosawa was taking place, with riderless horses plunging sideways and jockeys falling on their heads among thundering hooves.

12 April, 1981

Hail Columbia!

VISUAL thrill of the year was undoubtedly the space shuttle Columbia blasting off last Sunday. This event was heightened in its intensity by the fact that the space shuttle had spent several hours not blasting off the previous Friday.

The BBC *Tomorrow's World* team were there to keep us informed on both occasions. Or rather the team was *here* to keep us informed – the Beeb had nobody at the actual Cape except Kieran Prendiville, who reported by telephone, no face. All the British faces visible were emanating from London. In the great early days of space it would have been James Burke and a whole team of experts. The experts would have waved graphs while James Burke went up and down the gantry in a cage and crawled into a rocket socket. For the shuttle shot we were down to Michael Rodd and one expert, Geoffrey Pardoe. Geoffrey goes right back to the days when James Burke was blasting off every few weeks, but Michael, or Mike as he is usually known, is a new boy in a blow-wave haircut who normally spends his time telling you how some new computerised accounting system is going to put you out of work.

Mike and Geoffrey proved their collective cool on Friday, however. When the big moment came nothing happened. The space shuttle just sat there like the Taj Mahal minus the ornamental lake. It turned out that three of its computers were functioning properly, but the fourth was processing tax returns for the population of Pittsburgh. Covering brilliantly, Mike cued in Judith Hann, a *Tomorrow's World* pitchperson whose usual beat is demonstrating how the latest atomic-powered four-wheel-drive invalid trolley can climb sand-dunes. This time she explained how the shuttlenauts, in the event of an abort, would ride down a rope in a basket, jump in a hole, and wait there until the fuel finished exploding. Since the hole featured a two-day food supply, you got the sense that a conflagration of Biblical proportions had been envisaged.

What continued to happen, however, was nothing. Apparently the fourth computer had given up processing tax returns and started cataloguing old Bing Crosby 78 r.p.m. singles. 'For the latest on that situation,' flannelled Mike, 'over to Kieran.' But the fourth computer must have plugged itself into the satellite. 'Tweeng ping moot,' said Kieran, 'Wee wee wee wee. Pfft.' Geoffrey covered by talking about 'a very integrated system as such'. Finally the very integrated system as such was stood down until Sunday, while the engineers got on with the job of replugging the fourth computer, which by this time was counting all the cows in India.

By Sunday the newspapers were pretending to be blasé about the space shuttle. The Tomorrow's Worldlings, however, were still keen to go. As so often happens, naivety was rewarded. 'Something like the power of twenty-three Hoover dams' was promised by Mike as the force that would be unleashed. While you were still wondering whether the power of twenty-three Hoover dams was significantly different from the power of twenty-three million Hoover vacuum cleaners, the wick finished sizzling and up she went. Instead of replicating the stately tower-of-power effect created by the Saturn launch vehicles, the shuttle assembly yelled off the pad like a burning cat and headed straight for space in order to cool off. The thing was in orbit almost before Mike had finished being disappointed about how the satellite pictures conked out at the precise moment when the used-up boosters were blown free. 'We've lost the pictures, unfortunately. Let's look at what's just happened in animation.'

While we looked at cartoons of the boosters being dumped, Kieran tuned in from Florida with the information that the real pictures of the boosters being dumped were something to write home about. 'The pictures we saw here were *unbelievably* spectacular.' While Kieran was saying this on the telephone we were looking at pictures of Mike's face. Meanwhile the actual shuttle was already up there. It might still have been shedding tiles like an old housing development, but it was upside down in zero gravity while the two lucky men inside were seeing the world.

After a couple of days of that they were ready to come back, the fourth computer having presumably finished its digital rewrite of *Paradise Lost*. One of the treats in store for future viewers, when a television camera can be lifted to the atmosphere's edge and moved fast enough laterally to track with a returning shuttle, will be to see the ceramic-clad machine come screaming home all lit up like an incandescent bathroom. But for now there was plenty to be going on with. First you saw a white dot, then a white dot with wings. At 124,000 ft the shuttle was still moving at Mach 6, while the fourth computer nonchalantly whistled the adagio from Beethoven's Ninth symphony. Time for some steeply banked turns to damp out speed.

No mere projectile but a fully fledged aircraft, the Columbia tilted with an élan that reminded you all over again of why Leonardo wanted to fly like a bird – because the sensation was wasted on birds. 'Desperately trying to lose speed,' announced Mike, choosing the wrong adverb exactly. Out came the wheels, up went the nose, and the final few knots of all that enormous velocity were smoothed away to zero. Having proved itself to be the biggest fun ride since the prototype magic carpet, the space shuttle sat there in contented silence while the fourth computer started counting the stars.

The shuttle beamed down some beautiful pictures of Earth, but

one felt sour with envy of the men taking them. No such considera-
tion marred one's enjoyment of the pictures of Saturn in a special
two-part *Horizon* (BBC2), since they were taken by a robot camera
on an unmanned space-craft. Not only that, they had been compu-
ter-processed and enhanced in a way that made you feel a bit
inadequate to be looking at them with the unaided human eyeball.
Nevertheless the total effect generated fully human emotions,
perhaps the foremost of them being pathos. For a moment you felt
the way Einstein must have felt all the time.

In Einstein's great mind there was no distinction between
human creativity and the inspired order he saw in the universe:
that the laws and principles of nature should be so poetic was for
him no contradiction. He would not have been surprised at the
sheer loveliness of Saturn's rings and moons. For us lesser mortals
the spectacle is bound to be something of a poser. Luckily we have
Patrick Moore to help us. In *The Sky at Night* (BBC2) he telephoned
an astronomer called Dr Spinrad. 'I just wonder', wondered
Patrick, 'if and when we're going to be able to see all the way to the
edge of the observable universe.' Patrick held the telephone as if he
had never seen one before in his life. Looking like a baby smoking a
cigarette, he embodied the childlike curiosity which gives science
its indefatigable force.

19 April, 1981

Steve doesn't smoke

'**D**ELICATE little stun screw here,' whispered the voice-over in
World Championship Snooker (BBC2). One of those adolescent
Space Invaders champions who can shoot down sixty-four enemy
battle fleets, Steve Davis was so obviously unstoppable that the
tournament went a bit flat. Nevertheless I watched every day and
evening, since there was always plenty of tension attached to the
issue of which player would manage to smoke the most of the
sponsor's free cigarettes. The commentators refer to the 'Embassy
World Championship' at all times, but what really matters to the

Embassy people is the spectacle of a star player taking a drag on the product between winning breaks.

This year everything should have been rosier than ever for the sponsor. The Crucible Theatre, Sheffield, was jammed to the rafters with a snooker-crazed audience all ready to smoke like chimneys in emulation of their heroes. Presumably there were millions of viewers out there keen to do the same. But there was a joker in the pack. Steve Davis doesn't smoke. That was the sub-text during an otherwise unexciting final match, in which Doug Mountjoy was frozen out.

'This is a desperate situation for Doug Mountjoy,' whispered the commentators. But it was an even more desperate situation for the sponsor. With Davis not smoking at all, it scarcely helped that Mountjoy was smoking his head off. 'Watching the title drift away.' Mountjoy, the close-ups told you, was watching it drift away on a cloud of Embassy cigarette smoke. Still, as long as Davis didn't actually *mention* not smoking, the sponsors might still make something out of the day.

Davis won and was hailed by David Vine. 'Can I now ask', David bellowed, 'the presentation party to come out on stage? Managing director, W. D. & H. O. Wills . . . manager . . . Embassy . . .' Young Steve folded the cheque and put it in his pocket before accepting the trophy. 'I'd like to thank Embassy,' he said. The sponsors beamed. 'Unfortunately I don't smoke . . .'

26 April, 1981

Ho ho!

As Gore Vidal pointed out while bestowing a long and civilised interview on Melvyn Bragg during the leisurely course of *The South Bank Show* (LWT), 'Write about what you know' is the advice we give to people who shouldn't be writing at all.

What he meant was that writers without the capacity to imagine won't be very interesting even when reporting their direct experience, no matter how bizarre. He was deeply correct about this, but unfortunately television couldn't survive for a month if it had to depend on imaginative writers. You can't have many series like *Bread or Blood* (BBC2) because there aren't many writers who share Peter Ransley's capacity to take a book like W. H. Hudson's *A Shepherd's Life* and bring the past out of it. If your average hack were to adapt such a book he would, after completing prodigies of on-the-spot research, not only fail to bring the past out of it, he would put the present into it, so that you would hear starving shepherds saying 'No way.' They would say it in a flawless regional accent while wearing impeccably rural dung-cake make-up but the anachronism would be only the more glaring.

Nevertheless it is a good rule for a writer to acquaint himself with the local colour of any area he proposes to use as a setting. One of the things that made *Law and Order* so convincing was the authenticity of the speech patterns. You assumed they were authentic because they didn't sound like writing. Somebody had used his ears. He had also, alas, set a fashion, which after long travel through rusty pipes and around S-bends finally emerges in the form of *The Chinese Detective* (BBC1). The grainy look and the barely comprehensible East End argot are all there, except that they have somehow got mixed up with an old Charlie Chan movie.

Played inscrutably by David Yip, Ho is a cockney cop of Chinese extraction, presumably emanating from within audible radius of Bow Bells, although there is a possibility that he was born and raised somewhere around Rupert Street, and is therefore a Soho Ho. But whether a Soho Ho or a Bow Ho, Ho is a bozo with only a so-so capacity for delivering the tart witticisms foisted on him by the scriptwriter. Indeed Ho is a bit of a no-no: not, I hasten to add, through any particular fault of the actor, who does what he can with the immobilising problem of being expressive and impassive at the same time, thereby reducing his face to the status of a yo-yo that won't go.

A so-so no-go yo-yo from Bow or Soho, Ho is out to avenge his father, who was sent to jail for ten years after being framed on a drugs charge by a bent copper. But Ho has a hard row to hoe. His superiors regard him as a troublemaker, although it is hard to tell how they figured this out, since his face betrays nothing except a faintly yellow glow of woe at the latest low blow from the foe. The series might catch on, but for those of us approaching ninety years of age it can do nothing except induce an overwhelming nostalgia for Charlie Chan and his Number One Son. At one stage Charlie's Number One Son was played by Yul Brynner plus hair, but later Yul scalped himself and went on to greater things, most of which are already forgotten.

There were more detectives in *Man Alive* (BBC2), whose latest subject was shoplifting, billed as 'The Biggest Theft of All'. Michael Dean and the assembled experts strove dutifully to get excited about the depredations of the shoplifters, who in the big stores are apparently stripping the sales counters almost as fast as they can be filled from the vans. It rapidly became clear – indeed it instantly became clear – that there are three main types of shoplifter: crooked, sick and not guilty. The detectives seem to be catching about the same number of each kind.

Shoplifting, it is claimed, goes on at the rate of a Great Train Robbery every thirty-six hours. Meanwhile the glorification of Ronald Biggs continued on all media outlets. Nobody ever tried to arouse interest in the Great Train Robbery by saying it was the equivalent of thirty-six hours of shoplifting. Biggs's crime has always been assumed to have been innately glamorous. Precision of a military operation, etc. But if it was a military operation it was a pretty thoroughly bungled one, quite apart from the fact that a civilian got hit on the head and died of it. They love Biggs in Brazil and want to make him a television star. So that was what it was all for.

Gradually the television picture of Ireland is being filled in. The two big recent series on the subject helped a lot. To be informed on such a subject is an absolute good, even if you are still left relatively helpless: at least you know *why* you are helpless. *The Crime of Captain Colthurst* (BBC2) was an awkward mixture of dramatisation and studio interviewing but it cast a bit more light on what now seems in retrospect to be the period when England made its most catastrophic blunders.

In 1916, one is forced to assume, all the intelligent officers were away at the war, leaving Ireland to be garrisoned by idiots and bigots. Into which of these last two categories Captain Colthurst fell remains a moot point. Anyway, he shot the non-violent Irish journalist Francis Sheehy Skeffington for no reason at all, whereafter the army covered the whole thing up in a manner seemingly calculated to generate the maximum amount of bad blood.

Philip Bowen played Colthurst with a suitable air of virulent dementia: very bonkers, very low blink-rate. The question of why such a crazy bastard was ever allowed to walk around in uniform was partly answered by demonstrating that his brother officers were nincompoops almost without exception. One of the exceptions was Sir Francis Vane, who did his best to see justice done and came out of the business with honour, although not even he struck you as being exactly an intellectual dynamo.

Taxidermy was the subject of *Lion* (BBC2). It was, if you'll forgive me, great stuff. Two British Museum taxidermists looking like Mark Twain and Toulouse-Lautrec set about the task of turning a lion skin back into a lion. There's much more to it than you'd think. First you have to take a roughly lion-shaped armature of chipboard and bodge a lot of long nails through it in order to provide support for the plaster, which you go on applying until you've got a starved-looking small grey lion or else a large greyhound. This you wrap in wood-shavings, while taking frequent looks at a picture of a lion in an *Observer* colour magazine so as to ensure against inadvertently constructing an aardvark.

The head is entirely done with plaster in order to look as much like a lion as possible. Then you stretch the skin over the completed fuselage, which like a balsa aeroplane looks considerably more interesting uncovered. In go the glass eyes and Bob's your uncle, or rather Leo's your lion. The completed product looked unassuageably sad, no doubt because bored in advance by all the half-witted conversations it was fated to inspire. *Hockney at Work* (BBC2) was marvellous.

3 May, 1981

No kidding

On *Did You See* (BBC2) Kate Adie said all the right things about the soldier who had been ignited by a petrol bomb only a few feet away from her in Ireland.

Representing the clueless punters, Ludovic Kennedy asked the big question to which he already knew the small answer: why hadn't Kate and her team dashed forward to help? Because, Kate patiently explained, their help would have been useless and unwanted. All they had was cameras and microphones, not fire extinguishers, and the army gets impatient when amateurs interfere. Nor had the presence of her crew exacerbated the tension. The petrol bombing had been going on for three hours before she arrived.

Sincerely put by a good reporter who has had her eyebrows well singed in the cause of truth, this was convincing talk. Unfortunately it made the image of the burning man no easier to get out of your head. It will be a welcome day when the question of Ireland is far enough in the past to laugh at, but some things demand a lot of past between you and them before the pain they exude grows less alarming. My own view is that this necessary distance has not yet been established between us and the Nazi era, and that a supposedly comic series like *Private Schulz* (BBC2) would be an offence even if it were funny. In fact it is no funnier than a cold sore on the lip, so the point is hardly tested.

The great German historian Golo Mann has pointed out that the Nazis were opportunists: their destruction of the European Jews was not a matter of belief so much as a crime encouraged by bad literature. As cynical opportunists they were legitimate comic targets in the immediate pre-war years, when the great atrocity they were to commit was still in its first stages. But even then it took somebody as sophisticated as Ernst Lubitsch to raise an intelligent laugh, and even his wonderfully funny *To Be Or Not To Be* now seems imbued with as much pathetic innocence as dry wit. Subsequent history made the laughter hollow, and Carole Lombard's divinely frantic footsteps now echo through horrible long buildings in which ghosts still cry all night.

Anyway, *Private Schulz* is full of allegedly risible SS men, whose chief function is to have rings run around them by Schulz, an amiably feckless character who has been put in charge of forging £5 notes in order to wreck the British economy, which activity was in those days thought to require the intervention of an outside agency.

The series, written by the late Jack Pulman, gains what piquancy it has from the fact that the SS did actually get up to that very trick. A straight account of it might have made an informative and even funny documentary. Drawn out as a saga about a holy fool bamboozling the wildly saluting fanatics, it goes on and on like *Parsifal* but without the music, while constantly reminding you of *The Good Soldier Schweik* but without the humour.

But *Private Schulz* is merely bad comedy, which is easy to achieve, since hardly anybody is capable of the kind of concentrated effect needed to turn reasoned agreement into laughter. *People From the Forest* (BBC2) was bad drama – more difficult to forgive. Drama can be devoid of inspiration and still attain a level of elementary competence, but this production, although indefatigably artsy, somehow contrived to miss out almost entirely on the dignity of its subject, which was Sakharov and his heroic witness for freedom of expression. Sakharov was played by the excellent John Shrapnel, a fine-spoken actor with a noble head who in a better dramatisation would have made memorable casting as the scientific genius at war with his own Government. Alas, this time he was also at war with the script, the production and the direction.

I am sorry to sound peevish, but Sakharov is an important man whose cause deserves a better fate than to be made tedious by clumsy help. The dramatised political documentary is a dubious tradition which had its first big efflorescence in the 1960s, when scarcely a week went by without some pundit reinterpreting the recent past in terms of his own dullness. The form featured then, as it features now, direct addresses to the camera eked out with comatose dialogue scenes, heavy-handed symbolism and creaking epic devices. *People From the Forest* had all this and more, or to put it another way all this and less, because it wilfully threw away a dramatic plus which it had been handed on a plate, namely Sakharov's brilliance.

Sakharov's challenge to the Soviet Government went far beyond ordinary dissidence. Anybody brave enough – which means hardly anybody, but let that pass – can refuse to co-operate with tyranny. Sakharov told tyranny not only that it needed to change, but how that change could be brought about. He told the Soviet Union that it would have to either liberalise or else forfeit its status as a first-rate power.

Solzhenitsyn's moral condemnation of the Soviet past is comparatively easily dealt with inside the Soviet Union itself, where the Government controls the flow of information. But Sakharov's analysis of the Soviet future presents the regime with a real problem, since it becomes clearer all the time that he is right. This issue is of such towering historical significance that you would have thought it unlikely to be disregarded in a programme devoted to Sakharov's intellectual and moral stature. You would have been wrong.

24 May, 1981

Three dots for suspense . . .

A FIRST class two-part documentary about photography called *Snowdon on Camera* (BBC2) could well serve as a model for fledgling TV producers of how these things should be done. It was closely argued, richly filmed, tersely cut.

Above all it was quick. Without hurrying, the presenter did not hang about. He is shy on camera but gets a lot said, often by implication. Independent observers have suspected him for some time of being a severe sufferer from chronic honesty. Here was further proof. While being professionally scrupulous to a high degree, he is plainly sceptical about the pretentious talk which tends to attach itself to his subject. His conclusion, reached at the very end of the two programmes, was that photography has become inflated in every sense. On the way to this deduction a lot of territory was taken in, much of it beautiful to look at.

Kodak processes eighty-five million rolls of film a year, the overwhelming majority of them exposed by amateurs. Some amateurs carry $4,500-worth of equipment. Snowdon was shown examining a Nikon motorised camera the size of a Teasmade. If you pressed it in the right place it sounded like a machine gun. If you pressed it in the wrong place it would probably run you over. It was clear that equipped with one of these things even the most abject tyro might create a work of art by accident. So where did that leave the avowed artist?

Madame Harlip was the first artist to be interviewed. She does portraits. Snowdon was very respectful of her, which was generous of him, since it soon emerged that she thought his sort of thing was just taking snaps. What *she* did was paint with light, like Rembrandt. Helping to quell your mental image of Rembrandt blazing away with a Hasselblad was Madame Harlip's accent. 'And now I will giff you more artistic picture . . . giff me more feelings . . . keep zer mood on . . . I love zat very much . . . look at my rink.'

Her rink was on her finker. She defined her aesthetic philosophy as 'telling zer truce. Flattery is cheap. I personally couldn't do it.' Jesting Pilate would have had good reason to ask what zer truce was when some of Madame's portraits came swimming into view: if they weren't flattery, they were certainly fantasy. Karsh of Ottawa was a more formidable prospect. With the patina of memory, his portraits of the great are beginning by now to look monumental, an effect reinforced by those plain metallic backgrounds which echo Titian's Ariosto in thrusting the subject heroically forward, and which Snowdon echoed throughout the programme, regularly setting his talking heads against clean planes of cobalt and deep sea green.

Karsh was everything but funny. Terence Donovan is one of the funniest men in the world. Those who know him usually despair of the full effect ever being transmitted to those who don't, but Snowdon's editor trapped some of the torrent. 'Male jewellery,' sneered Terence, engulfing some Japanese device in one giant paw. 'They're for people to hang round their necks. You *sure* you're still a schoolgirl?' This last remark was addressed to a reclining fashion model, who warmed to the air of complicity, whereupon Donovan clicked away, while assuring us that the mood was what mattered – the machinery meant nothing.

Snowdon obviously sympathised with Donovan's approach. Nevertheless he gave the self-consciously dedicated American giants their due. Ansel Adams was shown making a few new prints from one of his classic negatives. Here was photographic art if such a thing was anywhere. Nor could there be any doubt that the carefully produced limited-edition prints of photographers like Penn and Adams are worth at least some of the high price they fetch at auctions. But once again Donovan's seemingly flippant attitude contained more of zer truce: the way to get rich, he averred, was to get into the authenticity business. Snap a few Portuguese birds in nineteenth-century peasant gear, hand the prints to a Frenchman with a Gauloise clinging to his lower lip, and send him into an auction room . . .

The Beeb has long wanted its own *Bouquet of Barbed Wire*, one of the all-time ITV ratings triumphs. Now at last they might have come up with something sufficiently rancid to stand the comparison. Called *Goodbye, Darling . . .* (BBC1), it will be in eight parts, of which the first part suggested that the three dots in the title portend a steadily accelerating build-up of tension in the viewer, possibly leading to migraine. There is a limit to how much drama the brain can take in before the cerebral cortex starts to boil. Who else, for example, is the heroine Anne going to get into bed with after she exhausts her current lover?

The moustached wimp of a lover lives in a caravan and waits wiltingly for Anne's visits. A Junoesque number whose hairstyle sometimes creates the impression that she is being impersonated by Benny Hill, Anne is the wife of a famous husband incapable of satisfying her demands. The caravan looks fairly light on its springs when the lover is in there alone, but Anne has only to join him and the suspension hits bottom. Meanwhile Anne's son, who is in love with her, is in rebellion against his father, whereas the daughter, who loves the father, has been traumatised by the sound of the caravan's shock-absorbers giving up the ghost.

Baroque casting among the peripheral characters ensures plenty of subsidiary interest, not to say fascination. There is a lesbian aristocrat called Lady Brett, who has a voice like a diesel locomotive and a wan companion called Maude. These two are either resting up for the next Fassbinder movie or else they are due to move centre stage, perhaps even into the caravan. Tune in soon or you'll never catch up.

Rod Stewart (BBC1) has an attractive voice and a highly un-attractive bottom. In his concert performances he now spends more time wagging the latter than exercising the former, thereby conforming to the established pattern by which popular entertain-ers fall prey to the delusion that the public loves them for them-selves, and not for their work. In *Rockstage* (Thames) Elkie Brooks looked to be some way down the same dreary road: if she had saved some of the energy she expended on strutting and put it into singing 'Lilac Wine' on key, she would have been fulfilling her promise instead of dissipating it.

Loretta Lynn's show was called just *Loretta* (Thames) and demonstrated that country music, for all its rhinestones and sentiment, is a real tradition that holds its performers within fruitful limits. She sang melodically, articulated cleanly, gave value for money and left you wanting more. How the rock stars ever came to think that self-indulgence was a superior way to behave is one of the great conundrums.

Roy Hattersley was the latest subject of *The Pursuit of Power* (BBC2), a chat series in which Bob McKenzie gives politicians such a rough time they must start wondering whether the pursuit of power is really worth the aggravation. 'I know no moment in the history of the Labour Party in modern times', gritted Bob, 'when it has got so near rock bottom as now. How have you managed it?' Hatters coped, but only just.

31 May, 1981

Two goals down

As episode two of *Goodbye, Darling* ... (BBC1) forcefully revealed, I was all wrong about Lady Brett and the wispy Maude being lesbians. They are just very, very good friends.

'We came out together,' one of them said, to which Anne's snobby husband riposted: 'Oh, you mean you were debutantes.' It is a measure of the sublime innocence underlying the script's air of sophistication that this interchange was evidently not seen as a joke by anyone concerned. Maude's problem, it transpired, comes in bottled form. As she became blotto the awful truth unfolded. Awful dialogue unfolded along with it. Lines the actors could do nothing with accumulated in heaps. The only way to play it would have been to get everyone into Scuba gear and do the whole thing underwater.

But back to the viewing week's beginning, marked by a particularly rich edition of *World Cup Grandstand* (BBC1). This took the form of a live telecast from Basle, where England had to defeat Switzerland in order to qualify for the World Cup. 'Tonight is a vital night for England in Switzerland. They must not only not lose, they must win.' So the writing was on the wall from square one, despite the facts – disgorged by John Motson at the touch of the usual button – that in 1963 England had won 8–1 at Basle and had never been beaten by a Swiss side since 1863, or it could have been 1763. You could take comfort from these statistics if you were an expert. If you were an ignoramus like me, you were too busy being overawed by the Swiss side as they lined up to face the camera.

They all looked like film stars. Clear skin stretched over rippling jaw muscles testified to yoghurt, muesli and mountain air. All the experts were agreed that the Swiss must lose, but for men haunted by doom they looked pretty calm, although it was always possible that the endless strains of their incredibly soporific national anthem had lulled them into unconsciousness.

The Swiss had lost at home to Norway – a good sign. Yes, it was practically in the bag for England. 'A defeat would be disastrous,' said Jimmy Hill. The whistle blew and it was instantly revealed that several of the Swiss could run very rapidly past the England defenders while yet retaining the ball. One of these Swiss was called Herman Hermann. A Swiss German rather than a German German, Herman Hermann was a real problem, but it took an ignoramus to see it. Experts like Bobby Charlton said that England looked 'safe at the back'.

Hardly were these words cold on Bobby's lips when the Swiss put the ball in England's net. 'He was given so much space.' Hardly had these words been uttered when the ball was in England's net again. 'England two goals down!' shrieked John Motson, translating the disaster into statistics. There was only one thing for the England fans to do – stage a diversion. Putting their Boy Scout badges in their pockets and artfully adopting fierce expressions, they pretended to riot. Alas, this imaginative tactic only half worked. England managed to score one goal while the Swiss team gazed puzzled into the stands, but one goal was two too few. Now England will have to beat Hungary 46–0 in order to get a match against San Marino.

Football hooliganism was one of the subjects in yet another riveting edition of *Question Time* (BBC1). Sir Robin Day, as he now is, ably contained a potentially explosive panel made up of Lynda Chalker, Denis Healey, Paul Foot and (deep breath) Admiral of the Fleet the Lord Hill-Norton. The contrast in forensic styles between the two last named pointed up the importance of manner on television. Paul Foot sat relaxed under his re-entry vehicle hairstyle and pithily made points. The admiral, burdening himself with that upper-class drawl by which near inarticulacy presumes to disguise itself as a stiff upper lip, could not convey even the simplest opinion in under five minutes and looked outraged when Robin cut him short.

Yet forced to a choice between the admiral's view of life and Paul Foot's most people would probably choose the admiral's, if only because it shows fewer signs of having been hatched in a cosy upper-middle-class incubator. Paul is absolutely certain that out-moded institutions must be swept away. You have to be brought up in sheltered circumstances to have that absolute certainty. Popular conservatism, which people like Paul always interpret as inertia, springs from a perception that society is too complicated for anyone to have all the answers.

Paul looks and sounds as if he has all the answers. His television manner might thus not be as effective as it is impressive, whereas the admiral, who bored you into the wall, probably succeeded in reinforcing the suspicion of a majority of viewers that when it came to hooliganism the idea of National Service might have something to it. Paul characteristically erupted into scornful cries about 'training them to kill', but most people would be prepared to give the admiral the benefit of the doubt and presume that he only meant keeping them out of Switzerland until such time as British society regained its sanity.

The week in politics, however, belonged to the man who calls himself Tony Benn. It remains a mystery why, having decided to adopt a revolutionary sobriquet, he did not go for broke and call himself, say, El Tornado or Tony Terror. Anyway, he had *Weekend World* (LWT) all to himself, with Brian Walden asking every question except the awkward one about just how democratic the new democracy within the Labour Party really is. Benn's absolute certainty on this point resembles Paul Foot's absolute certainty about everything and will result, I suspect, in a similar reluctance on the part of many averagely intelligent people to back up their admiration with a vote.

Billed as 'a Victorian comedy', *Landseer* (BBC1) took a superior line about the supposed frailties of its eponymous hero. Tableaux vivants and other elements of Victoriana were employed in order to bring out the old boy's unhealthy affinity with dumb animals, especially dogs. As a sworn dog-loather and lifelong enemy of anthropomorphic whimsy in all its forms, I would normally have been ready to go along with the programme's thesis, but in the event there was an air of arch self-satisfaction that left me resolved to look at Landseer with fresh attention: anyone who can attract that much condescension has probably got something to him.

Live from Monaco, *Grand Prix* (BBC2) was a thriller, especially after Alan Jones got into trouble. When Murray Walker shouted that it was 'all over bar the shouting' you knew Jones's long lead was due to melt away. Jones's car caught hiccups and Murray did his nut. 'I am going mad with excitement!' he told us – a necessary item of information, because even in moments of tranquillity he sounds like a man whose trousers are on fire. James Hunt tried to inject a note of sanity. 'Alan's car', he ventured, 'is doing something funny.' But Murray was beyond help. 'For once in my life I am at a loss for words!' he wailed, obviously never having realised that the reason why he continually screams like a bat out of hell is that he is always at a loss for words.

7 June, 1981

Forbidden kiss

D ES WILCOX gets the Sheer Guts of the Week award. On *Where It Matters* (Yorkshire) he played host to a discussion about race prejudice. The tumult in the studio sounded like a rough day in Beirut.

Luckily the bursts and salvoes were purely verbal, although there was a man in a bad shave and a beanie who looked as if he might produce a grenade at any moment and take Des hostage. 'Mr Ennals,' Des asked after a few dozen attempts to get beyond saying 'Mr Enn' and 'Mr Enna', 'is it possible to educate people out of prejudice?' Most of the noise, it should be pointed out, was emanating from people who were *against* prejudice. What they were fighting about was about what to do about it. The amount of fury available made daunting viewing. Des cultivated inner peace while the battle raged.

The tennis season got under way with Sue Lawley interviewing Billie Jean King on *Platform One* (BBC1). The main topic was Billie Jean's erstwhile Sapphic affair with a lady who eventually proved her selfless devotion by telling all to the gossip columnists, whereupon Billie Jean had the choice of either clamming up or else defending her civil rights. With the bravery of a true champion she chose the latter course, while the trash press got on with its self-imposed task of digging the supposed dirt on the female tennis circuit. A Saturnalia of orgiastic inverts was evoked, wherein grizzled veterans haunted the shower-rooms in order to descend without warning on fresh young virgins, tear the braces from their teeth, and imprint their trembling lips with the forbidden kiss of perversion.

Billie Jean did her best to tell Sue that not much of this sort of thing happens, but Sue, who otherwise got most of the points, didn't look too convinced. Yet it should have been clear enough from the rest of Billie Jean's utterances that what the tennis champions are chiefly passionate about is tennis. Only love of the game, Billie Jean averred, will get you to the top. The big, unspoken, unspeakable secret in the life of any star performer is that he, or in this case she, spends most of the time concentrating. A great truth that makes dull copy.

'You've said you like to keep your private life private,' Sue soothed, commiserating with Billie Jean on the unfairness of forfeiting your privacy just for being good at something. 'It's not fair but that's the way it is,' said Billie Jean stoically, apparently conceding that such treatment is the price of fame. Sue might have done more to speculate about why this should be so. After all, champions get famous by their own efforts, not because of coverage in semi-literate newspapers. What the junk journalist doesn't realise – or does realise, and waxes more aggressive so as to shout down his vestigial conscience – is that he is not really a party to the star's fame, which is based on solid public appreciation and would still be there even if the tabloid press disappeared overnight. I have always liked Billie Jean and after this interview I liked her even more. Those used to victory find it doubly hard to be gracious in defeat, but she has stuck up for herself in a classy manner and made her tormentors look the dunces they are.

Other things being equal, Billie Jean usually won, which made her hard to admire for those people who can only stomach excellence when it is well diluted with fallibility. On *Tennis 81* (BBC2) Dan Maskell made it clear that even in these professional days the old metaphysical distinction between gentlemen and players still applies. 'V. J. Armitraj, one of my favourite players, both as a man and as a tennis player.' When you scraped the flummery off that statement, what stood revealed was an enthusiast of the old school, who could never endorse Billie Jean's approval of the attitude to success in America, where the runner-up is rarely thought of as being more gallant than the loser. 'It was here, in the middle 1920s,' burbled Dan, surveying the vista at Queen's Club, 'that I served my apprenticeship to the lovely game.'

To Dan, God bless him. There is, after all, something to be said for the old attitude. But the gentlemanly air of not trying too hard tends to crack under the strain if it becomes tainted by resentment for the habitual winners. Some of these were on show at the pre-Wimbledon warm-up tournament, the *Stella Artois Grass Court Championships* (BBC2). Roscoe Tanner seems to have found a way of making his service go even faster, so that the ball is now quite invisible, like STEALTH, the American supersonic bomber which nobody has ever seen.

Indeed, just as we have to take the Pentagon's word that STEALTH exists, so we have only the noise made by Roscoe's racket to prove that there is an actual ball on the way. Perhaps he is faking the whole thing. John McEnroe, meanwhile, looks as endearing as ever. Let me make it clear, before Wimbledon is upon us to stifle all reason, that I like McEnroe's urge to win: indeed I can't see any other reason for playing competitive sports. What I don't like about him is his urge to lose – all that splurge of temperament which stops him being as good as his talent.

One of the plays that made Harold Pinter's name, *The Caretaker* (BBC1) showed itself to have a lot of mileage left in it, mainly because it features so many and such extended examples of Pinter's most resonant motif, the interrogation. It is hard to tell where Pinter's characters come from: all you know is that they are on the way to Sidcup and are well informed about the bus routes leading through the Angel. In Pinter the unplaceable new class that Orwell talked about found its theatrical voice. Yet what makes Pinter not just a post-war British playwright but a twentieth-century writer is the way he distils to an essence the characteristic modern political experience, which is to search, as if your life depended on it, for answers to questions that make no sense.

'Jenkins,' sneered Jonathan Pryce, interrogating a heap of rags which turned out on close inspection to be Warren Mitchell, 'Jen-kins. Sleep here last night?' 'Yeah.' 'Sleep well?' 'Yeah.' 'I'm awfully glad . . . what did you say your name was?' 'Jenkins.' 'Jenkins. Jen-kins . . .' A lot of this was like being sold a suit by a man with echolalia or interviewed on *Start the Week,* but there was humour in it too, albeit a bit mesmeric. The camera angles were not half flash in places – detracting from the claustrophobia rather than adding, I thought.

The Making of Mankind (BBC2) is much more interesting now that it has reached a stage where Mankind started leaving a few consumer durables lying around. The hunter-gatherer phase reached its peak during the last Ice Age, during which the hunter-gatherers, while waiting for the bison to show up, whiled away the time in deep caves by painting pictures of such astonishing accomplishment that you marvelled all over again at just how lousy our own artists were during the Middle Ages.

Unfortunately Richard Leakey and the programme-makers persisted in giving this material help it did not need. Animations of cave life appeared on screen. Cave-dwellers looking like the Grateful Dead or Hell's Angels sat around doing various conjectural things. 'In another corner the skilled tool-makers would be at work.' The animations couldn't have looked less convincing but it was better than having a mob of Equity card holders sitting there chipping flints. If you want to evoke things, though, the thing to use is the English language.

14 June, 1981

Them again

IT would have been comforting to start this week's television review with Wimbledon, but justice and a sense of proportion demand that the tennis-players should be displaced from top spot by the *SS* (Thames), back to haunt us in an excellent documentary produced and directed by Andrew Mollo.

The programme was a straight-up-and-down compilation of interviews, old film and narrative voice-over. What distinguished it was the quality of historical imagination displayed. Nazi organisations were deliberately constructed so that the various departments should duplicate one another. The chains of command are consequently very hard to unscramble, but by the end of the programme you knew that the *Waffen* SS, though it could lay claim to the odd spot of chivalrous conduct on those battlefields where it was up against a racially acceptable opponent, was fully implicated in the general SS programme of stark terror. Some of the old film adduced as illustration was enough to make you weep even at this distance. I thought I had seen all the footage in existence by now, but Mr Mollo found some more.

As the war ground on and the Nazis ran short of elite German man-power, suitable human material from the occupied countries was co-opted into the *Waffen* SS. This fact created an embarrassing difficulty for the victorious Allies, who very properly declared the SS a criminal organisation, but were then faced with the problem of deciding who were really guilty among the hordes of prisoners, some of whom had done no more than type laundry lists or deliver mail.

That there had to be some sort of reckoning should never be in doubt. The idea that the Nuremburg trials were a case of the victors punishing the vanquished is essentially trivial. The Allies were not half as victorious as the Nazis, who had wiped out whole populations of vanquished and would have walked away smiling if something had not been done. What was done was not perfect justice, but at least it was an attempt.

The attempt goes on, with the Germans themselves now in charge. In Düsseldorf the old Nazis who have recently been brought to book are practically senescent, but the smarter members of the younger generation have learned not to be carried away by compassion for their doddering elders. The evidence still cries out. As the Son of God once put it, those who have ears to hear, let them hear. The most heartening thing in a programme not long on heartening things was an ex-SS man saying that it was right for the message to be brought home and that any claims about the Nazi atrocities being, ordinary war crimes was blasphemy. The appropriate note of reverence was hit, and indeed never unduly departed from in the whole course of a powerfully sane documentary.

Wimbledon in a moment, but first a tiny wave of farewell to the first series of *The Levin Interviews* (BBC2), in which various, and variously, distinguished guests have been given the opportunity of listening to Bernard ask questions which reveal his personal obsessions. The latest interlocutor was J. Krishnamurti, revered by Bernard as a repository of Eastern serenity. 'What is the secret?' cried Levin, basking in the radiance of the guru's visage. 'Look at you! Serene, realised, content. What is the secret?' My own guess was that the old boy had attained serenity through being careful to let other people do the worrying, but this might have been an unworthy reaction to the sage's line of chat, a stream of platitudes which might possibly sound more challenging in the original language.

The secret of inner peace, it turned out, is to avoid conflict, which 'destroys . . . the whole sensitivity of awareness'. While pondering whether conflict ever did this for, say, Michelangelo, you could check out the wise one's contempt for the ego against his evident concern that his silky hair should cover his skull in the most impressive possible manner, even at the cost of its being parted remarkably low on the back of his serene head.

But if conflict was bad for serenity, thought was positively disastrous. Thought was the stuff to avoid at all costs. The aim was to be 'totally uncontaminated by thought'. 'Is thought the contaminant, then?' quavered Bernard. 'Yes,' said the holy man ineffably. He was wearing a very elegant shirt, into which a lot of thought had gone, starting with such elementary thoughts as how to make a hole for his serene neck to protrude from.

A moment's thought told you that it takes thousands upon

thousands of people, all thinking flat out, to support one guru while he sits there burbling on about the contaminating effects of ratiocination. From the occasional atavistic tone of impatience which crept into Bernard's voice you could tell he was still aware of this fact at some deep level, but by now the thirst for spiritual completeness has taken him over so thoroughly that his brain is almost in the same shape as Krishnamurti's – bland, moist and cloyingly sweet, like a lichee.

And now *Wimbledon* (BBC1 and II recurring), which Harry Carpenter is this year trying hard not to call Wmbldn, although he does not always reinsert the vowels in the right order. John McEnroe started badly, goaded by some obviously duff line-calls. There was much pontificating from the commentary box. 'And McEnroe, I fear, is indulging in a little bit of abuse of officials here.' 'Well this, I'm afraid, is par for the course.' Most of the time you couldn't quite hear what McEnroe said. 'Mwaargh nahg ahng ewarg,' he expostulated, 'Newn blarghing sarg!' 'Please behave,' said the umpire. 'Yah gahng shim! Shnargh!' Suddenly, catastrophically, McEnroe's voice snapped into focus. 'You can't be serious, man! You cannot be *serious*! How can you possibly say that ball was out? This man's an incarmpetent *fool*!'

McEnroe woke up next morning to find himself pilloried by Fleet Street. Journalists whose greatest athletic triumph had been to get back from El Vino's to the office without falling under a bus were calling him unworthy of his titles. It must have been gall piled on shame, but he controlled himself, and in the second round played an exemplary match against Ramirez. McEnroe has so much talent that nobody except himself can beat him consistently. All the other seeds in his half of the draw having volunteered for euthanasia, he should walk through to meet Borg, if Borg survives.

At that encounter temperament will probably tell. Borg has the same eyes as McEnroe, albeit placed more closely together. He is just as aware as McEnroe that some of the Wimbledon line judges need seeing-eye dogs. But Borg last threw his racket away in anger when he was a teenager. Noticing that the gesture had no result beyond its cost in energy, he never did it again.

28 June, 1981

Dan's winning lob

A TRADITIONAL feature of *Wimbledon* (BBC 1 and 2) is the way the commentary box fills up with British players eliminated in the early rounds. Mark Cox was first aboard, but was almost instantly joined by Virginia Wade, keen to launch her new career as a commentator.

She didn't make a bad start, when you consider that Ann Jones was already in the box and well established, with an armchair and an electric kettle. Ann had commented very politely during Virginia's only match. 'Ann Jones, how do you sum up the significance of this victory?' she was asked. The straight answer would have been that it was about to become very crowded in the commentary box, but she did not say so. Virginia was equally polite about Wendy Turnbull's match against Hana Mandlikova. She told us what Wendy was doing wrong, without mentioning that it wouldn't have made much difference if she had done everything right. Virginia stressed the word Mandlikova on the second syllable. The umpire stressed it on the first. Dan Maskell stressed it on the third and eventually wore his opponents down.

Dan's all-court commentating technique has by now reached such perfection that you would expect he had run out of surprises, but this year he unveiled a new trick of saying the wrong name just before saying the right one. 'Ann Jones, Anne Hobbs rather . . .' The effect was to wrong-foot the listener. Down at the receiving end against Mandlikova, Ann Jones, Anne Hobbs rather, did her version of the baseline bossa nova, a dance performed by British female players when they are about to receive service. It is designed to waste as much energy as possible. Sue Barker remains the most spectacular exponent, often bouncing up and down more than thirty times before lunging sideways to intercept the service and hit it out.

Ann Jones, Anne Hobbs rather, bounced almost as much as Sue, but Mandlikova was not impressed. Anne Hobbs, Ann Jones rather, sympathised with her compatriot. 'When she was in trouble against Virginia Wade she pulled out some real big ones when it really mattered.' Mandlikova went up against Navratilova for an all-Czech semi-final, with Dan Maskell as the chief voiceova, although everybody else was in the commentary box with him, including Virginia. 'She's very relaxed,' piped Virginia, referring to Martina, 'she *knows* she's won the title twice . . .' Martina went on to prove herself about as relaxed as it is possible to be when the new girl is wiping the court with you. Dan, meanwhile, was busily employing one of his favourite strokes, the one about the cold balls from the refrigerator. 'When the balls come cold like this from the refrigerator they really do skid away.' Nobody had anything to counter that.

David Vine doomily interviewed the defeated Navvy. 'I've never seen you so disappointed.' 'You're gonna make me cry if you keep talking like that.' Meanwhile, almost unnoticed, Mandlikova's eventual conqueror marched steadily towards the final, peppered with some brilliantly disguised backhands from Dan. 'Mrs Evert . . . Mrs Lloyd, I beg your pardon.' But by now the men's competition was boiling up. It had gone into a lull while McEnroe carved his way through the unseeded players left in his half of the draw and Borg revealed that he had hit form early, no cliff-hangers. In the commentary box there was a lot of speculation about how long McEnroe could contain his feelings or even whether it was good for him to do so.

As McEnroe squared up to Rod Frawley, Mark Cox was in the box for a lot of man-talk about the alleged necessity for the bad boy to uncork the boiling lava of his personality, lest his genius suffer inhibition. Some of this sounded more like vulcanology than wisdom. 'He's obviously not content with his form, and he *has* to *find* a way of getting rid of that pent-up emotion.' 'Yes, he has all this pent-up emotion . . . that pent-up emotion . . . his biggest problem is going to be to find out how to release it.' Nobody counselled the advisability of keeping the emotion pent up, although McEnroe had won his two previous matches with scarcely a murmur.

Frawley proving a tough nut to crack, there were early signs that the rift would soon spout lava. 'Wargh wharn whim glam heng,' whined McEnroe *sotto livello microfonico*, 'narf glahng shtum?' 'Will you please play on?' snapped the umpire. But something seismic was about to happen below that trembling crust. 'Ah chringh! Theeg ump glurg! GLARGH!' 'It's all pouring out now,' said Box and Cox. 'Unsportsmanlike conduct,' said the umpire. 'Warning, Mr McEnroe.'

'He needs these outbursts to get the negative tension out of his system,' explained Mark Cox. What was never explained was why Frawley should sympathise, especially when the negative tension happened to explode at the precise moment when he might otherwise have expected to be winning a set. 'Advantage Frawley,' said the umpire. 'Waagh fahgn blahg!' shouted McEnroe, holding things up. In the third set Frawley was robbed of a crucial point by a clearly bad line-call. In a civilised tone he made his only protest of the day. Shortly afterwards McEnroe suffered a call no worse and did his complete Krakatoa number.

Whether he called himself or the umpire 'a disgrace to mankind' remains problematical, but since he delivered the accusation while pointing in the direction of the umpire, whom he had been arguing with for an hour, he could scarcely complain about being miscon-strued. 'I wasn't talking to *you*, umpire. Do you *hear me*? What did I *say*? *Please* tell me!'

McEnroe shouted all this a few hundred times, as a child having a tantrum hopes to wear you down. The analogy is exact, because just as a child gets over the tantrum instantly but leaves the surrounding adults white-lipped, so McEnroe is all set to go within seconds of his latest eruption, while everybody else present, es-pecially his opponent, feels like a participant in the last act of a Greek tragedy. 'Frawley bore up *so well* under the most difficult circumstances.' Yes, and he lost. Whether or not McEnroe plans it that way, that's the way it comes out.

McEnroe went off to be reminded by the trash Press that the more he gives them what they want, the less they will respect him. Thus they get it both ways and leave him with nothing. Realising which people he appeals to might in the end be enough to help McEnroe clean up his act. The point was made academic when Borg and Connors (regularly referred to by Dan as Connors and Borg respectively) set about reminding you what tennis can be.

A physical throwback who crouches even when standing up, Borg examined his racket as if wondering what it was: some kind of club? Connors fired rifle-shots that left even the Swede standing. Two sets blew away while Borg played himself in. If you didn't know him, you would have said he had no chance. Connors, who did know him, knew that he had to be nailed quickly, since he gets stronger as he goes on longer. He went on longer.

At two sets all, even the McEnroe groupies must have been waking up to the fact that great sport, like great art, is more than just self-expression. Connors ('Borg, I beg your pardon') faltered and Borg ('Connors, rather') went through. As this column goes to press, the final is about to commence. McEnroe has the choice between playing tennis or the mad scene from *Lucia*. All those who admire his gifts hope it is the first.

5 July, 1981

Heavenly pink light

Police Commissioner McNee appeared briefly on *Close* (Thames), to put in a sensible bid for a respectful attitude towards the hard-pressed constabulary. Unfortunately he was appearing on the same night as a lot of pictures, liberally screened on both channels, which persuasively conveyed the impression that the hard-pressed constabulary's methods of searching houses in Brixton are likely to leave the householder wishing he had been looted instead. The most telling appearance of the week, though, was of a Brixton woman whose small shop had been obliterated. There wasn't enough left of the business to sell up and get out of. 'If anybody wants it,' she said bitterly, 'I'll give it away.' Here was a capitalist exploiter for the Left to make of what they could. Here, on the other hand, was an example of entrepreneurial initiative receiving its due reward under the shining aegis of Thatcherite monetarism. Here was a vote going begging.

At Warrington a great stack of begging votes found a patron in Roy Jenkins, thereby providing the biggest turn-up for the books since 1945. Back in the studio, Roy Hattersley nobly strove to dismiss the whole event as nothing but 'a media bye-election'. There may have been something to this contention: certainly the narrowly successful Labour candidate, Douglas Hoyle, looked as if he had been drawn by a particularly vicious caricaturist, while the Tory candidate had apparently been fielded in a cynical attempt to

snare the sympathetic allegiance of all those still weeping at Meg
Mortimer's departure from *Crossroads*. But whoofle and snort as
Hatters might, the fact was as glaring as the oil on Bill Rodgers's
hair – the Social Democrats had arrived. What was more, they
were expanding into a vacuum.

Meanwhile, back in the universe, *Cosmos* (BBC1) continued to
show how even Carl Sagan can make himself comparatively
uninteresting if he has enough help. Visiting us once upon a time
for a series of BBC lectures delivered to schoolchildren, Sagan
proved himself the best extempore speaker on science ever to have
appeared on television. Given a bench, a Bunsen burner, and a
steady relay of eager young assistants from the audience, he was
unbeatable. But *Cosmos* is a multi-national launch-vehicle with so
many hands on the controls that it travels in a tight spiral.

In the latest episode Sagan reached Mars, which he pronounces
Murruz. The planet Murruz is inhabited by Morshians. Behind
the Beeb's bench, Sagan had to stand still while he spoke. At large
in the Cosmos, he is free to accompany speech with action, but all
too apparently he has not grasped that beyond the trick of talking
on television there is a further trick of talking and walking
simultaneously, and that this trick must be mastered, not ignored.
He fills the screen with distracting gestures. He mugs something
fierce, often while standing on the bridge of a cut-budget version of
starship *Enterprise*, wherein his face is lit by the boudoir-pink light
of the heavens.

Nevertheless Sagan, though he has been more fascinating about
Murruz on previous occasions, managed to be fascinating about
Murruz all over again. We saw pictures of the doons of Murruz.
The unlikelihood was pointed out of any yoomans suddenly
appearing from behind the doons. As this series proves, Sagan
himself is only yooman, and yoomans make mistakes. But few
yoomans as clever as he share his gift of exposition. Next time he
should refuse all visual assistance except the barely necessary and
let his voice do the evocation. On television one good sentence is
worth a thousand dull pictures.

Introduced as being presented by Candice Bergen, *Rush*
(Thames) had only a brief intro from her and no presentation from
anybody. Instead you were supposed to draw your own conclu-
sions about what was allegedly going on during Rush Week at the

University of Mississippi. During Rush Week each new girl finds her ideal sorority, or soworty as it is known locally. Magically each soworty also finds the girl it wants. 'She *noo* that one of the biggest factors in me bein' happy was bein' in a soworty.'

Under the same pressure experienced by Party functionaries attempting to please Stalin, the girls progressed from test to test. Everyone, we were led to believe, ended up happy. Nobody looked sad except fat Angie, who will, one could not help hoping, develop a healthy neurosis out of her sense of rejection and write a scathing novel in which she shows up her contemporaries as a mindless pack of prestige-crazy jerks.

19 July, 1981

Wedding of the century

WITH camera shutters crackling around her like an electrical storm, Lady Diana Spencer, as she then was, had a little crisis. Off she went in tears with all the world's media in pursuit. Perhaps the whole deal was off. Perhaps she would become a nun.

Next day in Windsor Great Park Prince Charles told ITV that it was all nonsense about his betrothed not liking polo. 'Not much fun watching polo when you're surrounded by people with very long lenses pointing at you the entire time.' The place to be in such circumstances, it was made clear, was on horseback. 'Well, sir,' asked Alastair Burnet, 'what makes you play polo?' With the first chukka awaiting the swingeing thwack of the royal mallet, Prince Charles was eager to be away, but he gave the question his serious consideration. 'I happen to enjoy horse activities because I like the horse.'

An hour or so of horse activities duly ensued, apparently for the specific purpose of mystifying Mrs Reagan. 'Prince Charles with the ball . . . Prince Charles out on his own . . . playing for England against Spain just three days before his marriage . . . typically British . . . you can't get anything more British.' A British player who luckily turned out not to be Prince Charles fell on his head and went off streaming blood, thereby adding point to the snatched shots of Lady Diana carefully not watching the game. Princess Anne, more inured to horse activities, was, however, close by the side-boards to help her brother check his horse for loose steering and faulty brakes. 'And there's Princess Anne, who's of course a tremendous expert on horses . . . she is a real expert on horses if ever there was one.' Reassured, Charles scored a goal. 'And it's there! Prince Charles has scored for England.'

It became increasingly clear that Prince Charles had scored for England, Britain, the world, the solar system and the galaxy. Every human frailty manifested by Lady Diana only increased the universal conviction that the entire script was being written by the Brothers Grimm and that the Heir to the Throne had picked himself a peach. 'Are you looking forward to Wednesday?' the Beeb asked Mrs Reagan. 'I certainly yam. Isn't everybody?' The possibility was small that she would have said 'I certainly yam not, it's just another wedding,' but the enthusiasm was plainly genuine, although she still looked puzzled, perhaps from thinking about the horse activities. *Thames News* (ITV) and *Nationwide* (BBC1) both covered the coverage being laid on by the American NBC network. 'They've managed to bag these plum positions,' said *Nationwide* rather bitterly. All the rest of the world's television organisations were there too, including the Fuji company, now faced a thousand times daily with saying the two English words most difficult to a Japanese, 'royal family'. It comes out as 'royaroo famiree' but not immediately.

In *A Prince for Our Time* (BBC1) it was explained that 'Prince Charles is Colonel of ten regiments.' As a consequence he was well in command during *HRH the Prince of Wales and Lady Diana Spencer in Conversation with Angela Rippon and Andrew Gardner* (BBC and ITV), an all-channel, all-purpose interview in which the four partici-pants demonstrated various methods of looking uncomfortable in canvas safari chairs with high arm-rests. Lady Diana's pretty shoulders ended up around her ears, which might have helped her cope with the fatuity of the questions by making them inaudible. 'Literally fantastic,' said Prince Charles, describing the enthu-siasm of the people, 'so many people . . . overwhelming generosity . . . warm, affectionate . . . incredible kindness, I just can't get over it.' It was made clear that sacks of mail had more or less jammed the corridors of the palace, so that you had to take detours through pantries. Angela pretended to be stunned that children had baked cakes. 'Tremendous boost,' said Lady Diana tinily from between her shoulders. 'So many children crawling on top of me.' Prince Charles signalled his hopes that married life would be a calming influence. 'Getting interested in too many things and dashing abate, that is going to be my problem.' Lady Diana would help him solve it, but that wouldn't start until Wednesday. First there must be an evening of ritual separation. 'Not allayed to see me the night before, even by the light of exploding fireworks.'

Before the fireworks filled the sky, however, it first had to be filled by Frank Bough fronting *Nationwide* (BBC1). Frank was on top of a tall building, like a weathercock. He referred proprietorially to 'that famous old Cathedral here behind me'. Meanwhile Bill Kerr-Elliot pumped Lady Diana's famously unforthcoming flatmates. Still behaving like members of MI6 – except, of course, that they are almost certainly not working for the Russians – the flatmates nevertheless let slip the odd scrap. 'We often came back and found her dancing around the flat on her own . . . bopping.' The flat was a non-event without her. 'There's a general lack of Diana, really.'

Lady Diana had gone on to higher things, including the Archbishop of Canterbury. Interviewed by James Hogg, the Archbish predicted that with other people's prayers wafting him along he would soon get over his nerves. 'The ceremony being prayed over . . . you forget about the cameras.' Frank signed off with a necessary reminder. 'It's easy to forget that amid all the pomp and circumstance, tomorrow is all about the marriage of two *people*.' This helped put your mind at rest if you had been worried that it might be all about the marriage of two hedgehogs.

The Royal Fireworks (BBC1) were laid on in Hyde Park by Major Michael Parker, First Gentleman of the Rockets and Sparkler in Waiting. Raymond Baxter supplied the commentary, excelling even Prince Charles in the strain he put on a certain vowel, or veil. 'The Queen and twenty craned heads from other lands . . . bonfire built by Boy Skates . . . the Boy Skates, Sea Skates and Air Skates . . . the fuse darts ate across the grass.' Up went the rockets, but not so as to take your breath away. Billed as 'the most tremendous fireworks display since 1749', it looked a bit sedate. 'And neigh, the twenty-one guns of the Queen's Troop . . .' As the sky healed,

Prince Charles could be seen talking to Major Parker. What was he saying? 'A pretty average fireworks display, Major. Or should one say . . . *Sergeant?*'

Early next morning ITV stole a march by getting Leonard Parkin into position outside Lady Diana's window while the Beeb was still clearing its throat with a Bugs Bunny cartoon. 'She's just peeped out of her window . . . the famous hairstyle . . . The Dress is in there.' The BBC's coverage began with Angela Rippon sitting in a vast flesh-coloured Art Deco salesroom for pre-war cosmetics. 'We'll be speculating on The Dress,' said Angie. Michael Wood, now promoted, or demoted, from whizz-kid academic to all-purpose presenter, said, 'I'm going to look at some of the funnier moments,' a line not calculated to get you laughing. Both channels evoked a huge dawn security operation featuring underground bomb-sniffing Labrador dogs at large beneath the city, but already it was apparent that ITV, with a less elaborate studio set-up but more flexible outside coverage, had the legs of the Beeb, which was interviewing boring old buskers while the other side had success-fully tracked down the people who had made The Dress. Plainly they would reveal nothing even under torture, but it beat looking at a man with a mouth-organ.

'I've moved out into the Mall,' said Leonard Parkin, 'and this is the scene Lady Diana saw when she peeped out of the window.' If she peeped out of the window again, she would see Leonard, but no doubt she was busy climbing into The Dress. Meanwhile, back at the Beeb, Lord Lichfield told Angie how hard it was to get snaps of the Royals. 'The great thing to do is keep their attention because they tend to talk to one another.' Another BBC scoop was Herbie, the notoriously bad waiter from Costello's. He described a past catastrophe, pronounced castastrophe, which he had apparently visited upon a previous Prince of Wales. 'Zer banquet turned out to be a castastrophe for myself . . . zer soup went all over his leg . . . which he had to go inner zer barseroom and have it removed.' 'Do you have a message for the present Prince of Wales?' 'A present?' 'No, a message.' 'God bless zer Royal Family.'

On ITV, Andrew Gardner was with Barbara Cartland. 'What I believe in, of course, is Romance.' Twin miracles of mascara, her eyes looked like the corpses of two small crows that had crashed into a chalk cliff. They were equalled for baroque contrivance by the creation decorating the top lip of the BBC's next guest, Sir Ian Moncreiffe of That Ilk and That Moustache. 'No time is known', he explained, 'when there weren't these magic royal people.' On ITV, Judith Chalmers had the job of being enthusiastic about The Dress, sometimes called That Dress for purposes of emphasis. 'That Dress . . . The Dress . . . I'm looking forward to it.' Sandy Gall tuned in from Hyde Park Barracks, where the Blues and Royals of the Escort were already providing a formidable example of horse activities. Prince Charles was Colonel of every regiment in sight but actual power resided in the glistening form of Regimental Corporal Major Lawson, who would be the senior NCO on parade. 'The majority on parade', rasped the Corporal Major, 'will never ever see a parade of this enormity.' Filling the close-up, the hirsute extravaganza adorning the Corporal Major's top lip made That Ilk's paltry ziff look like a dust-bug.

ITV explored St Paul's to a well-written voice-over from Alastair Burnet, although later on he slightly spoiled things by calling it the Abbey. Katherine Yochiko of Fuji TV was interviewed. 'Royaroo famiree . . . so exciting reahree.' She predicted that The Dress would be 'just rike a fairy tayaroo'. 'It's just after nine o'clock,' said Andrew Gardner, 'so we've only got two hours to wait now before we see That Dress.' Aloft in the ITV airship, a camera watched the first soldiers march away to line the route. The air shots were destined to be a big plus for ITV throughout the day.

Back with Angela at the cosmetics counter, Eve Pollard the fashion expert was asked to predict what The Dress would look like. 'Cinderella dress .. real fairy-tale.' The first guests were arriving at St Paul's as ITV took its turn to hear from the Archbish about how prayers kept him going when the chips were down. 'Do you suffer from nerves on occasions like this?' 'I say some prayers.' The Beeb's chief commentator, Tom Fleming, clocked on for a long day. 'Once upon a time . . . what you will see now is no fairy story, but the story of two very real young people.' Never appearing in vision, Tom yet wears a morning suit in order to get himself in the right mood for dishing out the hushed tones of awe. 'Daunting journey that will carry her through this gateway . . . a new life of Royalty . . .' But ITV had caught the Earl Spencer, a natural star even in his infirmity. 'Are you a little apprehensive about today?' 'Not in the least.'

With fine young ladies poised beneath them, big hats were floating into the cathedral like pastel Frisbees flying in slow motion. 'I think it's going to be the most amazingly chic wedding of the century,' burbled Eve on the Beeb. 'It's because *she*'s such a knockout . . . endless huge hats.' For ITV Alastair Burnet did a voice-over about the buildings on the route. Gracing the proceedings with a touch of wit, his commentary was yet another plus for the commercial channel's coverage, which by now was making the Beeb's look and sound sclerotic. But Tom Fleming ploughed on. 'Queen Elizabeth, like Prince Charles, loves horses.' Spike Milligan, who loves whales, showed up after all: having learned at the last minute that Prince Charles was responsible not for whales but for Wales, he had temporarily shelved his protest on behalf of the threatened cetaceans and made it to Moss Bros just in time. 'Here is the King of Tonga,' said Tom Fleming, neglecting to add that the King of Tonga is roughly the same shape as the much-missed Queen Salote but lacks the bounce. Nevertheless the King of Tonga was an acquisition, looking rather like Lord Goodman giving one of those interviews in which the face is kept in shadow for security reasons.

The Queen's carriage left the Palace accompanied by the cheers of the multitude. 'There they are, all waving their flags,' said Tom Fleming as the people waved their flags. 'Hats,' he said, as the screen filled with hats. Lady Diana was dimly visible through the window of the Glass Coach. Tom was ready. 'A fairy-tale sight . . . that shy smile we've grown to know already . . . these bay horses look hale and hearty.' Lady Diana alighted to mass agreement that she looked like a princess in a fairy tale. 'Ivory pure silk taffeta!' cried the Beeb's Eve in triumph, her predictions fulfilled. 'Isn't it a fairy tale?' asked Judith Chalmers rhetorically. At least one viewer thought that the dress had been designed to hide the outstanding prettiness of its occupant's figure as thoroughly as possible, but to say so would have been treason and anyway the lady had only to smile in order to remind you that she would look good in a diving suit.

With all those present in the Cathedral and 700,000,000 viewers throughout the world dutifully pretending that her father was guiding her instead of she him, the bride headed down the aisle towards the waiting groom, Charles Philip Arthur George, shortly to be addressed by Lady Diana as Philip Charles Arthur George, a blunderette which completed the enslavement of her future people by revealing that she shared their capacity to make a small balls-up on a big occasion. 'Here is the stuff of which fairy-tales are made,' drivelled the Archbish, adding further fuel to the theory that he's the man to hire if what you want at your wedding is platitudes served up like peeled walnuts in chocolate syrup: he's an anodyne divine who'll put unction in your function. But the soaring voice of Kiri te Kanawa soon dispelled the aroma of stale rhetoric. Singing a storm, she even managed to make you forget what may have been the only surviving example of Maori national dress.

Spliced at last, the Prince and Princess headed for the door with Tom Fleming's voice helping you master the details. 'The cap-holder appears with cap and gloves,' said Tom as the cap-holder handed Charles his cap and gloves. Off they went down Ludgate Hill in the landau. While Tom told you all about the bells of St Clement's ('the bells that say oranges and lemons') Alastair Burnet recalled that Dr Johnson had defined happiness as driving briskly along in a post-chaise beside a pretty woman. By that definition Prince Charles was the happiest man alive, but Tom didn't want the horses to feel left out. 'These horses . . . certainly not reacting to the cheers . . . and yet perhaps . . .' ITV snatched the best shots of the bride. The policemen who were all supposed to be facing outwards spent a lot of time facing inwards. It would have taken a saint not to drink her in.

'And so, slowly,' intoned Tom, 'the horses find their way home.' For the balcony appearances ITV supered a shot of the Royals over a background of the cheering crowd. The BBC, perhaps because there were no horses on the balcony, showed less flair. While the Princess got on with the job of changing out of The Dress into her almost equally eagerly anticipated going-away outfit, the television companies went off the air for lunch. The BBC wedding party was still going on when they came back on the air at 3.30, with Frank reminding us that what was taking place in the studio was a true festive occasion, in case we thought it was a funeral.

In an open carriage weighed down with rose petals and buoyed up by balloons, the newlyweds headed for Waterloo. The Princess of Wales, wearing the kind of tricorne hat in which Edward VII's Alexandra was wont to wow the public, looked good enough to eat.

'It would be good,' said ITV's Alastair without any real hope, 'if people didn't intrude on their privacy at Broadlands.'

As the only clean train in Britain set off on its journey, the Beeb's Tom was ready with the words whose solemn gravity so exactly failed to sum up the occasion. 'Throw a handful of good wishes after them . . . from the shore as they go . . . may they carry these memories . . . to cheer them on their journey into the unknown.' But the people were less frivolous. Having put off the tone of portent until the inevitable day when it would come in handy, they were dancing in the streets.

2 August, 1981

The Bagwash speaks

INTRODUCING *The God That Fled* (BBC2), narrator Christopher Hitchens announced that 'the programme contains nudity and some scenes of physical and psychological violence'. No doubt the viewing figures were thereby enhanced. In the immortal words of Ronnie Scott, the bouncer was outside throwing them in.

Alas, despite a suavely written and delivered voice-over from Hitchens, the programme fell somewhat short of getting you suitably indignant about the doings of a character called the Bhagwan Rajneesh, who runs – or ran, until he recently did a fade – an ashram in Poona. To this ashram many Westerners come, or came, that they might prostrate themselves before the radiant wisdom of the Bagwash, as it is impossible not to call him if you have ever sat in a launderette and watched your tattered underwear revolve soggily for hours while exuding grey suds. The Bagwash talks the way that looks.

'Troot is eternally fress as the dewdrop in the morning,' droned the Bagwash, 'or the stars in the naiche. Troot . . . it is not a *ting*.' Sitting on the floor and on one another, his Western followers soaked up the enlightenment as it poured forth. A poignant instruction on a sign-board forbade them to go away. 'Friends, it is not possible to leave the discourse before it is over.' But – and this was the intractable 'but' against which the measured indignation of Hitchens pressed in vain – nobody showed any sign of wanting to leave the discourse. They couldn't get enough of the discourse. Far from looking as if they had been brainwashed into acceptance of the unalleviated tripe the hairy old boy was dishing out, they showed every indication of having searched for it all their lives.

The same applied to the ashram's other attractions. Not all the time on the ashram was spent listening to the Bagwash speak, only most of it. There were also opportunities to be touched by him physically. An activity which in any other context would have looked like a hirsute charlatan copping a feel of a pretty girl was known on the ashram as 'opening the third eye'. But the girls didn't just like it, they loved it. 'I'm happier here than I've ever been anywhere in my life,' said an obviously nice woman from England. Unless it involves the unhappiness of someone else, happiness is hard to argue with. 'It's an inner thing,' she added, looking enviably serene.

The men, of course, were better material for satire. Superannuated hippies in notably bad beards, they talked Californian balls about energy. 'A human being is an energy field,' said the sort of face which fifteen years ago would have been telling you about Timothy Leary. 'Nershing aspects of a one-to-one relationship . . . non-verbal levels of awareness . . . we do a lot of energy work.' Some of the energy work took the form of encounter groups, in which all present doffed their clothes and shouted hatred at one another, while somehow the shaggiest men with the most flagrant pudenda ended up sitting on top of the prettiest girls and loudly establishing an 'energy connection'.

The script was at its strongest when it pointed out that a mob of Western dropouts talking codswallop about spiritual values is something that poverty-stricken Poona needs like a hole in the head, or third eye. The suggestion that some of the participants in the energy sessions tend to finish up in hospital was not quite so unsettling. So do some of the participants in motor-cycle races. The injuries acquired while pursuing free activities are small cause for pity.

My own, perhaps hopelessly two-eyed view is that troot is indeed a ting, that human reason as we know it in the West is the only kind of thought there really is, and that the Wisdom of the East, to the extent that it exists at all, is at least partly and perhaps largely responsible for the fact that India can't provide a decent life for the majority of its people. But this conviction doesn't alter the fact that the West, precisely because it is both politically free and technically advanced, is bound to go on churning out a lot of inadequate personalities who are unlikely to find life tolerable without a spiritual leader who will at least pretend to do what anyone in his right mind so conspicuously fails to do – take them seriously.

In this regard the Bagwash seems a fairly benign example of his type. From private sources I understand that there were some nasty details which the BBC demanded be edited out of the programme, but I doubt if they would have convinced you that the Bagwash was the devil incarnate. He's just a talkative dingbat who manipulates the manipulable into manipulating one another – it's a closed circuit.

Wanly narrated, *Checkpoint Berlin* (BBC1) still came up with some fascinating data about the Berlin Wall. The year before last, for example, a girl got killed trying to cross it. Nothing startling about that, since the Wall has claimed a total of seventy-one victims to date. But this girl was born after the Wall was built. The thing has been there twenty years. Known to its creators as the Anti-Fascist Protection Barrier, it has so far been brilliantly successful in stopping West Berliners from staging a mass migration to the East, although if the whole of West Berlin youth is as blandly stupid as one or two of the examples interviewed then the day must surely come when democracy will have no remaining advocates.

Proposing that the Allied troops should pull out forthwith, one of them said: 'I'd say they have to *leave*. I'd say it's not very good, you know? As a matter of fact I do not believe that the Russians would want West Berlin, you know?' For those of us who didn't know, the speaker's face was a revelation. History hadn't happened to it. You needed all your Christian charity to hope that it never would.

The BBC might please the Government by withdrawing from E. P. Thompson its invitation to give the Dimbleby Lecture, but it won't please those of its supporters who want to see it given a proper licence fee in order that it might get on with the job of promoting free opinion. Free opinion includes E. P. Thompson's views on nuclear disarmament. To me they seem wrong-headed, but it wouldn't have hurt to hear them argued at length. If, however, the BBC's true destiny is to come up with a programming schedule that will offend nobody, they have made a good start with *Under the Weather* (BBC2), starring weatherman Jack Scott.

No longer confined to his fleeting half minute, Jack has now been given the bore's equivalent of a Heavy Goods Vehicle licence. 'What better than the wonderful British weather,' chortles Jack, 'which does have a bad name doesn't it, and all because of the good old low-temperature depression.' He fills us in on something called the Digby down-draught visco-static upsurge. 'Our imaginary cylinders extend upwards through the atmosphere.' It is children's television, except that children would not watch it.

9 August, 1981

Lindi's built-in barbecue

I N *Prostitute I Am – Common I'm Not* (Thames), several ladies of the night revealed all. Apart from the trade secrets, there was a beguiling emphasis on character. Lindi was the one who got you laughing. Fabulously successful at her chosen metier, she lives like Hugh Hefner, sharing his idea of good taste even to the extent of possessing a revolving bed with quadrophonic speakers, built-in barbecue, etc. 'I was very well developed,' she announced, explaining how the career began that had made all this possible. 'Always had a large bust.' The large bust seems recently to have been joined by the rest of her, perhaps as an inevitable side-effect of her lavish standard of living. Not that she doesn't give value for money. Her torture chamber has everything that opens and shuts, not to mention pummels and stabs. 'I got two different racks.' Proudly she demonstrated a large item of high technology which she described as 'an automatic rotating rack with motor and gearbox.'

MPs, QCs and peers of the realm apparently spend a lot of time swinging by the heels from the roof of Lindi's dungeon while she plies them rigorously with black-jacks and cured stingray tails.

Sheila offered a less comprehensive service than Lindi, but if you didn't mind her headmistressy expression would probably make a more intellectually stimulating companion. Kristina, an ex-Chelsea Set glamour queen, was so genuinely tasteful that you blushed for her and not just for yourself: plainly only her nervous breakdown had propelled her into these circumstances and it was hard to see what she was doing on screen except providing irresistibly good copy.

The gormless Liz was there to remind you of what prostitution really entails. Lindi, registered as a limited company and paying company tax, might seem to have got life well weighed up, but with Liz the truth was plain to see. For selling love to strangers you need partitions in the mind. But that was the minor message of the programme. The major message was that to legislate against prostitution is like drawing up laws against the sea.

The hookers' symposium was produced and directed by Judy Lever, one of three female programme-makers who all turned in good shows on the same evening. Chris Mohr produced *Ready When You Are, Mr de Mille* (BBC1), scripted and fronted by the redoubtable Barry Norman, who has by now got the documentary-about-Hollywood format running like a Rolls. The famous joke whose punchline provided the programme's title was told by various celebrities all delivering one sentence each, but this fancy idea unfortunately resulted in the gag being muffed.

Everything else, though, contributed infallibly to bringing out the old phoney's gimcrack greatness. If he had lacked energy, a talent for spectacle and the organising ability of Dwight D. Eisenhower, he would not have been such a problem. As it was, people couldn't decide whether they admired him or despised him, and still can't today. His amatory pluralism was decorous rather than otherwise; his severity with his minions got results that paid their salaries; his appalling vulgarity now looks like vigour. Basically he was an actor. In true existentialist style, he woke up each morning and played the part of film director. Acting better than his actors, he had all the personality that his films lack.

The third stand-out made-by-a-woman documentary was *Elvis Lives* (BBC2), produced by Sandra Gregory. Presented with the minimum of commentary but demonstrating the maximum of editorial judgment, this was really mind-bending stuff. Having unaccountably failed to rise again on the third day, Elvis is now buried under a mountain of souvenirs – a teetering peak towards which the faithful flock by the million, many of them dressed and hairstyled to resemble their lost hero. There was a stunning shot of half a dozen Elvis imitators crossing the road towards the camera. It made you feel that you had a many-faceted eye, like a fly.

But these were Elvis imitators only on their days off. 'Airs no way I can describe it,' said an Elvis imitator from Britain. 'I just love the man.' Other Elvis imitators work at it for a living. These Elvis imitators are best described as Elvis impersonators, since they hope, in the right light, to be taken for the original. Aspiring professional Elvis impersonators were shown auditioning. Some of them looked a bit like Elvis, but sang like dying dogs. Others could imitate his voice brilliantly, but looked like Lord Thorneycroft. The more desperate had had plastic surgery. A man looking like Elvis Presley injected with cortisone sang like Humphrey Bogart injected with cement.

Easily the most successful Elvis impersonator is Morris Bates, who hasn't had any plastic surgery but studies the video-cassettes until every sneer and pigeon-toed ankle-wobble comes as naturally as breathing. The sad thing with Morris is that he would be a tremendous rock 'n' roll singer on his own account. But he is humbly content to wear the Presley persona, as long as he can leave it behind in the dressing-room when he goes home. The fanatics want never to leave it behind. Larry Geller, billed as 'Elvis's hairdresser and spiritual adviser', made it clear, while addressing a rally-sized meeting of pilgrims, that the movement had reached a point where it must beware of traitors. It was revealed that a child has been born with its top lip curled, although whether it had emerged from the womb wearing blue suede shoes was not stated.

16 August, 1981

Ideological intervention, man

A N unintentionally wonderful programme called *A Town Like New Orleans* (BBC2) showed what happens when people whose proper concern should be some form of fruitful labour start mucking about with art. Few real artists despise business – in fact the more original they are, the more they tend to respect the workaday world – but it is a hallmark of the dabbler that he prides himself in being set apart, and so it proved here. Leeds, it appears, is crawling with jazz and pop musicians who have managed to convince themselves that they are contributing to the biggest explosion in their respective art forms since King Oliver met Louis Armstrong or Phil Spector invented the wall of sound.

The musical evidence adduced to back up this contention sounded pretty feeble, but perhaps the television crew had called during a bad week. 'Singing is one of the most important things in my life,' said a lady in a sad brown hat, 'it's a very deep need in me . . . I suppose I've never been lucky enough to have . . . the breaks.' A man with a beret, beard and spots played be-bop sax while one or two passers-by, stiff with cold and too many rehearsals for the camera, dropped pennies at his aching feet.

And that would have been the sum total of the action, if it had not been for a resident arts teacher endowed with a remarkable gift for improvising endless streams of free-form sociologese. 'Plurality . . . any viable activity as art . . . ideologically valid intervention . . . ideological intervention by a rock and roll band.' One of his pupils showed signs of outsoaring his master. 'We 'ave a lot of problems as a band . . . we see ourselves more as a working unit who are trying to locate ourselves as a working unit of production . . . criteria . . . validate . . .' It was the kind of talk which Duke Ellington used to say stank up the place. New Orleans had Storeyville and the sound of Buddy Bolden's cornet across the water. Leeds has ideological intervention in the back room of a pub. It follows with inexorable logic that Leeds is not a town like New Orleans.

Richard's Things (Southern) had everything by way of production values, up to and including the star producer himself, Mark

Shivas. Frederic Raphael wrote it. Liv Ullman was in it, playing the role of Kate. Her husband having been wiped out by a heart attack, Kate fell in love with his mistress, Josie, played by Amanda Redman and her very nice teeth. Josie (both breasts showing) lolled around on the lap of Kate (no breasts showing but face ecstatic) while the viewer, according to gender and/or proclivities, either marvelled at how tasteful it all was or gave thanks that so much crumpet had been assembled in the one place.

'I don't understand anything' moaned Liv the next morning. High on the list of things she didn't understand must have been how Josie's make-up managed to stay intact after a night of Sapphic sensationalism. Such frivolous considerations were hard to avoid, since the characters never began to live or even differ from one another. Frederic Raphael is clever but his characters all sound like him. Even the man who was supposed to be the bore spoke epigrams. Liv, as usual, looked on the point of tears all the time – an unvarying expression which the more gullible critics hail as expressive – which gave you some idea, but probably the wrong one, of why the deceased should have favoured Josie. A classily done piece of nearly nothing.

At the moment the channels are locked in a deadly competition to see who can screen the worst stretch of imported American trash. *Flamingo Road* (BBC1) is a chunk of junk aimed at the *Dallas* audience. 'Ah want it ol,' says a *Playboy* gatefold called Constance, 'and ah want it *nao*.' The town's straight-arrow hero and future State senator, an idiot called Fielding, does his best to evade Constance's warm clutches, but he is battered into submission by the Homeric similes of ruthless old Titus. 'Things don't just run,' opines Titus. 'Little wheels push big wheels. Big wheels push bigger wheels. Sooner or later those wheels need oil. So they don't squeak . . .' Meanwhile the beautiful Lane Ballou, languishing for love of the zero hero, sings plaintively in the cat-house. 'I know I shouldn't be acting like this,' says Momma, taking the words out of your mouth.

Nothing should have been able to counter that, but ITV fought back with a mini-series called *Condominium: When the Hurricane Struck*. Full of bad actors wearing wigs, the condo was totalled by a her-cane, but not before it had spent a lot of time being threatened by stock shots of big waves while the inhabitants held meetings.

You prayed for the her-cane to get there early and shut everbody up, but it insisted on travelling in a circle, as her-canes will. Finally the whole deal was underwater. *Towering Inferno* had met *The Poseidon Adventure*. Actors who had spent their whole lives on the feature list held on to their hair transplants and shouted the line that had been haunting them in their sleep for years: 'We'll never make it!'

23 August, 1981

Speer checks out

ALBERT SPEER, the only top Nazi to make it all the way through into the television era, died of old age practically on camera. He was making a programme for the BBC when he finally gave up the *Geist*, leaving one with some curiosity to see the as-yet unscreened tape, in order to ascertain how long his expression of innocent bewilderment stayed in place after his canny soul had departed.

Speer never made the mistake of saying there were no extermination camps. He said he didn't know about them. He impressed the gullible by declaring himself willing to accept responsibility for Nazi crimes even though he was not aware of their full scope. But as the man better informed about the Reich's industrial resources than anybody else including Hitler, Speer was in fact fully aware of the purpose and extent of the Final Solution and by pretending he was not he did the opposite of accepting responsibility.

Speer cheated the rope, cheated the world and yet further insulted the shades of innocent millions. Those of us who live by our brains should remember his example, which serves to prove that intellect confers no automatic moral superiority. Otherwise we will meet him again in the Infernal Regions, and be once more confronted with that look of puzzled concern, as if there were something difficult, ponderable and equivocal about the rights and wrongs of tearing children from their mothers' arms, piling their little shoes in heaps and pushing their twisted corpses into ovens.

To hell with him and back to the now-crowded schedules, which include a richly rewarding nonsense crafted by John Braine, *Stay With Me Till Morning* (Yorkshire). The luxuriously sensual title instantly evokes a milieu far from common experience, which might conceivably give rise to a series called 'Shouldn't You Be Going or You'll Miss the Last Tube?' We are in the North, but it is the North of rich wool-merchants driving Porsche 928 sports cars towards silk-sheeted appointments with vampy mistresses. Paul Daneman plays Clive. Handsome, powerful, wealthy, sophisticated Clive. Wearing a snakeskin shirt to indicate relaxation, Clive throws the kind of party at which vamps slide up the lapels of handsome, powerful, wealthy and sophisticated men. 'I do what I want and I say what I want and I never feel guilty.' Decadence is indicated by dancing very slowly with your hands on the lady's bottom.

But Clive's beautiful wife Robin, played by Nanette Newman, is upstairs being pinned to the quilt by her erstwhile admirer Stephen (Keith Barron), a media star who has come back from the South specifically in order to throw her about tempestuously among her hideous furniture. A tight head-shot of Robin must be intended to indicate either that she is having an orgasm or else that she has accidentally stuck a toe into a light-socket. A similar shot of Stephen suggests that he has just been bitten on the behind by a large dog. 'Yes! Yes! Don't be too kind!' cries Robin. 'Don't ever be too kind! Yes! I don't care!'

Meanwhile Clive is being vamped solid by a siren whose name I didn't catch, but whose dimpled chin vaguely evokes Kirk Douglas in a wig. With a roar from the Porsche they are off to her place and in bed together among decor outdoing even Robin's in its transcendental horror. As the camera zooms in on Clive's sophisticated features, Kirk's head drops meaningfully out of shot, perhaps signalling her vampish intention to make a meal of his pyjama bottoms. A symbolic champagne bottle gushes virile foam. Spume at the top.

Still on the subject of adultery, but subtracting the ludicrous and adding the terrifying, the latest ITV 'Bestseller' import was called *Murder in Texas* and just went to show that a television critic must be ever on the alert, even though his eyes grow corns from constant friction. After *Condominium: When the Hurricane Struck* you would have been excused for thinking that anything with the 'Bestseller' label on it must reveal itself when unwrapped to be a pile of fish-heads, but here was a well-scripted, well-acted mini-series which erred only in the direction of being too faithful to the facts. In the end it failed to make dramatic sense, but there was a lot to watch on the way, including a performance from Farrah Fawcett which proved that she is more than just a set of teeth.

Farrah was married to a rich plastic surgeon who did her in, employing for the purpose a syringe full of hand-reared microbes. He was a music-lover who turned out in the course of two absorbing evenings to be a complete nut, but if you discounted the strange attitudes adopted by his top lip it was plausible that he should draw first Farrah Fawcett and then Katharine Ross into the moiling toils of his obsession.

Nobody who saw the first instalment of *Fighter Pilot* (BBC1) is likely to miss out on seeing the rest. The opening sequence showed an RAF Buccaneer angling at zero feet along canals. Inside its black bubble the pilot's face must have been looking happy. No wonder there are two thousand applicants every year. Only one in five get through. We were shown the initial weeding. Apparently it is less crushing to be rejected for medical reasons than to be told you are all wrong mentally. What was more than mildly intriguing, however, was the fact that even the few survivors of the preliminary screening seemed to have little interest in flying as such. A boy with a beard who kept saying that he wanted to be in the Air Force 'should all else fail . . . as a last resort' got a surprisingly long way before being turfed out.

13 September, 1981

Hot pistils

DEALING with the sex life of flowers, the latest edition of *The World About Us* (BBC2) should have been fascinating, but a doggedly frolicsome commentary ruined it.

Somebody made the age-old mistake of thinking that all you have to do to be funny is to lighten your tone. It's a delusion characteristically harboured by those without humour. Addison once said you could tell the man with humour because he kept a straight face while those around him were in stitches, whereas the man without it split his sides while everybody else looked mournful. So it was here. 'The delights of the wedding night and breakfast next morning at the same moment!' chortled the voice-over, thereby destroying not just the beauty but the otherwise irresistibly comic effect of a particularly elaborate floral copulation involving wasps.

The flower, whose name I didn't catch because the commentary was making too much row, puts out a protuberance in the shape of a female wasp. A real male wasp – a bit of a boulevardier, judging by his snappy striped waistcoat – forces his attentions on the decoy, which thereupon precipitates him into a kind of small car-wash equipped with pollen-impregnated brushes. Carrying a yellow knapsack of pollen that makes him look like a Norwegian tourist and thus seriously dents his *flâneur* image, he staggers off through the air and eventually encounters the distaff version of the same flower, which strips him of the pollen while he is sucking up nectar.

Having it away by way of wasps was, in fact, one of the less elaborate methods of floral fornication on offer, but I found it difficult to follow some of the others because my fingers were in my ears – the very sort of posture which counts as an amorous invitation in the world of the stamen and the pistil. 'They are designed for one thing only . . . sex!' drooled the commentary. 'Sex in a hot climate!' it added, while the screen filled with what was either an Australian or an African water-lily.

By now I had a pillow wrapped around the back of my head to muffle the sound, but there was enough vision left to tell that the Austral-African water-lily has a pink and gold interior like a Hollywood boudoir. Everything is in there except Zsa-Zsa Gabor stretched out on a couch. In wanders a bee. Lulled by the indirect lighting and subdued organ music, it wriggles about sensuously among the multiple stamens. If the bee calls on the second day of flowering he gets out again alive, but on the first day the stamens secrete a slick fluid which drops him into the basement, where he is either converted into fuel for the winter or blackmailed by the flower's husband.

Once again, as with most programmes about reproduction, the lingering impression was of nature's supreme prodigality. Underwater flowers sent up pollen bubbles of which about one in a million got through, since there are small fish waiting around which eat nothing else. Similarly in an excellent episode of *Wildlife on One* (BBC1) there were evocations of helpless young fieldmice being thinned out by various predators, including a combine harvester. The mouse programme was narrated by David Attenborough and gained as much on sound as the flower programme lost. There was some amazing footage of Mrs Dormouse giving birth to five jelly-beans with whiskers. A small dormouse with a large acorn looked like the space shuttle on top of its fuel tank. The show could easily have succumbed to an attack of the cutes but managed to fight it off. Other investigators of the natural world please copy.

The latest venue for *Grand Prix* (BBC2) was Monza, where Nelson Piquet and commentator Murray Walker both blew up at the same time. Under James Hunt's exemplary tutelage Murray has quietened down considerably lately, so that you can almost hear the cars, but when things get tense he is still apt to go up an octave. No sooner did Piquet's Brabham gush smoke than Murray was outsoaring Maria Callas. 'Tremendous drama! What enormous drama!' The same sentiments would have been more appropriate to John Watson's high-speed shunt, in which nothing was left of the car except the driver, walking away. The running gag of the *Grand Prix* series is that whereas Murray, safe in the commentary box, sounds like a blindfolded man riding a unicycle on the rim of the pit of doom, the men actually facing the danger are all so taciturn that you might as well try interviewing the cars themselves.

For tantrums, you need tennis. In the *US Open Tennis Championships* (BBC2) John McEnroe was in fine form against Gerulaitis. 'Did you see it?' he asked the referee. 'Did you see it? I asked you did you *see* it? *Did you see it?*' Gerulaitis countered with a well-placed obscenity. 'It was a goddam foot over the fuckin' line!' But even with Dan Maskell helping ('Ooh, well played *indeed*, sir!') Gerulaitis lost. McEnroe went on to face Borg, whom he beat fair and square, no tricks. One hates to see Borg being anything except best, but time marches, although in his case there is no reason why it should not march with dignity. Look at Dan, still perfecting his clichés even in the twilight. 'A lot of work in front of McEnroe to pull this game out of the um, fire.' A vocal drop-shot like that needs more than talent. Only with a lifetime of experience can you hope to send the listener crashing to his knees in the wrong direction.

Apart from the opening sequence there wasn't any flying in the second episode of *Fighter Pilot* (BBC1), but there was still plenty of tension as you waited for even one of the trainees to betray some sign, no matter how hesitant, of actually being interested in aeroplanes. Even the young man who has already served time in the RAF as an aircraftman could offer no account for his motivation beyond a desire for better conditions. At the end of the instalment he was judged not to have what it took and was told he had failed. He was told this in front of a BBC camera and God knows how many millions of viewers, which argued for unusual openness of character on his part. Off he went home while the others marched unimpressively around the parade ground. One of them was moving his right arm forward with his right foot. It was either hard to imagine him at the controls of a Phantom or else easy to imagine him flying it at supersonic speed into your back yard.

Luckily the whole question of East-West confrontation was rendered academic by Ms Anna Coote, who in a *Labour Party Political Broadcast* (all channels) revealed that the Soviet Union is not a threat after all. Only the media makes people think that. Disarmingly sincere though she patently is, Anna seems seriously to have underestimated the extent to which she is a media person herself, and nowhere more so than in her assumption that the media can make people think things.

20 September, 1981

Blinding white flash

'MAYBE what we're doing is God's will,' said Sophia Loren in *The Cassandra Crossing* (ITV). 'Who knows?' The big film of the week, it was directed by George P. Cosmatos, whose creations are much valued by insomniacs, since it is impossible to view them for long without becoming George P. Comatose.

In *The Cassandra Crossing* the TransEuropean Express has been hit by a plague of bad acting. NATO attempts to shunt the train off into Poland and isolate it there until all the bad actors have either died off or recovered, but their plans are foiled by Richard Harris in the role of a famous surgeon, Sophia in the role of his estranged but adoring wife, Martin Sheen as a drug-addict mountain-climbing gigolo, and numerous others. Some, although not all, of those mentioned are good actors in normal circumstances, but even Martin Sheen finds it difficult to turn in an Oscar-winning performance when he is pretending to be a drug-addict mountain-climbing gigolo with plague.

In command of the NATO forces is Burt Lancaster, striding about purposefully in front of lit-up maps of Europe which convey no information at all beyond a rough outline of the Atlantic coast. His hair magically changing from black to grey between shots, he makes the Tough Decision by which the train is sent over the Cassandra Crossing to destruction. Thank God, we laugh, that reality isn't like this.

Then we turn on the latest instalment of *The Defence of the United States* (BBC1) and find out that it is. High-ranking American officers preparing for nookoola war in Europe seem to be equipped with the same sort of maps as Burt. They also share his daunting capacity for Tough Decisions, such as the decision to send a plague-stricken train over the Cassandra Crossing, or the decision to start lobbing 10-kiloton warheads in a battle zone where the centres of human habitation are two kilotons apart at the most.

The Soviet Union seems purposeful and monolithic mainly because we know very little about how its forces behave at operational level. The Red Army looks wonderful in the training films if you can forget those tank commanders who arrived in Prague under the impression that it was Minsk. Meanwhile the United States forces are largely open to inspection by the lay viewer, with appropriately unsettling results. Russian tank commanders might not be able to tell one country from another, but American tank commanders, we can now be certain, don't realise, when asked, that a blinding white flash in the sky signifies the detonation of a nuclear weapon.

We saw a referee in a war game asking an American tank commander what a blinding white flash in the sky signified. He looked puzzled. The referee helpfully rephrased the question, asking what a nuclear weapon would look like if it went off – wouldn't there be a sort of blinding white flash? The tank commander still wasn't sure, so the referee declared him dead. The tank commander retaliated by ordering the CBS television cameraman to get off his tank. The whole scene could have been out of a movie by George P. Cosmatos. It had everything except Sophia Loren.

Anyway, the *Labour Party Conference* (BBC2) reached its climax last Sunday evening, with Tony Benn and Denis Healey fighting it out on the roof of a plague-stricken train as it hurtled all unheeding towards the Cassandra Crossing. David Dimbleby was in charge of the communications room, with Robin Day as chief interrogator. To carry out this role, Robin had been equipped with a chair higher than anybody else's, so that the person he was talking to showed above the table only from the chest up, whereas you could practically see Robin's flies.

Thus enabled to look down on Neil Kinnock, Robin tried to get him to say whether he would abstain or not, but Kinnock stalled. A Bennite was asked why, if the TGW membership vote had gone to Healey, the TGW delegation's vote would go to Benn.

The Bennite answer was that the TGW vote hadn't *really* gone to Healey, although it might have seemed to do so if you lacked the sophisticated measuring techniques available to the Bennites.

Roy Hattersley asked Michael Meacher to be specific about what sounded like a campaign to intimidate MPs. Neil Kinnock said: 'This isn't doing the Labour Party any good at all.' Robin asked: 'What, this discussion or this election?' The plague victims were attacking their guards. There was some hope that the oxygen-enriched atmosphere inside the sealed train would cure the plague all by itself, but would it happen before they all arrived at the Cassandra Crossing? Cut to the roof of the train, where Healey finally managed to flatten Benn, but probably not for long.

Next night on *Panorama* (BBC1) the warring forces within the Labour Party were to be seen at their least ambiguous. It was Scargill versus Kinnock and Hattersley, with David Dimbleby as referee. All present were smart enough to know that a blinding white flash in the sky signifies the detonation of a nuclear weapon. It wasn't really two against one because Kinnock is meant to be on Scargill's side. But Kinnock had abstained in the vote. 'The abstention tactic', said Scargill from under his increasingly diaphanous baldy hairstyle, 'was a dishonest tactic.'

Kinnock told Scargill off, informing him that he, Kinnock, had held Left positions for a lot longer than Benn, and had been in the Labour Party a lot longer than Scargill. Hatters, who made out that he had been in the Labour Party pretty well from its inception, asked Scargill what he, Hatters, having been in the Labour Party for several hundred years, should now do. Leave?

This should have been a decisive blow, but Scargill knew how to retaliate. Yes, he said, if you don't believe in Clause 4 you should leave. Hatters was slow to parry, mainly because he doesn't believe in Clause 4. Nor, probably, does Kinnock – not as an article of dogma, anyway.

In *The Bob Hope Golf Classic* (LWT) the participation of President Gerald Ford was more than enough to remind you that the nuclear button was at one stage at the disposal of a man who might have either pressed it by mistake or else pressed it deliberately in order to obtain room service. There was many a shout of 'Fore!' or perhaps 'Ford!', as the President's tee-shots bounced off trees or bombed into the crowd. A droll commentator remarked that the President had turned golf into a 'combat sport' and that the security men were coming in handy to keep track of the ball.

But if ever we needed reminding that even though the world is an epic movie by George P. Cosmatos the people cast as expendable extras really die, a *Panorama* (BBC1) report on Vietnam was there to remind us. Fronted by the excellent Willy Shawcross, it was a short version of his thoughtful report for the *New York Review of Books*, but where words had been taken out pictures had been put in, and some of them were sad beyond expression. 'She has lost both eyes through vitamin deficiency,' said a doctor holding a child, 'and she has tuberculosis.' Maybe what we are doing is God's will. Who knows?

4 October, 1981

Borgias on my mind

BACK from Las Vegas with what should have been decisive evidence that the Americans are all crazy, I switched on the set and came face-to-face with Britain's very own Barbara Wood-house, starring in *Barbara's World of Horses and Ponies* (BBC1). It was a bit more than the already boggled mind could absorb.

Already established as the world's leading authority on dogs, Barbara now emerges as even more magically authoritative about horses. She can get a horse to do anything. All she has to do is breathe up its nose. As yet untrained, the pony stands waiting, its knees slightly atremble. Barbara approaches confidently, bends down, applies her capacious mouth to its wet nostrils, and breathes up its nose. After that, the beast will do her bidding, and so would you. Apparently Barbara learned this technique in Argentina from a Guarani Indian who is either a very rich horse-trainer or has spent much of his life in hospital, I didn't quite catch.

Breathing up the pony's nose is a form of praise. Barbara is keen on praise as the foundation of her reward system. 'We always do praise.' She also does sugar. Sugar cubes are handed out with a frequency that makes you worry about the horses' teeth. But they are not always *handed* out. Sometimes they are mouthed out. 'Would you like to take a piece out of my teeth?' Barbara asks the horse. Since the horse has just found out by the empirical method that Barbara is strong enough to push it sideways, it is in no position to demur.

The horse nods. Barbara leans forward intimately with a sugar lump poised in her bared teeth. The horse bares its own teeth and takes the sugar lump. From behind your chair you watch the programme end. 'Barbara Woodhouse', says a voice, 'suggests that you do not give a pony sugar from your mouth unless you know the pony very well.' Or else, the voice forgets to add, you will get half your head bitten off and no horse will want you to breathe up its nose ever again.

No doubt *The Borgias* (BBC2) also breathed up horses' noses, along with all their other debaucheries. Out in the middle of the American desert, with nothing to watch on television except hysterical evangelists and the sort of used-car salesmen who slap each offering vigorously on the bonnet to indicate that it will not fall apart when you insert the ignition key, I often wondered how the Borgias were getting on. The answer is that they are getting on famously, especially with one another. After only three episodes, each Borgia has already been to bed with all the other Borgias. It is like an Andrea Newman series wrapped in red velvet, with ermine trimmings.

Pope Rodrigo Borgia is played by Adolfo Celi, looking like Lord Weidenfeld dressed as Father Christmas. The Pope is the only male Borgia without a codpiece. All the other male Borgias have codpieces. There is Cesare Borgia, Juan Borgia and their tennis-playing youngest brother, Bjorn Borgia. On the distaff side, Lucrezia Borgia wears pearl-encrusted brocade when she is not in bed with His Holiness. Exhausted from breathing up Lucrezia's nose, the Pope has trouble with his diction. Referring to a trip taken by Juan and Cesare, he says: 'They got nipples together.' Eventually you figure out that he means they go to Naples together.

Cesare and Juan got nipples together and Cesare kills Juan on the way. Thus Cesare takes another step towards supreme power. The intricacies would be hard to follow if the dialogue were not so explanatory. 'As Vice-Chancellor of the Holy Church, should you not be here to welcome the King of France?' The arrival of the King of France and his bad shave is indicated by an expensive sequence showing several extras carrying spears into Italy. 'All Rome is as darkened by a great fear.' It seems there is no hope, but the Pope copes. He employs soft soap. Nope, he doesn't just mope. But Juan's death breaks his heart. 'By the bones of Christ!'

Producer Mark Shivas has probably several times been heard to say something similar by now. *The Borgias* is a pretty ramshackle vehicle to be bearing his illustrious name. But you have to take a chance, and it probably seemed like a good idea at the time. The material is, after all, potentially very strong, and not just on the level of the family that sleeps together slays together. Cesare had a political intelligence sharp enough to fascinate Machiavelli, who, in examining the implications of Cesare's success, raised permanent questions about the compatibility of means and ends.

Meanwhile the biggest and still the best ever Renaissance in the arts was going on full blast. For a series, the subject is ideal: any amount of strong characters and events, opportunities for visual splendour thick on the ground, and above all no literary master-piece to clog the works. Dreaming up a story line of your own is not as easy as it might seem, but it's a breeze compared to adapting a great book.

If *Brideshead Revisited* (Granada) is not a great book, it's so like a great book that many of us, at least while reading it, find it hard to tell the difference. In my own mind there is no doubt: Evelyn Waugh is the most important modern novelist in English and *Brideshead Revisited* is one of his most important novels. But the irascible young have a point when they call the book a ruin, so for the moment one should perhaps acknowledge their case. Yet if the book is a ruin it is a magnificent ruin, with the remains of a strict architecture beneath the ivy.

Waugh was severely correct in his use of the English language. It was a nasty surprise, then, to hear the television version of Sebastian Flyte asking, 'Would you care to dance with my friend and I?' John Mortimer, the adapter, is almost certainly aware of the difference between the nominative and the accusative. Derek Granger, the producer, is likewise an educated man. Yet somehow the solecism slips through, showing up all those prodigies of set-dressing for what they are – props at a seance in which a lost spirit resolutely declines to appear.

'Would you care to dance with my friend and I?' ranks as additional dialogue. Most of the words, it must be conceded, come straight out of the novel. But so much of Waugh's original narration is read out over the pictures that you can't help wondering why they didn't just read out the whole book, and thus solve the evidently nagging problem of how to retain its nuances of style. Somebody obviously realised that *Brideshead* without its texture would lack substance too. So they have borrowed some of its texture, as a man hard of hearing but good at whistling might reproduce accurately the loud parts of a song.

Frederic Raphael's *Byron* (BBC2) had a strong script. Mr Raphael himself featured largely, wearing an open neck shirt like the late Dr Leavis. Byron was played by an actor far too thin for conveying Byron's weight problem. On the other hand he did not look particularly vigorous either. A disembodied actorly voice was entrusted with the task of reading out Byron's Spenserian and *ottava rima* stanzas. They were made to sound listless. Mr Raphael emerged as being more intelligent and energetic than his hero, which might be true but was surely not the intention.

1 November, 1981

A man called Insipid

WHISTLING in from Brisbane to Sydney last Friday week on a TAA airbus, I was on the flight-deck beside the pilot flogging him onward, lest I be too late back to my hotel for *Miss World*, which arrives in Australia after bouncing off half a dozen different satellites.

In ten years as a television critic I had never missed *Miss World* and nor did I this time, but it was a near run thing. Richard Boston dealt admirably with the subject last week, but you could tell that his was the view of the detached intellectual rather than the experienced fanatic. You have to be able to remember the way Miss Spain almost fractured an ankle in a previous competition if you are fully to appreciate the way the current Miss Venezuela can't move any distance, no matter how short, without tripping at least twice. Similarly it takes a fond scholarly appreciation of how Michael Aspel used to handle the job of emcee if you want to assess Peter Marshall in the same role. Michael Aspel was an intelligent man pretending to be interested in the surrounding nonsense. Peter is not pretending.

Assisting Peter to marshal the traffic, Judith Chalmers was chiefly remarkable for the way she combined her time-honoured hockeysticks manner ('What a jolly difficult decision to make!') with a women's liberation bodice that was much more up to date, not to say down to earth. Her patter was hardly epigrammatic, but compared with Peter she sounded like Wittgenstein. In fact Peter, if Wittgenstein had ever encountered him, might have inspired the Viennese genius to a third position on the nature of words. Wittgenstein started off by believing that each word meant something. Later on he believed that words meant something only in relation to each other. It never occurred to him that someone could speak endlessly without meaning anything at all.

Yet that is exactly what Peter can do. In all cases except his, the secret of vivid language is to set up a tension between the expected and the unexpected. Nothing Peter says is unexpected. Yet it is all so expected that it startles. When one of the girls comes weaving along the esplanade, Peter says: 'Yes, she does like to be beside the seaside.' When another girl leans awkwardly against the hull of a beached yacht, Peter says: 'Well, it's hello sailor to contestant No. 4.'

Normally this level of prose is obtainable only in Fleet Street, where experienced journalists, after a few decades of having their brains pickled in alcohol, are allowed to work out their time writing captions for the photographs on page three. But Peter has got there in a single intuitive leap, while still young enough to enjoy his sense of mastery. The young Beethoven, when improvising at the piano, would sometimes laugh at the audience as they sat there petrified by his demonic powers. In just such a way Peter smiles slightly to himself when he thinks of a question to ask Miss Zimbabwe. 'You like to watch soccer. Ever tried playing it?'

Since the next thing I saw on Australian television was Barbara Woodhouse appearing live on a chat show, there seemed no reason not to get back here as quickly as possible. I arrived just in time to see the latest episode of *Brideshead Revisited* (Granada). Once again I found it very worthy, even estimable, but still inexorably en-slaved to the stylistic beauty of the original text. Waugh is the greatest modern master of elision. How can you fill out a scene which he has deliberately compressed to a single line? The answer is: awkwardly.

When Julia gets engaged to Rex Mottram, Waugh writes the whole thing down in a few words. 'So Julia went into the library and came out an hour later engaged to be married.' Here John Mortimer has no choice but to write some dialogue, since Charles Ryder's voice-over has already gone on too long. Mortimer is a skilled dramatist, but not even he is up to the task of supplying extra lines for Rex, a character who draws his whole force from being left elliptical. Julia and Rex exchange a few lines indicative of very little. Then Julia comes out of the library while Charles intones: 'So Julia came out of the library an hour later engaged to be married.' What lasts seconds on the page has taken minutes on screen. The net effect is to make the series windier than the novel.

It should go without saying that some of the acting is very good. From British actors, who, mainly thanks to regular television work, are in a high state of training, one expects nothing less. But I can't believe that the principal casting has been either very appropriate on the one hand or notably adventurous on the other.

Charles Ryder need not look like Evelyn Waugh, but it is a bit much to make him look like Alan Quartermaine. If Charles looks more aristocratic than the aristocrat, where does that leave Sebastian?

A really adventurous choice for the character to look like the author, incidentally, would have been Mr Samgrass. John Grillo plays him well, but as Uriah Heep. Actually Waugh was in precisely Samgrass's position, getting himself well in with the great. He did it with ease, but because of his genius – the thing he valued least in himself. He wanted the gentlemen to take him for a gentleman. Some of them told him that the aristocratic society portrayed in *Brideshead Revisited* was a fantasy, but he didn't listen, probably because he already knew but preferred the myth to the reality. He knew everything about himself, transmuting his own anguish into the serenity of an art which condenses substance into style and therefore ultimately defies adaptation. The series is a Fabergé curate's egg.

The latest *40 Minutes* (BBC2) was all about gorillas in a zoo on Jersey. The starring gorilla was Jambo, billed as 'the most virile gorilla in the world'. Looking like a Russian weightlifter in a grey satin leotard plus blue mink bolero, Jambo enjoys enviable success not just at attracting female gorillas but at impregnating them, which is apparently a difficult trick, even for a gorilla. Jambo himself, for all his macho strut, can't do it alone. He needs the help of Dr Seager, or it could have been Dr Eager, who extracts Jambo's semen and tests it for fertility.

The process of extraction was the Bad Sight of the Week. 'Dr Seager has perfected a method of extracting semen from gorillas. He calls it electro ejaculation.' Jambo was knocked out and examined by the doc. 'Look at the size of his testicles,' murmured the probing medico, 'they really are remarkably small.' It was also remarked that the size of Jambo's penis was nothing to write to Africa about.

But Jambo's humiliation had only begun. 'Dr Seager smears a probe with lubricating jelly and inserts it into Jambo's bottom.' Ten-volt charges were then transmitted to 'certain nerves', a technique which, we were assured, 'brings about erection'. It worked at least as well as showing Jambo some old eight by ten glossies of Fay Wray. 'We've got full erection here now.' Dr Seager meant that Jambo had full erection. Up Jambo's defenceless fundament went the test tube to catch the sperm. 'During the operation Jambo was to orgasm four times.' I was to spasm with terror at least twice that many times, but my eyes never left the screen. 'Unlike chimpanzees the gorilla appears not to masturbate.'

The gorilla is more dignified than the chimp all round. Not only does it not wank, but it keeps most of its genital equipment to itself, instead of wearing its engine externally like an old motor-cycle. In fact the gorilla was a model of decorum until it met man. 'They're a very private animal . . . a lot of their display to man is bluff.' But ours to them is in dead earnest. All Jambo does is beat his chest like a set of flaccid bongoes and make with the face. But if we threaten to shove a probe up his bum and plug his poor inadequate little dingus into the mains, we actually do it, don't we? Good old us.

22 November, 1981

Signals from the void

THE recent death of the great psephologist Bob McKenzie left a sad gap in the Beeb's coverage of the Crosby by-election on *Newsnight* (BBC2). In two hours of political analysis there were none of Bob's beloved hand-signals.

Instead, the hand-signals came from anchor-man John Tusa and computer operator Peter Snow. But the whole point of Bob McKenzie's hand-signals was that they were precisely illustrative, so that if you stuck your fingers in your ears – which during Bob's more excitable moments you could be excused for doing – it was still clear what he was talking about.

If Bob wiggled the index finger of each hand in a spiral and brought them slowly together, it meant that the two main parties were converging on the major issues. If he bunched his right hand into a fist, opened it, tilted it vertically and moved it slowly sideways across the screen, it meant that the percentage swing would probably continue throughout what he called the Battleground. Bob, although much smarter than President Ford, fell into

the same linguistic sub-group. (When Ford talked about arma-
ments he made a little gun with his thumb and forefinger, and
when he talked about armaments increasing throughout the world
he drew a circle in the air.)

John and Peter have inherited Bob's impulse to make hand-
signals, but with them the old realism has declined into abstrac-
tion, in keeping with the tendency of any art form to approach
decadence through technical advance. As we waited for the dec-
laration, John helped pass the time by gravely mixing metaphors
about the by-election being an assault course to determine the
temperature. Was the SDP's popularity a flash in the pan? He
illustrated 'flash in the pan' by holding his hands near each other
and moving them vaguely outwards. With Bob, one hand would
have been a pan and the other a dramatically ascending puff of
smoke.

Sitting at his computer terminal, Peter Snow said that if Labour
lost its deposit the result would be one that we could perhaps
'slightly discount', since with Labour in a hopeless position the
vote would be squeezed. For 'squeezed' Peter made a hand-signal
as broadly and indeterminately significant as a green sunrise by
Rothko. But the computer drew gripping high-tech pictures of
hexagonal columns. These columns were based on poll projec-
tions, rather than the not-yet-forthcoming actual facts, but they
were still very impressive. The SDP column was up there like
Trajan's tribute to himself. The Tory column was less vertiginous
but still had the proportions of the national headquarters of a
reasonably prosperous bank. The Labour column looked like a
poker chip, or perhaps, at a generous estimate, a Wimpy. Peter
explained that Michael Foot's popularity was 'lower than that of
any Opposition leader since polling began'. To illustrate this, Bob
would probably have drawn a grass-hopper in the air and pointed
to its knee, but Peter just sat there tapping his keys.

Apart from the hand-signals, Bob McKenzie combined a first-
class analytical brain with the rare gift of being able to question
politicians closely while not sounding aggressive. He *was* aggres-
sive, but he didn't sound it. Vincent Hanna, *Newsnight*'s inquisitor
at large, sounds so aggressive that you start sympathising with the
poor harried politicos, even when they are being evasive. Vincent
achieved the difficult feat of making Eric Heffer sound hard-done-

by. Eric was trying to explain that the Labour voters hadn't deserted, they were merely voting tactically in order to get the Tory out. That this argument was the product of wishful thinking would have been patent if Vincent hadn't interrupted it with such vigour and so often. But at least Vincent doesn't make any hand-signals. With one hand holding a microphone and the other grasping the lapel of his opponent, there is nothing left mobile except his mouth.

Studio guests were Leon Brittan (Tory), Gerald Kaufman (Labour) and Bill Rodgers (SDP). Leon fought his corner with some skill for a man who has trouble keeping his eyebrows on his forehead. Explaining that such a brilliant government was bound to suffer a mid-electoral dip in popularity even though its tough policies were already on the point of ushering in a new age of recovery, Leon sat relaxed while his eyebrows took off like a pair of jet fighters scrambling for a dawn interception. Also his baldy hairstyle presented a bit of a credibility problem, since no matter how long you grow the hair at the back of your head and no matter how carefully you arrange it over the depilated cranium, the television lights penetrate the screen and bounce off the glabrous dome beneath.

But if Leon had been wearing a tutu and holding a wand he would still have been less implausible than Gerald Kaufman, who said that if Labour lost now it would be because its faithful voters wanted it to win later. 'What the electorate is telling us is that we should do something about it so that they can turn back to us.' With the air of a horse already home and hosed, Bill Rodgers suavely insisted that the SDP was not a media party and that it did indeed have policies. He had only just started explaining what these were when John cut him short and switched the scene to Crosby.

As if to emphasise her status as a media darling, Mrs Williams was discovered pushing her face into the camera, no doubt as a joke. Actually the idea, on which Leon and Gerald seemed agreed, that Shirley Williams had an exceptionally powerful personal appeal was of a piece with the larger idea that the SDP is a media party. With at least two albatrosses around her neck – education and Grunwick – she had, on the personal level, at least as much going against her as for her. Her overwhelming asset was membership of the Liberal-SDP alliance. Only an expert could fail to see that the alliance would have won Crosby even if it had fielded Barbara Woodhouse. Supposedly short of policies, the alliance has the only policy that currently matters – the policy of not having the policies of Labour or the Conservatives.

Her victory having been announced, Mrs Williams spoke of 'an idea that has found its time'. Roy Jenkins, who first had the idea and explained it in his Dimbleby lecture on television, fought off Vincent's suggestion that he might be envious. 'Twemendous wesult . . . forms part of a pattern . . . Cwoydon . . . Cwosby . . . bwoken thwough . . . acwawse the nation.' Tuning in from Olympus, David Steel patiently explained to John that for the Liberal candidate to stand down was in his party's long term interest.

The alliance plainly has at least three Prime Ministers to choose from; even more plainly the will of the country is behind them like a tide; and most plainly of all the whole thing is happening precisely *because* what they stand for can't be summed up as anything else except general intelligence. The image faded on Peter at his keyboard, providing a 'detailed breakdown' of the result. Somewhere out there in the sleepless night Mrs Thatcher and Michael Foot must have been having detailed breakdowns of their own. Further away still, the ghost of Robert McKenzie was describing with his rotating left forearm an imaginary tunnel, at one end of which he was rapidly opening and closing his right hand, to indicate a light.

29 November, 1981

More Borgias

NEVER drawing breath, *The Borgias* (BBC2) bores on, like a bore at a party who, having bored everybody else into the wall, stands alone in the kitchen and bores himself.

Borgia dialogue is a closed circuit in which the output exactly equals the input, since everybody in it tells everybody else nothing except what they must know already. 'Send my brother Jofre to me,' says Cesare Borgia to his father, Rodrigo Borgia, alias the Pope. But even in the hectic procreative whirl prevailing among the Borgias, the Pope would have had time to notice that his son Cesare had a brother called Jofre.

The reason Cesare tells Rodrigo that he, Cesare, has a brother called Jofre is so that we, the audience, may be informed. When the dialogue is not informing us about the genealogy of the Borgia family it is informing us about the geography of Italy. 'Rimini has fallen. We must take Ferrara unaided.' 'Ferrara unaided! Are you mad?' 'Surely you know that the Duke of Ferrara's sister Isabella della Pella is the nephew of your cousin, Giotto Grotto-Blotto?' 'For your sake I hope you speak the truth.'

After a short pause for the torture, strangulation, poisoning and beheading of their latest guests, the Borgias all get back into bed and resume the activity which has made their name terrible in the annals of European history. Rival families ambush them, France invades them on a regular basis, but nothing can stop them talking. 'Help me retake Urbino.' 'Retake Urbino! Are you mad?' 'My friend the King of France advises me to be rid of you. Do you plot against me, Romeo?' 'The Duke of Milan attacks Bologna and the Duke of Bologna attacks Milan. God is good to us, my friends.' 'The man lies!'

Unable to tell his own sons apart, the Pope is in his cups. But the wine has been spiked by the agent of some rival family who want a series of their own. Or perhaps Rodrigo's sons have grown sick of hearing the dialogue mispronounced, especially when you consider how hard it is to follow even when pronounced clearly. 'Barf! Yark! Whok!' shouts the Pope, but on past performance he could be reciting the Gettysburg Address. When he clutches his cassock and takes a nose-dive into the mixed salad, however, the matter is beyond doubt. 'GARF! BWUP! THWORK!' But Cesare, too, is stricken. He writhes in his bed as if suffering from a maladjusted cod-piece. 'Your horse and foot await.' 'My horse?' 'And your foot.' More next week, and every week, forever.

Photographed with the clean-edged richness of colour that you get only when the cameraman is knocked out by the subject, *The Shogun Inheritance* (BBC2) has been the visual treat of the season, partly because it has a commentary, delivered by Julian Pettifer, of a delicacy to match its looks. Having been twice briefly to Japan, I consider myself an expert, because the place is so odd that if you have been there even for five minutes you are miles ahead of someone who hasn't been there at all, even if he has been studying its history all his life. But I have learned a great deal from every episode I have watched, and by now am even inclined to modify my earlier conviction that the Nips are weird. The Nips are *very* weird.

Jazzing up that otherwise intractably rebarbative subject, the Japanese traditional theatre, Pettifer said: 'Sodomy, which was already commonplace among the soldiers and clergy, now began to interest the common people also.' This caught my attention, which the puppets, beautiful though they were to look at, had temporarily lost. I once asked my young interpreter in Japan how often he went to see Kabuki or Noh and he said he wouldn't touch either of them with a ten-foot ceremonial sword.

The otherwise inexplicable popularity of crude Japanese science-fiction movies, and of interminable television series about men in dressing-gowns kicking each other, can perhaps be understood in terms of the boredom induced by the traditional art-forms from which they represent the only escape. Also the enormous success of Western music in Japan is perhaps no accident, Japanese music having so little in it except subtlety. Phoowee-phut. Tick. Plonk.

It will be understood that these are frivolous estimates, arising from a profound, and indeed disturbed, recognition of Japan's abiding strangeness. Pettifer and his production team have done much to induce the appropriate sense of alienation. A Japanese master swordsmith was shown putting a lot of effort into constructing a sword which will probably never be called on to actually do anything except rest in its scabbard. For two weeks he melted the metal, doubled it, tempered it, annealed it, melted it, doubled it . . . All the time he was sitting cross-legged while wearing the joke hat of an honorary Samurai.

Meanwhile Dr Sen was putting young ladies through a three-year course in the tea ceremony. The tea ceremony does not last much less than three years anyway, so during the course the trainee gets only a couple of chances to go right through it. 'You are rejuvenated,' said Dr Sen, 'ready to continue the fight.'

Those of us who dimly remember what the fight was like the last time the Japanese were using their swords in earnest are glad that the fight nowadays is being conducted by peaceful means, even if they are now winning instead of losing. This excellent series gives you some idea of the reasons for their triumph. They are a rice culture with the emphasis on collective dedication. Most of us in the West are not very fond of collective dedication and in our case we are probably right. But over and above that the Japanese have chosen to sell goods wanted by people instead of guns wanted by governments. The United States, which is selling guns, is being outsold by the Japanese. In the long run people have more purchasing power than governments. It should have been a simple lesson, but for the Japanese it took a shattering military defeat to teach it.

The winners have learned more slowly. *Zone of Occupation* (BBC2) has been telling – in a lugubrious manner, alas – the story of how Britain did everything wrong when occupying its zone of Germany after the war, but how the Germans, having learned their lesson, did everything right. The consideration that Britain must have done *something* right, or else the Germans would never have got started again at all, is seldom allowed to arise.

The latest episode of *To the Manor Born* (BBC1) was billed as the last instalment of the series, but will no doubt be merely the prelude to another, since the two leading characters are now married. Now at last she will be able to do something about his clothes. One imagines that those slanting pockets on his tweed jackets are meant to indicate an *arriviste*, but surely he arrived long enough ago to have noticed by now what everyone else is wearing.

6 December, 1981

Midwinter night's dream

CHOPIN loved his country but resisted all appeals to go home, on the principle that whereas in Paris art was eternal, political turmoil in Poland was merely endless.

Perhaps the only appropriate response to the week's events, for those of us who could do absolutely nothing about them, would have been to put on an old record of Rubinstein playing Chopin's second piano sonata and slowly consume a bottle of whatever they used to drink in Poland when they could still get it. But the television set did its best to remind us that there are other forces at work in the world besides power and despair.

It was a nice coincidence that in Jack Gold's *A Lot of Happiness* (Granada), a brilliantly directed documentary showing the choreographer Kenneth MacMillan conjuring sculptural beauty out of a couple of human beings in long socks, the aforesaid Chopin had a leading role. To some piercingly lovely fragments from the third piano sonata, MacMillan, himself shambling around in a pair of baggy pants, pushed Vladimir Klos into various positions so that Birgit Keil could wind around him in several directions at once, with results that looked like a warmer version of that statue in which Giambologna successfully showed how many Sabine women a Roman could rape at the one time without moving his feet.

Drawing on an apparently fathomless supply of ideas, MacMillan told the dancers what to do. Sometimes he told them to show him what they felt like doing next, whereupon he either kept the notion if it fitted or thought of something else. Gold's main camera fluently filmed all this happening. A second camera filmed the first camera. When MacMillan took the completed short ballet from the rehearsal room into the television studio, the film camera was there again to show what happened.

In any other director's hands this might have been an emptily intricate approach, but Gold's coherent mind had obviously made sense of it in advance. In addition, the editing could not have been more subtle or sensitive. The completed job was a fully adequate television tribute to that most organic of artistic events, the MacMillan *pas de deux*. In fact if MacMillan's dance numbers got any more organic you would have to ring the police. 'I'm trying to get a bit sexy now,' he confided, tying Vladimir and Birgit into a reef-knot.

Further down the ladder of ambition and higher up the scale of decibels, the *World Freestyle Dancin' Championships* (Thames) had a lot to offer this year apart from the usual migraine. On a set like a huge pin-ball machine the solo dancers separately pursued their doomed but delightful aim of getting it all together while shaking themselves to pieces. There was the sinisterly named Klaus Praetorius from Germany. Spyros Chrysos from Greece wore a

Snappies Clingfilm playsuit that threatened to produce a chrysos all by itself.

All favoured the flat-foot spin, but there were variations in the amount of contortion gone in for, with some dancers just vibrating on the spot like a blender and others, notably Michelle Thomas from South Africa, uncorking prodigies of corporeal plasticity. Michelle could dive backwards and come up smiling before her feet left the ground.

Michelle won the singles, but even she was nothing compared with the winners of this year's big innovation, the doubles. A pair of Italians called Luca and Paola did an adagio number that would have left Kenneth MacMillan worrying about their physical safety. Paola spun around Luca's neck like a propellor before zooming through one of his armpits and reappearing under his crotch on the way down to his ankle. This would have looked difficult even if Luca had not currently been imitating a man trying to remove a pair of trousers full of ants while putting out a fire in his hair. Then a pair of Americans came on and made everything you had seen before look static. The set pulsed, the cameras zoomed, tilted and raced sideways, and everybody had a good time.

One of the many nice things about *A Midsummer Night's Dream* (BBC2) was that a good time was had by all. Contrary to general belief, Australian media folk spend as little time as possible rolling logs for one another, so it is with some reluctance that I call my compatriot Elijah Moshinsky an outstandingly stylish director of drama. Having persuaded the Beeb to let him build a pond in the middle of a studio, he staged half the action around it and in it, with no more than two or three other sets accounting for everything else.

But as so often happens when television directors shoot tight in a carefully dressed small space, the general effect was of a richly populated frame. Trevor Nunn pioneered the technique with his *Antony and Cleopatra*. Moshinsky took it a step further, keeping his carefully angled cameras static as often as possible, so that the occasional move startled. The whole scene in which the rude mechanicals planned their one and only theatrical appearance, for example, was done with one low camera angled upwards to show them all sitting at a tavern table. But the camera script would not have meant much without Moshinsky's imaginative handling of actors, which in this particular scene included the coup of getting

Peter Quince to talk and behave like the retiring Director General of the BBC.

As Theseus, Nigel Davenport spoke with the noble relish befitting a part which almost as much as that of Hamlet seems to give you the sound of the author's voice. Meanwhile, back in the forest, Puck looked like Pete Townshend of the Who made up as Dracula and behaved like Johnny Rotten. The fairies were clearly out of hand, mainly because of Oberon's sticky involvement with Titania. As Oberon, Peter McEnery sported an Alice Cooper hairstyle and did a lot of sly doting on the recumbent Titania, played by Helen Mirren at her most languorously plush.

Powered by Titania's slumbrous fertility, the whole area burst into flower. The part of Helena was taken by Cherith Mellor, who equipped herself with a pair of Cliff Michelmore glasses and did some very funny little moves. She said 'Oh, excellent!' after falling in the pond, which was a nice twist of the words. The design, by David Myerscough-Jones, drew on the whole romantic visual tradition all the way back to Mantegna, and with the possible exception of a moon out of Maxfield Parrish it worked a treat.

On *Question Time* (BBC1) the word 'subsidisation', meaning subsidy, was used by Sir Robin Day and immediately echoed by other members of the panel, except for Lady Antonia Pinter, who talked more sense than the other three panellists put together. They were Harold Lever, Edward du Cann (called Mr Buchanan by a member of the audience, which is apparently recruited right off the street) and Bernard Levin. Formidable men all, but the lady had the gift of common sense. Poland was the main subject. Lady Antonia movingly stated the only possible sane view, which was that the events were horrible and all the more horrible for being inevitable – tragic, in fact.

20 December, 1981

Man of marshmallow

A THIN week started with a fat weekend, which included two movies by Andrjez Wajda, *Man of Marble* and *Man of Iron* (both on BBC2). The second, I thought, was a lot better than the first, but either separately or together they told you a great deal.

During the rare periods of tolerance in his country Wajda makes films in batches. Of necessity some of them are a bit scrappy. For much of its length *Man of Marble* looked like the story of a girl who had been driven mad by the responsibility of owning the only pair of flared jeans in Poland. There were films within the film to prove that official films about bricklaying are boring, but the films within the film were so very boring that the film proper got boring too.

When the girl reappeared in *Man of Iron* she had calmed down, forming part of a much more integrated story, of which the main thread dealt with a drunken journalist who had sold his soul to the regime, was sent to infiltrate the initial Solidarity strike at the Gdansk shipyard and there, perhaps too late, got back in touch with his own soul. 'If we don't put things in order,' said one of the man of marshmallow's superiors, '*they* will come and do it.'

They have not come yet. There is a school of thought which says that the Polish army is doing the job for them, but even under the harshest military rule, so long as it is Polish military rule, there is some chance of the Poles retaining their historical memory. Every year, at a certain date, the Russian newspapers tell the story of how Dubček was a CIA agent. They will undoubtedly tell the same sort of stories about Walesa. But in the countries which they tell such lies about, the truth only tastes all the sweeter. That's why Wajda's great first masterpiece, *Ashes and Diamonds*, gives off its heady perfume of romance. It isn't just because of Cybulski's dark glasses or the little flames burning on the bar counter to mark the passing of the doomed young heroes. It's because the texture of reality is more satisfying than any simplification which can be made of it.

Another big event of the weekend was *Aida* (BBC2), in a production beamed to us from San Francisco, where they have a stage which can take two hundred extras in the triumph scene and still not buckle under the strain when Pavarotti comes striding on as Radames. Nor could the girl in the title role be accurately described as a sylph. A few weeks earlier *Samson et Dalila* (BBC2), designed and produced by my gifted countrymen Sidney Nolan and Elijah Moshinsky, had entirely ravished the eye, not least because Shirley Verrett had looked the part as well as singing with such maddening beauty that Samson was no longer able to keep his hair on. Television transmissions of that visual standard rather spoil you for the suspension of disbelief which in the opera house is so often necessary.

But if the principals look the part it should be thought of as a bonus, not as a basic. The best-looking Aida I ever saw was Sophia Loren, star of a Cinecittà movie version in which somebody else supplied the voice and a large disc of white cardboard represented a full moon over the Nile. Second best-looking was Galina Vishnevskaya, appearing at Covent Garden in a frock of her own devising. It was a scarlet sheath slit to the lower ribs and she did a lot of Egyptian posing on one knee, thereby distracting attention from the fact that her vocal manoeuvrings in the upper layers of the *tessitura* were a trifle approximate.

Other Aidas at the Garden have been given the Dress with the Stripe. It has a white stripe going down the middle and is meant to make large girls look narrow. Combine that with the regulation pair of platform sandals and a new soprano fresh in from Finland is likely to be thrown. Perched one night in the top row of the gods – your ears pop going up the stairs – I sweated with sympathy while a visiting Aida, hugely in evidence even at that distance and obviously mortified by the striped dress, forgot all the words of 'O patria mia', fell off one of her clogs and made an unscheduled exit sideways.

There was comparatively little of that in San Francisco. Pavarotti looked like R2-D2 wearing a roulette wheel for a collar, but when he opened the small hole in the bottom half of his large face the sound that came out must have brought Verdi up out of the grave saluting. Having soaked up a quarter of an hour of applause after each aria, Pav would either embrace Aida for a duet or else crunch off to the dressing room for a leisurely plate of pasta.

The blandishments of Amneris had no effect on him. This was a bit of a wonder, because although on the substantial side herself, she had a torchy voice and a cleavage calculated to make a sacred crocodile roll in the mud. Amneris, amid much noodling from the oboes, offered Radames her all, but he nobly chose to croak in the dungeon with Aida at his side.

The production, by Sam Wanamaker, looked utter nonsense on the tube, but no doubt was more impressive in the opera house,

although to make the ballet scene look less ridiculous you would
have had to turn the lights off. In the old Covent Garden produc-
tion, now alas replaced by something no more tasteful but much
less fun, the ballet dancers indicated their African provenance by
wearing baggy brown leotards and in the triumph scene the
warriors came shambling down the ramp, headed off stage for a
change of helmet, sprinted around the back of the cyclorama,
climbed the ladder and came shambling down the ramp again,
short swords held valiantly upright. Meanwhile the music was
thrilling you to bits.

In *Dallas* (BBC1) the cast finally got the news that Jock would
not be back. Theoretically he would return home from the Interior
of South America in order to attend the annual Ewing Barbecue,
but we all knew that he wouldn't make it, since the actor playing
him had been for some time no longer among the living – the
reason why Jock had gone to the Interior of South America in the
first place. Nevertheless there was much talk of Jock's imminent
return. 'Everybody, that was a cable from daddy . . . He wouldn't
miss the Ewing Barbecue for *anything*.'

Miss Ellie concurred. 'Jock's going to be there.' The Barbeque
began and Jock had still not arrived, but Lucy, dancing with her
nose buried in Mitch's navel, was confident. 'My granddaddy is
coming back from South America. His plane's due in two hours.'
Then Miss Ellie got the phone call. She stood silent. It took a while
for her children to notice, since she looks equally tragic if told that
the laundry has not been delivered. 'Jock was flying in from the
Interior by helicopter. It crashed. They say . . . they say . . . that
Jock is dead.' Is JR falling in love again with his own wife? Is Dusty
impotent, or just afraid that Sue Ellen is no longer in control of her
mouth movements?

In *The Star-Maker* (Thames), which was malodorously spread
over two nights like a witch-doctor's poultice, Rock Hudson played
Danny Youngblood, film director. 'I've got to find out if I'm me,'
said various starlets in succession, 'or just a figment of Danny
Youngblood's incredible imagination.' Rock finally checked out on
the casting couch. On *Nationwide* (BBC1) Frank Bough asked a girl
streaker who had just pointed her bare chest at a rugby match
whether she was an extrovert. 'No, I don't go around throwing my
clothes off.' Nobody was going to accuse *her* of being undignified.

She reminded you of Herostratus, who suicided in order to become famous.

10 January, 1982

Nobody understands all

A REPEAT series of *Shoestring* (BBC1) and a brand new series of *Minder* (Thames) helped convince the viewer, by way of these two deservedly popular vigilantes, that good triumphs over evil in the end.

Back in the real world, a rapist was let off with a £2,000 fine because the girl brought it on herself by hitch-hiking after dark. The news that you can rape a hitch-hiker for only two grand will no doubt soon spread. A victim would be very foolish to co-operate with the police if she had nothing in prospect except to compound her agony and watch her tormentor get a small endorsement on his credit card. She would be better off ringing up Shoestring or Minder. They don't exist, but at least they don't disappoint you. They always come through with the goods, even if the goods are only dreams.

One of the most satisfying daydreams is to imagine yourself apparently defenceless in the presence of powerfully armed foes. They laugh at you. They mock and deride. Har har har. But you have taken a vow not to use your super strength. The only trouble is, if you never use your super strength nobody will ever know you've got it. Then they dare to interfere with your girl. At this point your code of silence allows a certain discreet demonstration of martial arts. The heavies don't know what hit them. They go backwards through windows. They hang upside down from trees.

An archetypal fantasy which males start having at about the age of six and are in many cases still having on their deathbeds, this daydream provides the plot outline for at least half the American vigilante series made for export. In *Kung Fu* (BBC1), now being repeated in 'selected episodes', the enchanted reverie can be examined in its pure form. Kwai Chang Caine, played by David Carradine, is an oriental monk with martial arts training, a shaved head and an infinite capacity to remain immobile when taunted, mocked or derided. He roams the Wild West of America, in perpetual search of a group of heavies who will not taunt, mock and deride him. They all do, however, and he must suffer in silence until they make the mistake of taunting, mocking and deriding someone else. Then he erupts into a series of flying kicks which keep all the stuntmen in Hollywood busy falling into horse-troughs, going backwards through windows, hanging upside down from trees, etc.

During the long wait before he unleashes his secret knowledge, Kwai Chang is chiefly occupied with looking thoughtful, in a multitude of reaction shots which are probably all secured in one long take, cut up into short lengths and spliced in throughout the programme. Sometimes the pensive look dissolves into a flashback. Suddenly we are in the temple where he received his training. 'Ah . . . I am not *worthy*.' Bong. Ancient monks transmit nameless secrets to young adepts, such as the secret of how to shave your skull without nicking it and having to staunch the flow of blood with styptic pencil or small pieces of toilet paper.

The latest episode was one long flashback and so gave you a good idea of the layout. Disciples are trained in the use of every conceivable weapon, but only on the understanding that to Take Human Life is the ultimate sin. They are also trained in the ancient art of speaking their dialogue as if each sentence had a full stop every few words. 'I have seen. Something which. I cannot. Hold back.' The occasional rush of eloquence is allowed, but it must sound like a poem. 'The one at the gate you call a man. He is more than a man and less than a man.' 'If it is written, then it will be so.'

The man at the gate is possessed by evil. He has come to Take Human Life. Disciple Wu gets the job of fighting him. 'Disciple Wu is beyond any in the use of the lance.' As Wu and the hairy challenger join battle, Kwai Chang strides off in the company of a beautiful princess to find the castle in which evil has set up headquarters. 'You will. Think me. Foolish.' The evil spirit calls itself the Force, but doesn't say whether or not this is by arrange-ment with *Star Wars*. 'I am the Force. Know too that I will be the destruction of your temple. You think I could not destroy you where you stand? You are an ant that crosses my path." Using contemplative techniques, Kwai Chang totals the Force, where-

GLUED TO THE BOX

upon the man at the gate recovers his sanity and apologises for having attempted to Take Human Life. 'Forgive me, master, for bringing violence to so holy a place.' 'It is over,' says the old man. 'Master,' says Kwai Chang, 'I do not. Understand. All that has. Happened.' 'Nobody understands all.'

17 January, 1982

Rebarbative reverberations

Anyone who isn't watching *The Bell* (BBC2) must be crazy. On the other hand, watching is no guarantee of staying sane.

Having read the novel when it came out, one remembered that Iris Murdoch had been brilliantly successful in evoking a religious community consisting exclusively of dingbats. Where the series has improved on the novel is in finding visual correlatives for the various forms of lunatic self-obsession. There is a chap in a beard, for example, who hardly ever says anything. The beard says it for him. It is an entirely shapeless beard that grows straight out from his face at forty-five degrees. His arms are folded proudly under it while he sits listening to one of his fellow inmates deliver the daily pious lecture.

One by one each of the devotees gets a chance to bore all the others for an hour on end, instead of just intermittently as usual. The competition is fierce, but Michael, played by Ian Holm, has no trouble emerging as the most tedious. 'In each of you there are different talents, different propensities.' One of Michael's propensities is for lusting hopelessly after young Toby. But Toby has been eyeing the joyous poitrine of Dora, flighty wife of the particularly demented Paul.

If Toby is worried about his manhood, he has come to the right girl. She is restless, she is full-blooded, and she has a yo-yo for a husband. 'It is, of course, a fact that you are indeed my wife,' says Paul, sounding as always as if he is translating at sight from an ancient Chinese manuscript. 'To say that you are my wife is to state the obvious.' Understandably alienated, Dora flees into the night with Toby.

252

Down at the lake, Toby dives into the pitch-black water and attaches a cable to the bell. Together he and Dora winch the enormous bell out of the mud and hatch a plan to substitute it for some other bell due to arrive tomorrow. There is no reason why this plan should not succeed, since a religious community which has not been woken up by the roar of the winch's motor is unlikely to notice a couple of young people carrying a two-ton bell ten feet high into a position of concealment. Pleased with their idea, Dora and Toby lie down naked together under the bell as it hangs suspended over the little jetty.

While Dora and Toby are boffing beneath the bell, there is a rustle in the shrubbery. It is the misanthropic Nick Fawley, he whose sister Catherine is about to become a nun. Now he has the power to break Michael's heart and drive Paul loopier than ever. All he need do is let slip the information that he has just seen Dora and Toby copulating under the clapper. But when the big day of the bell ceremony dawns, it finds Michael and Toby hand in hand. Dora's tabloid journalist boyfriend arrives from London. Pig-ignorant and crass (the plot's solitary, fleeting contact with realism), the journalist tramples all over the community's jealously guarded privacy. He is determined to report the arrival of the new bell.

Back in Fleet Street, that is the sort of scoop that every news editor dreams of – a red hot story about a religious community installing a new bell. Will Dora and Toby get out before they, too, go bananas? Will the leggy if lethargic Catherine disappear into the nunnery, or will she find her true destiny as a dancer with Hot Gossip? Is the quiet, thoughtful, infinitely boring James Tayper Pace the biggest head-case of the lot? Why does everybody keep using the word 'rebarbative'? Next week it will be revealed unto you.

Already a booming success, *Wood and Walters* (Granada) should be there forever. The basic strength of the show is the avalanche of high-quality material provided by Victoria Wood, but on top of that there is the bonus that she is an engaging performer in her own right, and on top of *that* there is the further bonus conferred by the participation of Julie Walters, who can give even a dud line an interesting reading and who lavishes on a good line the sort of inventive attention that makes writers think there must be other compensations in the television business besides money.

In the latest episode Julie was a security-conscious shop assistant carrying a machine pistol. 'We don't usually let obese people into the cubicles in case they sweat on the wallpaper.' Fatness figures large in Victoria's writing. 'My mother lost three children before she was twenty,' Julie confided. 'They weren't *hers*, of course.' Another of Victoria's preoccupations is marriage, which she seems to be mainly against. Her witty song 'Don't Do It', sung by both girls with a live band in attendance, was obviously deeply meant.

Victoria was a guest critic on the latest instalment of the continuously interesting, and indeed by now compulsory, *Did You See?* (BBC2), hosted this time by Mavis Nicholson because Ludovic Kennedy was off with flu. Ludo fronts the show to perfection, but Mavis took over without a hitch, thereby indicating the robustness of the format. One of the programmes up for discussion was *OTT* (Central), which Victoria was generous enough to rate as highly original, even though it counts as a competitor.

When it was put to Victoria that *OTT* lacked edge, she asked why edge should be thought of as something a comedy show needed to have. At least one viewer gave a small yell of agreement at this point. The word 'satire' got into the minds of showbiz journalists back in the 1960s and no amount of subsequent experience has been able to get it out. At that time parallels between *TW3* and eighteenth-century English literature were drawn by hacks who thought a couplet was an article of clothing. Nowadays a new generation of hacks compare anything new with what they fondly imagine *TW3* to have been like. Anybody engaged in television comedy, of however patently unsatirical a stamp, soon gets used to being asked why he is not more *savage* – the question invariably being put by someone who has no historical sense to speak of and scarcely two political ideas to rub together.

The cruel fact is that 'satire', as it is commonly referred to in the context of television, was, even at its funniest, almost always palliative. The true subversives are people like Victoria, who with such a song as 'Don't Do It' has a good chance of actually changing how young people live, and in a direction their parents won't necessarily like. As for *OTT*, encouraged by Victoria's backing I stick by my judgment that it is an innovation. Indeed the only thing predictable about it is Alexei Sayle, who has a large reputa-

thing predictable about it is Alexei Sayle, who has a large reputation as a New Wave comedian, but whose routines so far have proved to be strings of stand-up one-liners distinguishable only by their frame of reference from the hit-or-miss patter of the average warm-up man. On stage he is more free to use foul language, but foul doesn't necessarily mean strong.

The token male on Victoria's programme, Rick Mayall, is also a New Wave star, but his monologues are thought right through. Mayall started off doing guest spots as half of an act calling itself 20th Century Coyote. It was clear even then that the television camera would lap him up, but he has since learned to give it even more to feed on. In *Wood and Walters* he impersonates a male chauvinist piglet called Mitch. His expressive hands tell a different story from the one coming out of his mouth, while his eyes search sideways for hidden threats, like Kenneth Griffith hiding from the Gestapo, or just waiting for a bus. The time for television comedy is now. Those days when the young David Frost read out other people's gags were only a portent.

31 January, 1982

Guardians of party orthodoxy

IN the first of a new series of *Not the Nine O'Clock News* (BBC2), Pamela and the boys once again raised the roof and lowered the tone. 'The only good Pole is a deed poll,' they cried, meaning to debunk an American television compilation, starring Ronald Reagan among others, which had allegedly been extremely vulgar on behalf of Poland.

Unfortunately the American programme was not shown here except in a few extracts, so the *Not* lot were the ones left looking vulgar. Apparently the switchboard was jammed with protests from people who thought that the breezy young comedians were being unforgivably insensitive about Poland. It takes only half a dozen people to jam a switchboard, especially if they are all poised over their telephones just begging for a chance to miss the point of what they see.

Nevertheless it can't be denied that Poland is currently a dodgy subject for humour, and is perhaps best left alone. The extracts from the American compilation looked gruesomely twee, but I suspect that the complete programme might have been touching for its sincerity. After all, the Americans are bound to be naive about freedom: they've got it, and thus don't realise what a tricky subject it is. The main reason why we were all so eager to condemn the American programme unseen was probably out of a deep-seated fear that it might result in the United States cavalry, inspired by the voice of Frank Sinatra, actually riding to the aid of Poland. Which in fact is the second last thing anybody wants, the last thing being the Russians doing the same.

If you wanted to jam a switchboard on the subject of Poland, *News at Ten* (ITN) would have been the place to ring up. Their coverage of the whole sad sequence of events has been far better than the Beeb's from day one, but a few nights ago their camera crew filming in Poland might have done more to black out the face of the balaclava-clad young Solidarity pamphleteer they were talking to. His features were easily distinguishable by anybody with normal vision, a category which presumably includes the Polish security police, who could soon be in receipt of videotapes by a not very circuitous route. If anonymity is offered, it should be delivered. That apart, ITN deserves credit for biting deep into European politics, almost as if Britain's destiny were bound up with that of the Continong.

Footage of Suslov's funeral procession suggested that the Soviet authorities were trying to put one soldier on parade for every innocent civilian that the murderous old hack had caused to be rubbed out, but if that was the intention then they ran out of soldiers long before reaching the proper total. On *Newsnight* (BBC2) one of the guest experts called Suslov 'a guardian of party orthodoxy'. If guarding orthodoxy means adapting orthodoxy so that it justifies whatever crime the Central Committee might want to commit next, perhaps he was. Anyway, the point is moot at best, since nobody ever doubted that Suslov's main task, as the party's chief ideologist, was to make sure that the State's monopoly of wisdom could never be challenged by the independent human imagination.

His imagination now more alive than ever, Osip Mandelstam

was the subject of a patchy but considerable edition of *Arena* (BBC2). Arty shots of cigarette smoke could not detract from the awesome dignity of the topic. D. M. Thomas spent an inexplicable amount of time climbing rocks in Wales, but you still did not hurl imprecations at the screen, mainly because Joseph Brodsky might reappear at any moment to say something else that was both perceptive and resonant, while there was also a chance of seeing a few more precious seconds from a filmed interview with the late and truly great Nadezhda Mandelstam, who wrote the best book of prose that is likely to be published in my lifetime, *Hope Against Hope*. Her book is made doubly tremendous by the consideration that you would dearly like the circumstances undone which led to its being written.

Brodsky was interrupted when he was just about to air his key point about Mandelstam, which is that his work was subversive not just in the occasional satirical poem about Stalin, but in its lyrical essence. The point is fully made in one of Brodsky's fine critical essays, and would have been made in the programme if he had been allowed to talk longer. The moral is: when you get a talker of Brodsky's stature and eloquence on screen, let him talk, and save the cigarette smoke for a programme about climbing rocks.

As a weekly critic I don't have to attend previews, which fits in with a personal conviction that a preview theatre is a bad place in which to judge a programme. The true picture is not up there on the big screen, but over there on the little one standing in the corner. Not, however, that the ambience of Sylvia Clayton's first play, *Preview* (BBC2), is entirely strange to me, since in olden days I wrote and fronted thirty-nine separate editions of Granada's *Cinema*, meaning that I ate egg mayonnaise sandwiches in the dark for months on end while watching movies which had the same chance of release as Rudolf Hess. You meet some weird, doomed types in those places, most of them critics who made their names praising the documentaries of Robert Flaherty, who now resent the new names which have replaced theirs, and who are kept alive only by alcohol and the desire to see those new names become obscure in their turn.

Preview had some of that and would have had more if the pace had not been slower than Suslov's funeral. There was an agreeably eerie film-within-the-programme in which the assembled scriveners saw themselves acting out their fates, but before you got to that there was a lot of dull dialogue about Fleet Street being a cut-throat place where bright young critics angle for the jobs of tottering crocks. The truth would have been more interesting. Crocks keep their jobs until well after death and are far less likely to check out from a cut throat than from cirrhosis of the liver compounded by sclerosis of the brain.

The crock in the play turned up his toes without ever having got around to writing that novel, but probably that was just one more bad novel we had been spared. Cherie Lunghi, as the nice young critic who thought life in China was more meaningful, unintentionally aroused the conviction that there would be more than one reason to join her on a slow boat heading for that area of the world. Among the many things they have not got in China is Fleet Street. They haven't got freedom either, so I suppose there is a connection.

The George Formby Story (BBC2) was a reminder that British popular culture is finally impenetrable by anybody not born and raised in these islands. Here was a man with a silly face who flailed away at a ukulele while singing, in a gratingly high voice, ditties burdened with leaden innuendo. He was loved by everybody from the King and Queen on down to the bottom of the coal-mine. The programme tried to cast his wife Beryl as a manipulative ogre, but she seems to have managed his career with unfaltering brilliance, considering the material she had to work with. A great puzzle.

'I have a gift for disaster,' said Richard Burton in *The Medusa Touch* (ITV). 'I am the man with the power to cause catastrophe.' He spent the whole movie taking the words out of your mouth. *International Snooker* (BBC2) was yet another nightmare for the sponsor, Benson and Hedges. Steve Davis, who doesn't smoke, won. Terry Griffiths, who does, lost. 'And Terry can do nothing about it,' said the voice-over, as Terry sat there helplessly smoking. Smoke and lose, that was the message.

7 February, 1982

Terms of reference

MERELY by his presence, Robert Kee confers distinction on *Panorama* (BBC 1). But not even he could make sense of the resulting uproar when the three leading voices in the British Rail dispute all got together in the studio for their first meeting of any kind since the imbroglio began.

Kee was the baritone in the background. Weighell was the bass sitting impressively to one side. Sir Peter Parker and Ray Buckton were the two competing tenors, singing their hearts out into each other's faces. 'The ACAS understanding . . . as indeed it should be dealt with,' sang Ray, 'productivity initiatives . . . through the machinery.' This was impressive but incomprehensible. One trusted Sir Peter not only to match Ray's legato line, but to provide clarity of diction. 'The terms of reference were from ACAS,' Sir Peter sang when his turn came, 'taken to ASLEF.' 'The terms of reference,' bellowed Ray. 'The terms of reference,' shouted Sir Peter. 'Gentlemen, if I may,' came Robert's voice from the background, followed by a low, sad phrase from Sidney: 'Let me make this clear.'

There was a tangible pause, a dynamic silence, a kinetic hiatus like the one towards the end of the sextet from *Lucia* just before they all get going again. Then they all got going again. 'The ACAS terms of reference.' 'Constitutional arrangements.' 'The established machinery.' 'Violated and abrogated.' 'The terms of reference.' 'The terms, the terms of reference.' 'Let me make this clear. Let me make this clear. Please *let* me make this clear.'

But perhaps it was time to start yet another week of feeling bad about Britain. After all, the weekend had left us feeling rather good about Britain, and too much of that would be dangerously unrealistic. Chief cause of the euphoria was, or were, the British ice-dancers Jane Torville and Chris Dean, who won the European ice-dancing championship against stiff opposition from the Russians. In fact the Russians were sensationally good. Ice-dancing is at a peak right now and will thus almost certainly soon decline steeply, because the abiding handicap with the art-sports is that when they run up against their technical upper limits, then the range of possible aesthetic effect is soon exhausted.

Pairs skating, for example, has never really advanced as an art since the Protopopovs: Rodnina and Zaitsev were merely more technically daring, although Gardner and Babilonia, if their career had not been hobbled by injury, would perhaps have achieved a new synthesis. Nobody has equalled Peggy Fleming's accomplishments in women's free skating and it is doubtful if anyone ever will, since there is nothing left to do except work variations on the technical vocabulary that is already established. Triple jumps are as far as you go: there will never be a quadruple jump, not even for the men.

Ice-dancing has the aesthetic advantage of severely restricting the possible athletic manoeuvres in the first place, so that the trainers are obliged to look for pleasing effects rather than encourage their dancers to try triple toe-loop death-spirals upside down. But even then there is a limit to how many beautiful moves you can make, and Jane and Chris have probably already hit it. Watching them skate was a perfect pleasure, even if the gold outfits they chose for their final programme made them look like a cigarette advertisement.

OTT (Central) continues to be miraculous for the way it maintains its shape even when melting. The same could be said for a brick of cheap ice-cream, but *OTT* is more nourishing – a real television breakthrough. Much of the breaking through is into areas where at least one viewer doesn't particularly want to be dragged, such as nudity, which scarcely ever looks good even on the young, and at my age gets to be an offence.

Nevertheless the latest performance from the *OTT* dance group Greatest Show on Legs was one of the funniest routines I have ever seen on television. The premise was that a certain number of naked men had to cover up their vital areas with the same number of balloons, so that when the balloons started bursting there was a lot of sleight of hand, spinning around and defensive crouching.

Just in case some nervous executive gets the urge to kill *OTT* off, it is perhaps worth mentioning that when the BBC pulled *Quiz of the Week* off the air it effectively lobotomised itself as a purveyor of intelligent humour. *Quiz of the Week* was a witches' brew with Ned Sherrin doing most of the stirring. Chris Tarrant, an equally quick-witted performer and producer, is doing the same with *OTT*, where if the participants blow a link they have to busk until the tape rolls or else just sit there while the egg piles up on their faces.

The fully written script, however, will always be the basis of television humour. *Les Dawson* (BBC1) is such an engaging fellow that you might wish he could be more adventurous, but his audience probably likes him for sticking to what he knows, which is mainly a verbally evoked Orc-sized mother-in-law and a wife who has to be transported in a cage. The show starts each week with Les seated at a disaster-prone piano and never fails to get you in. But for what a written script can give rise to you have to watch Julie Walters doing her 'Dotty's Slot' number in *Wood and Walters* (Granada). Oscar Wilde would have swooned with envy. Every line is an epigram that comes shining through Dotty's cloud of talcum like a shaft of moonlight.

14 February, 1982

Spirit of Bishop's Stortford

THERE have always been plenty of reasons for even the most case-hardened television critic to contract a terminal case of nitrogen narcosis, but Ray Buckton of ASLEF is the most potent yet. He has a beautifully modulated voice with which he says nothing intelligible at all. Listening to him is like lying tranked in a cradle while being crooned to by a nanny.

On *Nationwide* (BBC1) Ray was as incomprehensible as ever. As far as I could tell, Lord McCarthy's ACAS inquiry had found against BR and told them to pay the vexed 3 per cent, no strings. This decision left Ray looking good. Unfortunately it did not leave him *sounding* good, except in the aforementioned sense of deploying a bass timbre as mellifluous as Chaliapin's. Ray's rival Sidney Weighell not only has eight times as many members, he is capable of enunciating whole sentences that you can understand, whereas you feel that if you were to ask Ray for directions to the nearest railway station (or, more likely, the nearest coach station) he would tell you to turn left at the terms of reference and wait until the decision of the traffic lights had been ratified by his executive committee, through the machinery.

Sidney Weighell was one of the panellists on yet another excellent instalment of *Question Time* (BBC1), by now established, under the brusque chairmanship of Robin Day, as the nearest equivalent television has ever come up with to the Athenian agora. Sid recommended the merging of unions, which sounded like good news for most of us, although it no doubt sounded to Ray Buckton like the kind of proposal which his executive committee, after due deliberation, might feed into the machinery in such a way that it would never come out. The Government's Norman Tebbit, who turned out to be a dab hand at this kind of debate, slyly said he was all for mergers if the unions could arrange them. Meanwhile a man in the audience who was trying to shut himself up kept apologising for not being able to. 'No need to apologise,' barked Robin, 'just keep quiet.'

The Prime Minister was on *TV Eye* (Thames), pointing out, as if to an assembled school of not very bright children, that no responsible adult could possibly *think* of reflating. She made reflating sound like a synonym for flatulence – something which rude small boys did and only the sillier girls giggled at. 'Of *course* we can't reflate. It would be *morally wrong*.' Llew Gardner did his best to dispel the air of devotional sanctity. 'But Prime Minister, the CBI thinks you should reflate . . .' He went on, while she nodded with weary understanding, to give a quick list of people who thought she should reflate, but the second that he ran out of breath she pounced, saying that it all depended what you meant by reflation. For people who thought that Ray Buckton had already handed the English language all the punishment it could take, here was a chance to see it being worked over by an expert.

But if you were to put Margaret Thatcher and Ray Buckton on a desert island and wait patiently for their progeny to be born and grow, you still wouldn't come up with anything to equal Michael Foot in the sheer ability to detach language from meaning and set it free in some abstract realm of its own. On *Panorama* (BBC1) Robert Kee strove heroically to pin the Leader of the Opposition down with specific questions, but it was like trying to drive a nail through a blob of mercury. Freely invoking 'the Spirit of Bishop's Stortford', Foot answered Kee's contentions that the Labour Party might be seriously disunited by saying that it was very important for the Labour Party to be united. 'Absolute importance of us combining together to win that election . . . the spirit of Bishop's Stortford.'

Kee kept trying. 'Can you win an election by simply saying you're going to win an election?' But Foot, it transpired, wasn't just saying that they were going to win the election. What he was saying was that they were, in fact, going to win the election. Because they were united. By the Spirit of Bishop's Stortford. Kee brought up the name of Arthur Scargill. 'I'm not saying for a moment', said Foot, 'that it's all got to be done in the old pattern.' But Kee's point was that Scargill *does* say it's all got to be done in the old pattern.

'Of course, ha-ha,' laughed Foot, with the little laugh which points out that the question is too obvious to be worth answering, 'there have *always* been such differences.' But Kee's point was that the differences might this time be decisive, since the left wing of the party believes in the nationalisation of everything and the Right doesn't.

Cleverly photographed and directed by Chris Menges, *East 103rd Street* (Central) showed a New York Hispanic family being consumed by heroin, all except the beautiful daughter, who lectured the others on their folly. She did this in a monotone which might have driven anyone to seek oblivion, but her strength of mind could not be gainsaid. The programme took it for granted that social deprivation was the culprit. To harbour such an assumption is the director's prerogative, although it begs the question of how some other cultural groups in the same city have managed to lead industrious lives in conditions even worse. The son, Danny, whose sole achievement to date has apparently been the growing of a moustache, proved himself an adept at getting into profile and brooding gracefully. 'What do you want, son?' 'Be somebody.' It can't be done without doing something.

Flashing back, *25 Years Ago – 'Tonight'* (BBC1) justifiably enjoyed a nostalgic wallow. Cliff Michelmore was in charge. He deserves credit for having pioneered the relaxed manner. Cy Grant sang a freshly composed Topical Calypso, thereby reminding you how awful the Topical Calypso invariably was. Only the filmed reports are left to be cherished: the studio stuff, which was the real staple, is nearly all gone. But from the patter of the reporters in the field you got some idea of the show's flavour. Whicker's virtuoso talk-and-walk number about the weirdly numbered houses in Northumberland still looked good. What happened to *Tonight*? It became *Whicker's World, TW3, The Great War* – it vanished by expansion.

21 February, 1982

Make mine Minder

A LWAYS the best thing of its kind on the air, *Minder* (Thames) has been particularly nutritious lately, with George Cole's portrayal of Arthur Daley attaining such depths of seediness that a flock of starlings could feed off him.

Not that Arthur Daley is a scruff. Indeed his standard of living is quite high. But he is very dodgy, very furtive. 'Mr Daley?' someone asks. 'Depends,' he replies. His past might catch up with him. The future looms. He deals in cash. Small amounts of cash which he takes in, and even smaller amounts which he gives out. By far the smallest of these latter he gives to Terry, his Minder. Played by Dennis Waterman, Terry is honest to the core, but works for Arthur because there is nothing else going. Hence he is always being dropped in it.

That is the basic scenario each week: Arthur drops Terry in it. But the outline is filled in with richly tatty detail, like one of those Japanese woodcut series about the Floating World, the life on the verge of criminality, where nothing is nailed down. In the episode before last, Arthur's niece was getting married on the same day as he needed to shift a consignment of pornographic magazines. The bride found herself sitting on the magazines while Terry drove the limo.

In the latest episode Terry looked on with alarm while Arthur tried to get more than his fair share of a quarter of a million quid that an old lag was supposed to have tucked away in a bank, pronounced bang-k by Max Wall, who was playing the old lag. The standard of the casting is high each time. Maurice Denham and Rula Lenska were among those chasing the quarter million.

As well as looking like four times that much, Rula caught acting from everybody else, so that by the end of the story you hoped she would be back. But if Terry had a classy girl-friend in a white Porsche he would be out of character. Strippers are more his weight. In *Minder,* luxury is a vodka Slimline in the local boozer. This is the best low-life comedy series since *Budgie*, which was likewise conceived under the aegis of Verity Lambert. Her sure touch for this kind of thing is something of a mystery. Perhaps she used to be a gangster's moll.

Looking at shows like *Minder* and *Shoestring*, you can see what happened to the British film industry. Television left it standing. Apart from the concerted effort represented by Ealing in its best years, very few British films got within a hundred miles of authentic low life. They didn't get within the same distance of authentic high life, either. They were made, on the whole, by people who knew very little about any kind of milieu except the perennial one in which bad movies are made. Wanting that kind of film industry to return is like wanting the restoration of the Bourbons. In Britain, the only real reason for turning an idea into a feature film instead of a television programme is if the small screen and a low budget would combine to cramp it.

Postponed because of the Polish crisis, *Isadora* (Granada) at last hit the screen, and soon told you, if you needed telling, that Kenneth MacMillan is a man of genius. Either something is out of whack about the way theatrical events are reported, or else MacMillan's creations for the ballet are transformed between stage and screen, so that what starts out as a grudgingly praised semi-inspired sprawl arrives in my living-room like a revelation.

Not that the story was without hiccups. As well as being a woman of towering originality, Isadora was a bit of a fruitcake, and in her late years spent a lot of time being messy and boring – qualities never easy to convey without being messy and boring in your turn. Also I thought the death scene went for nearly nothing: a Bugatti can't dance, but Isadora might well have danced for a while with the scarf that got caught around its wheel and broke her neck.

As things were, the car came down the ramp, her head snapped back and the lights went out. MacMillan is not always successful in giving his works a final, simple, climactically satisfactory dramatic shape. But what he invents along the way is so rich there is no point carping. The first *pas de deux* with Gordon Craig was even more dementedly erotic than the best things in *Mayerling*, and the lurching, starkly sculptural dance of grief in which Isadora and Paris Singer mourn their dead children was like nothing else I have ever seen.

The preliminary programme, *A Lot of Happiness,* which showed MacMillan in rehearsal and was screened in December, was directed by Jack Gold. This one was directed by Derek Bailey. Between them, Gold and Bailey have done a lot to convince me over the past ten years that to review television is to have a front seat for the main action.

Both directors have responded to MacMillan with the gifted attention that his work deserves. Granada and the ITV network in general can also be commended for devoting the best part of two whole evenings to an artistic enterprise with no guaranteed appeal for a mass audience.

If the fly is clever, the fly on the wall technique can occasionally generate such a multi-faceted view of life as *Hot Champagne and First Night Nerves* (BBC2). An amateur dramatic society of British expatriates in Monaco were shown struggling with their latest annual production, *The Heiress.* 'There's not a lot to do out here, so most of us become preoccupied with the group.' One way or another they all felt that Monaco lacked something. 'I long for winter.' They were huddling together for cold. But the awful thing about provincial art is the way that its exponents must stew in their juice. Confiding in the camera, they ratted on one another right and left. 'For the last four days anyway I would have given my right *arm* to get out of this part.' 'She hasn't got the first idea of the part *anyway*.'

Josephine, who was having trouble remembering her lines, never wanted to be in Monaco in the first place. 'Close the door, Gerald. *Gerald* wanted to leave England. *I didn't.*' The producer's approach was perhaps not best calculated to calm the nerves of amateurs. 'A major prop wasn't there. *A major prop*. How DARE you?' The actual first night performance was not shown, but the conversations overheard in the dressing-room afterwards sug-

gested that it might attract mixed reviews. 'I'm sorry.' 'Forget it.'
'I'm *sorry*.' 'You were fabulous.'

28 February, 1982

Rumpole recollects

T HE forensic verve of John Mortimer made *A Voyage Round My
Father* (Thames) as unswitchoffable as a courtroom drama,
even though it was nominally about a man who refused to admit
that he couldn't see.

Having your blind father played by Laurence Olivier is no doubt
a big help. As Olivier has got older and, dare one say it, feebler, his
energy has only become more apparent. When his magnificent
athlete's body could no longer vault up stairs like the young
Hamlet or fling itself about like Richard III, his energy transferred
itself to his voice, which grew even stronger. When the volume of
his voice began to lessen, his elocution became even more sculp-
turally exact. Forced now to work within a much narrower dyna-
mic range, he is twice the actor for the screen that he was fifty years
ago, when he had more fizz than the camera could absorb. Not that
he ever hammed it up. But he swamped everyone else just by
standing there. People who tell you that Olivier overacts are telling
you about themselves. He is just over-alive.

Here was a good chance to watch a senior great actor do one of
his best tricks, namely, doddering impatience. The old man's wife,
played by Elizabeth Sellars, had to read him the sordid details of
upcoming divorce cases while they were travelling together on the
train to London. 'What was that? Do speak up, dear.' 'Stains.'
'What was that?' 'STAINS.' It would have been easy to play such
scenes as farce but the temptation was resisted. Alan Bates was the
young John Mortimer and Jane Asher, by now a valuable actress,
played his first wife.

An even younger version of John Mortimer, played with be-
spectacled sensitivity by Alan Cox, was incarcerated in the manda-
tory weirdo prep school, staffed exclusively by fruitcake masters of
whom the dippiest was the man in charge. Incarnated by the droll

Michael Aldridge (who was one of the many things about Michael Frayn's play *Noises Off* that caused me to leave my seat and roll in the aisle), the headmaster laid down the law to the new boys even to the extent of telling them what nicknames the masters were to be known by. 'I'm Noah. This is Mrs Noah. You are the animals.'

Mortimer has always been so prodigal with his gifts that one tends to look in the wrong place for his best work: the *Brideshead* adaptation, for example, was nothing like as good as the Rumpole scripts. But *A Voyage Round My Father*, generally agreed to be a fine thing, actually is a fine thing. It was in two minds about whether the old man was a paragon or a monster, and it left you convinced that to be in two minds was the only way to be.

The new arts centre at *The Barbican* (BBC2) was opened by the Queen, who was obliged to put in a pretty tough evening. The music was composed by such dependable regulars as Beethoven, Wagner and Elgar, with Handel being heard intermittently during the fireworks. Also the building itself must have been pleasant for her to make a tour of, even if full of people bowing low, dropping suddenly to one knee, or making speeches. She made a speech of her own, very properly assessing the new place as one of the wonders of the modern world.

But the art exhibitions must have put a considerable burden on the royal patience. 'The Queen is a great lover of visual art,' said Richard Baker. Boy, had she come to the wrong place. Apart from the Picasso sculptures the post-war French art couldn't have been duller, and to clobber the regal visitor with a load of Canadian tapestries was to risk a diplomatic incident. 'Tapestry is a great tradition in Canada, especially French Canada,' said Richard Baker with patently attenuated enthusiasm. Her Majesty did not flinch. It's a tradition in the family: when the Germans drop bombs, you stay put, and when the Canadians send tapestries you pretend to look interested.

One of the strengths of British television is that its style has been set by people overqualified for the task. Robert Robinson, for example, had more than it took for writing and presenting a programme like *The Auden Landscape* (BBC2), since he has a literary background himself. What television will be like when it is staffed throughout by people with nothing but a television background is a worrying question, but it is a safe prediction that programmes as off-handedly intelligent as this one will be hard to come by.

Robinson nailed his colours to the mast by calling Auden 'the most distinguished poet to have written in English since the death of Tennyson'. If the average presenter had said this he might have left you wondering if he had ever heard of W. B. Yeats or T. S. Eliot, but coming from Robinson it was obviously a conscious provocation. I think he's right, but the programme helped demonstrate that greatness does not preclude childishness. The homosexual ambience was amply evoked, and sounded as bitchy as hell. There can be no doubt that Auden loved Chester Kallman but one look at him told you that that must have made two people who loved him, Auden and his mother. The word 'mother' figured large in Auden's private vocabulary. His own mother knew all about his proclivities but never condemned. He rewarded her by being a man of genius.

An actor read Auden's verse with no observation of the line endings whatsoever, thereby transforming some of the most vitally rhythmic poetry ever written into spineless mush. Robinson himself should have read it all. He recited from 'The Fall of Rome' with just the right measured vigour, although he should not have done so from memory – the reindeer don't *run* across the miles and miles of golden moss, they *move* across it. Anyone who believes that Auden's gift for evocation vanished after the war should read 'The Fall of Rome', but *caveat lector*: you will never get its slide-show of phantasmagorical images out of your head.

If you scoop *Dallas* and *Flamingo Road* together, move them north to *Knot's Landing*, and then transport the whole shebang west to San Francisco, you've got *Falcon Crest* (Thames) and you're welcome to it. Starring Jane Wyman, it was obviously meant to be entitled 'The Return of the President's Wife' but the White House disapproved. The plot turns on the inability of a preternaturally stupid family to realise that their Aunt Angela is screwing them up. There is a lot of technical talk about the growing of grapes, by which we learn that grapes are susceptible to a fungus called bunch rot.

Forged Papers (BBC2) told you what happened to some of the English residents of the South of France who stayed on during the Vichy regime. Some of it was very nasty. Your average French anti-semitic 'expert on the Jewish problem' was just aching to get started on solving it, so you didn't have to be a secret agent to be in deadly danger – your ancestry could be enough.

A snooty-looking woman called Lady Henderson looked as if she was going to commandeer your help at the local gymkhana. When she talked, though, it was a quiet litany of unendurable horror. 'People were tortured all night. You could hear it all going on. Unfortunately I saw my dear husband and I only recognised him by his coat.' Her husband suffocated on the way to Dachau. She survived Ravensbrück. 'People say, "Was it really like that?" and I say "Yes, haven't you read the books?"' The titles listed her medals for valour. Here was reality if you could take it. Switch *Falcon Crest* back on, quick.

7 March, 1982

Ernest Hemingway Schopenhauer

A FANTASY sprayed with dirt from an aerosol can, *Hill Street Blues* (Thames) allows you to travel in a bubble of wish-fulfilment through the grim reality of New York crime.

Actually the city is never specified, but if it is not New York it is certainly not Richmond, Virginia. Teenage gangs maraud, torture and kill. Heroin addicts fall face down in the street. Hispanic families, their numbers thinned only by attacks from giant cockroaches, pullulate in crumbling tenements. In the middle of this nightmare is a precinct station full of more wisdom than Periclean Athens ever knew, more kindness than ever obtained in the ambience of Francis of Assisi or Vincent de Paul. All the policemen are philosophers. All the policewomen are female philosophers. The female attorney who invigilates the premises in order to ensure that the Bill of Rights is fully upheld looks like a fashion model.

Captain Furillo is the man in charge. Not only is he a philosopher, he is a sad philosopher, a Schopenhauer who has seen too much of war and has just finished writing *A Farewell To Arms*. Not only is he Ernest Hemingway Schopenhauer, he is extremely good-looking in a sensitive way. He is Robert De Niro Ernest Hemingway Schopenhauer. But if he were twice as good-looking as he is already, he could not begin to be as beautiful as his mistress, the vigilant attorney Joyce Davenport. She has Clarence Darrow's sense of justice, the figure of Cyd Charisse and the face of an angel. Furillo's wife has conveniently taken herself off, leaving Furillo and the knockout legal eagle to agonise about whether they should cement their relationship further, or merely go on lying around without any clothes on while the city burns down outside their window.

Are these two entitled to go on indulging themselves in love without responsibility? Why yes: because their responsibilities are so great. At any time Furillo could be summoned from his fleeting ecstasy in the percale sheets and transported by a howling car with a flashing light into the middle of a pitched battle between extras of various colours. Essentially he is alone, separated by the glass partition of his office even from the other cops whom he must send into battle, like Gregory Peck in *Twelve O'Clock High*. And what a swell bunch of guys they are, a team of wild young talents watched over and guided by Sgt Esterhaus, the most extraordinary philosopher of the lot!

Sgt Esterhaus is tall, rugged, witty and profound. He can ask the Socratic question and lay down the Aristotelean precept. He speaks of the precinct station as 'a tenuously balanced social microcosm'. Thus Lucretius spoke of the Universe. In addition to his mental powers he is sensationally attractive to women. When the pearls drop from his lips, all these love-hungry broads are on their knees lapping them up. But his heart, however reluctantly given, belongs to a luscious, self-proclaimed nymphomaniac who waylays him regularly behind the filing cabinets in order to slake the insatiable need aroused by his image burning in her mind.

Not an American series but a British series about Americans in Britain, *We'll Meet Again* (LWT) is about another swell bunch of guys who have come here during the Second World War in order to bomb Germany to its knees. By my count they are attempting to accomplish this with only two aircraft. But the two aircraft are B-17s in spanking condition. You see one of them taking off towards you while the other one taxis to the end of the runway. Then you switch to stock footage of a formation of the Eighth Air Force streaming its condensation trails on the long, hard road to Schweinfurt. More stock footage shows an FW 190 making a flank attack from three o'clock up. Stock footage of a B-17's .50 calibre waist guns takes on the stock footage of the FW. Flamer! Great shooting, Buzz. Take us home, skipper.

Back on the ground things are, well, earth-bound. Susannah York is the lady of the manor. The squire is away somewhere pointing his stiff upper lip at the Germans. If he never comes back, Susannah might marry the wonderful young American major, who is made doubly wonderful by being almost the only real American on the base. Most of the other Americans are either British actors with variously inadequate American accents, or else actors of North American (i.e., Canadian) origin who sound like British actors imitating Americans.

The best thing about *We'll Meet Again* is a terribly strict and foolish father who hates Americans. His daughter is the first girl in the district to get pregnant. A philosophical pub-owner helps guard her from her father's wrath. There is a lot of talk about the material wealth of the Americans in comparison to the war-weary and flat-broke Brits, but not much of this discrepancy is actually shown. In reality it was a burning issue. The American enlisted men were better dressed than the British officers. It was two different worlds colliding. But to bring out the full poignancy of the collision would take much more penetrating writing than anything on offer here. *We'll Meet Again* is a cliché with four engines. A sucker for machines, I usually watch, but am not improved, only diverted.

The latest Andrea Newman bouquet of barbed whatsit, *Alexa* (BBC1), had a surprisingly deep first episode in which a free-lance journalist, played by Isla Blair, moved in to help her distraught friend, who had given up her career in favour of having babies. The friend's frustration and her husband's deadly wetness were thoroughly evoked. Unfortunately in the second episode Isla, who if she were an American actress would be a prime candidate to play a wildly beautiful attorney haunting a precinct station full of peripatetic philosophers, showed signs of falling for the deliquescent husband of her friend. Understandable on the level of human fidelity and betrayal, this seemed physically unlikely. But Andrea Newman is coming on, and at this rate we will have to look elsewhere for overwrought sludge.

In *A Week With Svetlana* (BBC2) Malcolm Muggeridge played host to Stalin's daughter, but surprisingly little got said. 'It's terribly hard to understand his character,' Muggeridge said of Stalin. This was an odd thing to tell Svetlana, who understands her father's character very well. But if there was not much talking there was a lot of walking, along those muddy paths in which ruts have been worn by the editor of *Private Eye* and others among Muggeridge's attendant galaxy of deep thinkers.

In *World About Us* (BBC2) Julian Cooper dealt with Futebol Brasil. In Brazilian futebol there are apparently only two clubs that count, and one of them is called Atletico. A supporter of this club is thus known as an Atletico supporter. Cooper's main challenge was to find a non-attention-getting way of saying this. 'There is a tropical exuberance about these Atletico supporters.' The programme suffered inevitably from a depressing monotony of theme, since there is only one fact about Brazilian futebol that matters – the country is so grindingly poor that futebol is the sole escape from reality.

While still in South America, however, I should mention *The Flight of the Condor* (BBC2), a series now concluded. The condor itself emerged as a gutless snob who hangs around gracefully waiting for something to die, but it and all the other creatures were photographed in a way little short of miraculous, and the sequence of a bat catching a frog at dead of night *was* miraculous.

14 March, 1982

Stop treading on the rug*!*

THE latest film for television to be devised and directed by Mike Leigh, *Home Sweet Home* (BBC1), was assessed by an unusually obtuse *Times* critic as having nothing in it. It had everything in it.

With *Abigail's Party*, Leigh's unique talent was firmly hinted at, but not, I thought, fully confirmed. He obviously had a terrific eye and ear for human banality, but you wanted to be sure that the observations would shape up: art, after all, is more than just registration. In *Home Sweet Home*, the gripping story of three postmen and how practically nothing happened to them, every tortured inarticulacy took its place in a fearfully symmetrical confection.

There were arias of loneliness and struggling pretension, in which daydreaming wives haltingly poured out their anguish. 'It's like a band of steel pulled tight across my temples.' There were passionless duets in which hang-dog husbands were brought even further to heel. 'Stop treading on the *rug*! You're *squashing* it!' There were long, Mozartian, end-of-the-act ensembles in which everybody said nothing.

If you can imagine *Così fan tutte* with the music taken out, and then with the words taken out, and then with all the decor and costumes replaced by the tackiest fabrics and furniture known to mortal man, you've got a movie by Mike Leigh. That there should be two such original artists as him and Bill Forsyth loose in Britain at the same time is a remarkable thing.

In one of Forsyth's films about hopeless Glasgow youth, *That Sinking Feeling*, there is a small but resonant sequence showing the boys sitting in a car. It has already been established that the boys are skint and have no prospects, unless their projected robbery of a warehouse full of stainless steel sink-units pays off. How could they be sitting in a car? And then the camera pulls back to show that the car is an abandoned wreck. The single camera movement that advances the story is a mark of Forsyth's work and equally of Leigh's. *Home Sweet Home* was full of invisibly precise long shots that told you about the isolation of the characters without anybody having to say a word – which was lucky, because nobody in the story could tell you much about himself or anyone else.

A more noticeable piece of directorial flair happened when the second most hopeless postman took some time to park his bicycle. You knew it would not stay upright, but the question was when it would choose to fall down. The camera panned with the postman and the bike fell gently somewhere off screen. Tati used similar tricks in *Mr Hulot's Holiday*: the image of the swing door that went *sproing*, for example, was often conveyed merely by the sound-track.

Craft on this level of subtlety is a particular delight to watch at a time when some young directors, through no fault of their own, are being called geniuses for having their names on vast adaptations full of star actors and historic buildings. Such generalship should never be undervalued, but it is not necessarily the same thing as creative talent. Mike Leigh is making something out of nothing – or, rather, showing you that what superficially looks like nothing is really something.

His communities of zombies speak clichés when they speak at all, but their emotions are real. Even if they feign passion there is genuine deprivation underneath. The inability to talk is revealed as a kind of language, into which any half-way normal utterance must be translated before it can be understood. 'So it was a mutual separation.' 'Nar, she just run off with some geezer.' Even more hopeless than the second most hopeless postman, the third most hopeless postman was incapable of taking in the news that his wife was having an affair with the first most hopeless postman. 'Why?' he asked. He couldn't see why anyone would want to.

The first most hopeless postman's daughter was in care because he did not know how to look after her. He knew he did not know how and worried about it, but did not know how to turn the worry into action, mainly because he did not have the words. The social workers had the words, but they were all the wrong ones. A terrible girl called Melody was full of uncomprehending cheer. 'Fair enough?' Finally she ran off to London and left them all to it.

Melody's boyfriend, another social worker, ended the film with an extended sociological recitative about 'contributing infrastructural causes'. Not a word he said meant a thing, but the first most hopeless postman did not know that. We knew it was nonsense, but to him it was a blank. Mike Leigh is conducting the most daring raid on the inarticulate yet. Harold Pinter is Christopher Fry beside him.

While in an expansive mood, let me record my, and I hope your, gratitude for *Manon* (BBC2), the Kenneth MacMillan ballet transmitted from Covent Garden. Lately I have spent quite a lot of time hailing MacMillan as a man of genius and won't pile the bouquets any higher here, but it still needs to be said that Jennifer Penney and Anthony Dowell in the first *pas de deux* were enough to make you hope that Manon would see sense and stick with Des Grieux, instead of screwing everything up and being shipped off to croak in Louisiana.

The Manon story is perhaps to be appreciated in its ideal form by seeing the English National Opera production of the Massenet version at the London Coliseum, but not everyone can hope to do that, whereas with the ballet all you had to do was touch a button and there they were, dancing their little hearts out.

So did Jane Torvill and Christopher Dean in the *World Figure Skating Championships* (BBC1), but the Beeb got its skates twisted. Our couple danced first in the final group and were interviewed in depth ('Did the cup of tea help?') while the next pair were dancing, thereby depriving us of a chance to compare. British champions bring television madness in their train. Robin Cousins used to be a victim, but now he has joined the persecutors. If he is to go on commentating, he must try harder not to describe what we can already see. 'Look at the flowers! It's almost like a florist's shop!'

The whole style of Esther Rantzen's *That's Life* (BBC1) affects me like being trapped in a lift with a warm-up man, but her marathon programme on how to have a baby was almost certainly a boon for millions of women. There were harrowing stories of visits to the clinic in which nothing was accomplished except a long wait and an insulting word from the doctor. One woman overheard a consultant tell his students that her baby might be dead in there. 'He told me I had big ears and that it didn't concern me.' A nurse who thought, correctly, that her baby was in distress was told by the doctor that she was over-reacting because she was a nurse. For those of us who have been well-treated in this respect, here was a shaking up.

Colin Welland would not be the first name that sprang to mind if you were compiling a list of people suffering from excessive humility, but from now on he should assert himself and never go on screen unless he is writing his dialogue. In beer commercials it does not matter so much, because while uttering other people's lines his moustache is under the foamy surface of the product. But in the *Labour Party Political Broadcast* (all channels) his mouth was clearly visible, coping with such locutions as 'a carefully thought-out package of radical alternatives'. It transpired that the package of radical alternatives would be financed by borrowing money.

21 March, 1982

One last look

TERRY WOGAN, currently hosting the best radio show on the air, hosted the worst television show just to stay in practice. *A Song For Europe 1982* (BBC1) plumbed new troughs.

Most ghastly development is the tendency for every other singing group to field a sub-Hot Gossip group of leather fetishist dancers. The song 'Dancing in Heaven', featuring a lot of space talk about radar and countdowns, was delivered by a squad of people in American uniforms and pressure-suits who gyrated to what they hopefully described as orbital be-bop. In all songs there were frequent mentions of U and R, as in 'U and R have just begun.' U might have been able to put up with this, but R couldn't stand it.

A series deservedly honoured, *Arena* (BBC1) profiled author Salman Rushdie with a subtle thoroughness which incidentally told you a lot about his strange homeland. 'You literally aren't alone, ever,' was his most telling comment. Trains are a very big deal in India. During one train journey Rushdie looked out of the window and counted the amounts of time between people. Even in the most desolate stretches of countryside there was never more than a 15-second interval. Here was the governing factor of subcontinental politics laid bare.

If you subjugate India to the extent that the Indian ruling class will want to educate its young in your public schools, eventually you will get the occasional Salman Rushdie ready to take on the job of explaining his own country to you in terms you will understand. But who will do the same job for Britain? It is a country far weirder than India. From the window of a British Rail Intercity train the gap is often more than 15 seconds between people, especially if the train is stuck a mile outside Macclesfield 'owing to the engineering'. But in every other respect Britain is a teeming, jostling daydream of sacred cows, holy men, thugs, curry-merchants and people who will write letters for you in return for money. How, for example, do you begin to explain the mere existence of someone like Tony Benn?

In India the Tony Benns sit semi-naked under gnarled trees and pull greased cords through their nostrils while inhaling water through the penis. But in Britain they are prominent in what was, until last Friday, the leading political party of the opposition. *Newsnight* (BBC2) was already predicting victory for Jenkins just after 11 p.m., basing its estimate on a poll taken of voters leaving the booth – the only kind of poll, experience suggests, on which you can even begin to rely. Vincent Hanna was *Newsnight*'s man on the spot in Hillhead, with John Tusa anchoring in the studio. In charge of discussions: Sir Robin Day. Biffen, Hattersley and Shirley Williams represented the big three. 'If Roy Jenkins does win,' asked Robin, 'is the mould of British politics really broken?'

'No,' said Hatters, adding that even if the SDP did win it would in fact be a disappointment for them, because they would have won by much more had they not been morally defeated by a 'much underrated candidate', meaning the mysteriously taciturn Labour candidate with the beard. Robin's incredulity at this was beautiful to see, but far stranger things were happening on the commercial channel, where Tony Benn was now out of his tracksuit and warming up.

Alastair Burnet was in charge of the ITN studio, with Peter Sissons out in the field. Sissons convincingly argued that Jenkins had peaked at the right time and not by accident: he was a 'very, very astute campaigner' who had personally met twice as many constituents as any other candidate. Back in the studio, however, Benn knew that Jenkins was really just Reg Prentice in disguise and that the people had been fooled. Benn's propensity for going on television and telling the people that they are easy to fool could well bring about, in the course of time, the utter destruction of the Labour Party, but tonight he wasn't going to let a consideration like that slow him down.

'I'm absolutely amazed by Tony Benn,' said Jim Prior, representing the Tories. Dr Owen of the Alliance contented himself with a few rational statements while Benn mimed incomprehension and stoked his pipe, another of his delusions about television being that it is a medium which favours histrionics. Actually it exposes them ruthlessly, but some people are hams to the core.

'CND is four times as big as the SDP,' Benn announced, forgetting to add that the RSPCA is four times as big as CND. 'It may be that the SDP is past its peak.' On BBC2 they were interviewing local Scots politicians. Back to ITN, where Benn was saying, 'I believe the SDP is now past its peak.' He had gone from 'it may be' to 'I believe' in half a minute. 'I think what we're witnessing', he went on, 'is Jeremy Thorpe reappearing in the guise of Roy Jenkins.' Back to the Beeb, before Benn could suggest that what we were witnessing was Flash Gordon reappearing as Ming the Merciless of Mongo, Emperor of the Universe.

Hatters was telling Robin that if Jenkins won it would really be a victory for Labour, because in the general election an SDP led by Jenkins would take votes from the Tories, whereas an SDP led by Shirley Williams would have taken them from Labour. 'I genuinely believe that this is an encouraging vote for Labour.' This was a pretty mad moment for Hatters, but he still sounded as judicious as Thucydides compared with what was going on back at ITN. 'I personally', Benn was saying, 'think that the SDP has passed its peak.'

He could say that again and was plainly determined on doing so, but there was a big blur as both channels switched to Hillhead for the announcement. A total of 282 people had voted for the other Roy Jenkins, but in the end it was the real Roy Jenkins who stood up. Back in the BBC studio, Shirley Williams threw away her walking stick. 'We've got back into Parliament the man who will lead that Alliance.' On ITN, Owen said, 'Fantastic.'

If this wasn't real generosity in both cases, it certainly sounded like it. If they were fooling the people about their own disappointed hopes, at least they had paid the people the compliment of employing a fairly high level of acting. Benn, on the other hand, the man who goes on endlessly about how the media manipulates the people, went on manipulating to the end. 'I think this means we'll have a Labour government . . . the SDP is on the way down . . . the SDP will disappear.'

Which is my cue. Last year in Las Vegas I met a blackjack dealer who told me there are only two kinds of gamblers, the dumb ones and those who know how to quit while they're ahead. After ten years of writing this column I still face the gleaming tube with undiminished enthusiasm, but with increasing frequency I find my own face looking back at me. It is time to quit my chair, before I find myself reviewing my own programmes. Creativity and criticism, in my view, are more continuous than opposed, but there is such a thing as a conflict of interest. There is also such a thing as making way for fresh talent. By standing up and moving aside for my gifted successor, Julian Barnes, I avoid the possibility of finding him suddenly sitting in my lap. No doubt he will slag one of my programmes first chance he gets, but by then I will be in the habit of damning all critics as fools.

28 March, 1982

Clive James
Visions Before Midnight £2.50
TV criticism from the *Observer* 1972–76

The first selection from the newspaper column that made TV criticism an entertainment in its own right. The 1972 and 1976 Olympics, *War and Peace*, the Royal Wedding, the Eurovision Song Contest, the exit of Tricky Dick – the favourites are all here.

'Clive James's television reviews . . . turn the pale glimmers on the set into something like a gaudily lit portable theatre of clacking wooden puppets . . . his stunning pieces readjust horizontal and vertical holds almost before there is time to blink away the images that were actually transmitted'
DENNIS POTTER

The Crystal Bucket £1.95
TV criticism from the *Observer* 1976–79

'His contribution to the art and enjoyment of TV criticism over the past ten years has been immense. His work is deeply perceptive, often outrageously funny and always compulsively readable.' Thus the judges of the British Press Awards, in naming Clive James Critic of the Year for 1981. *The Crystal Bucket* offers a further selection of his inimitable 'visions before midnight'.

'One of the few columnists who make you laugh aloud . . . if there were angels he would be on their side: and that would certainly include Charlie's Angels'
MELVYN BRAGG, SUNDAY TIMES

Unreliable Memoirs £1.95
The Kid from Kogarah tells all.

'You had better not read the book on a train, unless you are unselfconscious about shrieking and snorting in public' OBSERVER

'The public's favourite wit and pundit, reduced in imagination to short-trouser size, wrestling with snakes and aunties and mutual-masturbators in the bush-bordering suburbs of postwar Sydney . . . called up in the familiar two-fisted prose. The old boy may be 40, but he times a punchline disgustingly well' RUSSELL DAVIES, LISTENER

Clive James
From the Land of Shadows £2.50

'These literary-critical essays . . . have a kind of freshness about them . . . in the tradition of Hazlitt, Bagehot and Desmond MacCarthy, with a gusto worthy to succeed theirs and a philosophy well set out in the introduction' JOHN BAYLEY, OBSERVER

'James' main strength as a critic of contemporary fiction lies in his wry description . . . we can only be grateful to him for caring, and for keeping us smiling while we learn' TABLET

'His outstanding talent is as a cicerone, guiding the ignorant traveller with patience, knowledge and wit round some favourite literary edifice' THE TIMES LITERARY SUPPLEMENT

Vladimir Nabokov
Lectures on Literature £3.95

'With a pleasure which is both sensual and intellectual, we shall watch the artist build the castle of cards and watch the castle of cards become a castle of beautiful steel and glass.' For nearly twenty years Nabokov taught a university course on the masterpieces of world literature. An orator, a novelist, a lepidopterist of world renown, he examined literature with a scientific exactitude as well as with a writer's appreciation. Here are his legendary lectures on the Europeans: on Jane Austen, Dickens, Stevenson, Joyce, Flaubert, Proust and Kafka. With an introduction by John Updike.

Lectures on Russian Literature £3.95

'Literature must be taken and broken to bits, pushed apart, squashed and then its lovely reek will be smelt in the hollow of the palm, it will be munched and rolled upon the tongue with relish.' Nabokov left his native Russia at the age of twenty to escape what he called 'the bloated octopus of the state'. In this volume are published his lectures on the great nineteenth-century Russian writers: Gogol, Turgenev, Dostoevsky, Tolstoy, Chekov and Gorki.

'I cannot imagine a more rewarding hardbook for anyone who appreciates, or hopes to write, fiction' FREDERICK RAPHAEL, SUNDAY TIMES

'A great Russian talking of great Russians' ANTHONY BURGESS

'Unique in the history of literary criticism in its power to grip, astonish and occasionally infuriate' GUARDIAN

Joyce Johnson
Minor Characters £2.50

Girl met boy on a blind date arranged by Allen Ginsberg. It was January 1957. The girl was Joyce Johnson, the boy Jack Kerouac. It was nine months before *On the Road.* Like Robin Hood's and Peter Pan's, Jack's was a boy gang – women were minor characters at best.

'Joyce Johnson summons up the mythic Greenwich Village of jazz, poetry and black-stockinged Bohemia with infinite ironic grace' ANGELA CARTER

'The love story of Joyce from the Upper Westside who journeys to the Village on the subway . . . and Jack, the confused, mother-tied, suddenly famous road poet . . . a first-rate memoir, very beautiful, very sad' E. L. DOCTOROW

Hunter S. Thompson
The Great Shark Hunt £3.50

strange tales from a strange time

Here is the first British publication of the best of Gonzo in one volume. From Private Thompson in trouble with the air force, to a devastating portrait of the ageing Muhammed Ali – taking in the Kentucky Derby, Nixon in '68, McGovern in '72, Fear and Loathing at Watergate, Jimmy Carter: a compendium of decadence, depravity and horse sense.

'No other reporter reveals how much we have to fear and loathe, yet does it so hilariously' CHICAGO TRIBUNE

Tom Wolfe
In Our Time £2.95

America in her 'Elizabethan period, her Bourbon Louis romp, her season of rude animal health and rising sap!' – Tom Wolfe's prose and drawings in *In Our Time* define the dog years of the twentieth century with a telling eye for the style of the moment and a Pantagruelian appetite for the zaniness of its cockeyed landscape, introducing us to the inhabitants of this shifting moral terrain: the New Cookie, 'the girl in her twenties for whom the American male now customarily shucks his wife'; the Jaded Teenager, burnt out by eighteen; the Jogger, driven on mile after mile by his feeling of superiority over his fellow citizens. *In our Time* is Tom Wolfe at his most acid and most diverting.

Jan Harold Brunvand
The Vanishing Hitchhiker £1.95

urban legends and their meanings

The take-away chicken that was really a batter-fried rat . . . the carnivorous spider hidden underneath a well-lacquered hairdo, busily eating away at the scalp – these are the stories that always happened to a friend of a relative of the man in the pub. But as Jan Harold Brunvand demonstrates in this entertaining book, they're a great deal more. These tales form the folklore of modern man, some gaining enough credibility to appear regularly as genuine news-stories. So sit back and enjoy the myth and legend of the fast-food joint and the parking lot, the executive lifestyle and the urban jungle, the alligator in the sewer and the madman and the babysitter.

Hugo Williams
No Particular Place to Go £1.95

Hugo Williams went looking for the America he'd been dreaming of most of his life – B-movie, back-lot, rock 'n' roll America. He found it in bars and Greyhound buses, clubs, beds, record stores and mean streets. With the excuse of a poetry-reading tour, he zigzagged across the country, missing nothing with his watchful poet's eye, and coming back with a freight of strange, hilarious, unforgettable impressions.

'Rich scraps of lunacy which seem to promise some imminent insight into the much plundered American psyche but, in the meantime, are simply very funny' TIME OUT

Bruce Chatwin
In Patagonia £2.50

Patagonia – 'the uttermost part of the earth' – at the tip of South America. The name calls to mind giants and outlaws, Magellan's dog-headed monsters, natives whose heads steam. This book is a quest, a wonder voyage – about wandering and exile. The narrator's quest for a strange beast is marked by encounters with other people whose stories delay him on his road.

'A brilliant travel book' OBSERVER

'Pure pleasure – full of incident and anecdote and the oddest facts imaginable . . . vastly enjoyable' PAUL THEROUX, THE TIMES

introduced by Jill Tweedie
Letters from a Fainthearted Feminist £1.95

'Dear Mary, Sorry I haven't written for a while, but back here in Persil Country the festive season lasts from November 1 (make plum pudding) to January 31 (lose hope and write husband's thank-you letters). I got some lovely presents. A useful Spare Rib Diary. A book called The Implications of Urban Women's Image in Early American Literature. A Marks and Sparks rape alarm . . .' So begins the first of Martha's weekly letters to her more liberated Sister, Mary. Thirty-eight, fulsome wife and mother, she longs to put into practice the precepts of the women's movement, and is thwarted at every turn.

'Humorous and often hilarious . . . the more human face of feminism'
DAILY MAIL

'Read it . . . and it's worth reading for its serious message as well'
EMMA TENNANT

A. G. Macdonell
England, Their England £2.50

The classic comic novel is now in Picador.

'Mr Macdonell's book is a joy to read. I recommend it impartially to Englishmen, Scotsmen and Welshmen alike . . . The first two pages are sufficient to show the excellence of the fare that will be set before you and you settle down to enjoy its gaiety and its droll satire and general sparkle'
SUNDAY TIMES

'Macdonell has hit off the peculiar foibles of the educated Englishman and the strange meanderings of his existence . . . from the last ball of the cricket match, which takes over four pages to catch, to the inimitable description of the Great Central Railway at Marylebone' GUARDIAN

'In a universe entirely mad no one thing can be more lunatic than any other . . . one of the most amusing satires it has ever been my luck to read . . . extravagantly funny' DAILY EXPRESS

Picador

☐	**The Snow Leopard**	Peter Matthiessen	£2.95p
☐	**Rolling Stone Illustrated History of Rock and Roll**	ed. Jim Miller	£4.95p
☐	**Lectures on Literature**	Vladimir Nabokov	£3.95p
☐	**A Short Walk in the Hindu Kush**	Eric Newby	£2.50p
☐	**The Best of Myles**	Flann O' Brien	£2.95p
☐	**Autobiography**	John Cowper Powys	£3.50p
☐	**Hadrian the Seventh**	Fr. Rolfe (Baron Corvo)	£1.25p
☐	**On Broadway**	Damon Runyon	£1.95p
☐	**Midnight's Children**	Salman Rushdie	£3.50p
☐	**Snowblind**	Robert Sabbag	£1.95p
☐	**Awakenings**	Oliver Sacks	£3.95p
☐	**The Best of Saki**	Saki	£1.95p
☐	**The Fate of the Earth**	Jonathan Schell	£1.95p
☐	**Street of Crocodiles**	Bruno Schultz	£1.25p
☐	**Miss Silver's Past**	Josef Skvorecky	£2.50p
☐	**A Flag for Sunrise**	Robert Stone	£2.50p
☐	**Visitants**	Randolph Stow	£2.50p
☐	**Alice Fell**	Emma Tennant	£1.95p
☐	**The Flute-Player**	D. M. Thomas	£2.25p
☐	**The Great Shark Hunt**	Hunter S. Thompson	£3.50p
☐	**The Longest War**	Jacob Timerman	£2.50p
☐	**Female Friends**	Fay Weldon	£2.50p
☐	**No Particular Place To Go**	Hugo Williams	£1.95p
☐	**The Outsider**	Colin Wilson	£2.50p
☐	**Kandy-Kolored Tangerine-Flake Streamline Baby**	Tom Wolfe	£2.25p
☐	**Mars**	Fritz Zorn	£1.95p

All these books are available at your local bookshop or newsagent, or can be ordered direct from the publisher. Indicate the number of copies required and fill in the form below   10

Name_____
(Block letters please)

Address_____

_____

Send to CS Department, Pan Books Ltd, PO Box 40, Basingstoke, Hants
Please enclose remittance to the value of the cover price plus:
35p for the first book plus 15p per copy for each additional book ordered
to a maximum charge of £1.25 to cover postage and packing
Applicable only in the UK

While every effort is made to keep prices low, it is sometimes
necessary to increase prices at short notice. Pan Books reserve
the right to show on covers and charge new retail prices which
may differ from those advertised in the text or elsewhere